An Areal Typology of Agreement Systems

Surveying over 300 languages, this typological study presents new theoretical insights into the nature of agreement, as well as empirical findings about the distribution of agreement patterns in the world's languages. Focusing primarily on agreement in gender, number and person, but with reference to agreement in other smaller categories, Ranko Matasović aims to discover which patterns of agreement are widespread and common in languages, and which are rather limited in their distribution. He sheds new light on a range of important theoretical questions such as what agreement actually is, what areal, typological and genetic patterns exist across agreement systems, and what problems in the analysis of agreement remain unresolved.

RANKO MATASOVIĆ is Professor of Comparative Linguistics in the University of Zagreb and a Fellow of the Croatian Academy of Sciences and Arts. He has published thirteen books in Croatia and abroad, including *Gender in Indo-European* (2004) and *Etymological Dictionary of Proto-Celtic* (2009).

An Areal Typology of Agreement Systems

Ranko Matasović

University of Zagreb

CAMBRIDGE UNIVERSITY PRESS

CAMBRIDGE
UNIVERSITY PRESS

University Printing House, Cambridge CB2 8BS, United Kingdom

One Liberty Plaza, 20th Floor, New York, NY 10006, USA

477 Williamstown Road, Port Melbourne, VIC 3207, Australia

314–321, 3rd Floor, Plot 3, Splendor Forum, Jasola District Centre,
New Delhi – 110025, India

79 Anson Road, #06-04/06, Singapore 079906

Cambridge University Press is part of the University of Cambridge.

It furthers the University's mission by disseminating knowledge in the pursuit of
education, learning, and research at the highest international levels of excellence.

www.cambridge.org
Information on this title: www.cambridge.org/9781108420976
DOI: 10.1017/9781108355766

© Ranko Matasović 2018

First published 2018

Printed in the United Kingdom by Clays, St Ives plc

A catalogue record for this publication is available from the British Library.

Library of Congress Cataloging-in-Publication Data
Names: Matasović, Ranko, author.
Title: An areal typology of agreement systems /
Ranko Matasović, Univesity of Zagreb.
Description: Cambridge, UK; New York, NY: Cambridge University Press, 2018. |
Includes bibliographical references and index.
Identifiers: LCCN 2018000225 | ISBN 9781108420976 (hardback)
Subjects: LCSH: Grammar, Comparative and general – Agreement.
Classification: LCC P299.A35.M38 2018 | DDC 415–dc23
LC record available at https://lccn.loc.gov/2018000225

ISBN 978-1-108-42097-6 Hardback

Contents

Figures

Maps

Tables

Tables

Preface

Quid velit et possit rerum concordia discors?
(Horace, Epistles 1.12.19)

This book is the result of over a decade of investigation. It all began in 2004, when I wrote a monograph on gender in Proto-Indo-European (Matasović 2004), a synthetic treatment of the development of that category in one of the largest and best-studied language families in the world. One of the conclusions of that book was that gender, as a grammatical category, has an unexpected distribution in Eurasia, in that the languages and language families in the south and west of Eurasia are gendered, while those in the north and east are not. Moreover, gender agreement is mostly adnominal in Indo-European, while it is shown on verbs in all other gendered families of Eurasia. This led me to extend my investigations to other forms of adnominal agreement and to other linguistic areas. In a paper published in 2014 (Matasović 2014a) I argued that there was a fundamental areal–typological opposition between languages with adnominal agreement and those without it, and that languages with adnominal agreement generally also have verbal agreement, while the converse does not hold. However, the sample of languages on which the 2014 paper was based was too small and it was somewhat biased, as too many languages from Eurasia were included; moreover, the definition of verbal agreement used in that article was objectionable, as it was taken for granted that only languages with argument indices coded by affixes should be taken to instantiate verbal agreement. Clitics were disregarded, and the relationship between clitic and affixal agreement was not properly discussed. Therefore, a larger and more carefully constructed sample was needed, and several methodological problems had to be addressed. This book grew out of that effort.

I have reported on the progress of my work at several conferences, including "Syntax of the World's Languages V" organized by myself and my colleagues in Dubrovnik in 2012, as well as at "Syntax of the World's Languages VI" in Pavia in 2014. I would like to thank the participants of these conferences for their discussion of my papers, and especially to Tena Gnjatović, who helped me with the Pavia presentation. Part of the research carried out in preparation of this book was supported by the Alexander von Humboldt Foundation (Bonn), to which I am very grateful for helping me not only now, but at several points in my career.

I would like to thank Martin Haspelmath for being my host at the Max Planck Institute for Evolutionary Anthropology in 2015, where I used the magnificent resources of the Institute's library – probably the largest collection of grammars of "exotic" languages in the world. I am also grateful to Greville Corbett, whose work on gender and agreement provided a lot of theoretical framework for this book, and who offered me advice and help on several occasions. Robert D. Van Valin, Jr. and his colleagues from the Institute of Linguistics in Düsseldorf University invited me to present the first results of my investigations in December 2015 and I would like to sincerely thank them for the stimulating questions and discussion that followed my presentation. Some of the most difficult chapters of this book were written in the winter semester of 2015, while I was a visiting professor in Heidelberg University, and I doubt that I could have finished them were it not for the intellectually stimulating atmosphere and good academic resources of that university. I would also like to thank my research assistant, Jurica Polančec, who has kindly read the first draft of this book and suggested some corrections and improvements, as well as to Goran Pavelić for a number of corrections.

Finally, the greatest thanks of all go to my wife, Maja, and to my three sons, Mavro, Lujo and Fran. Writing good books matters, but living with good people while doing it matters more.

Abbreviations

Almost all the abbreviations for grammatical morphemes were taken from the sources in which the original examples quoted in the text appear. However, some regularization was made where there was absolutely no doubt of confusion, e.g. f. for feminine gender was consistently changed to fem. Leipzig glossing rules (www.eva.mpg.de/lingua/resources/glossing-rules.php) were used throughout the book, whenever our sources allowed it.

abl.	=	ablative
abs.	=	absolutive
acc.	=	accusative
adj.	=	adjectivizer
aff.	=	affirmative
all.	=	allative
a.obl.	=	associating oblique
art.	=	article
aux.	=	auxiliary
caus.	=	causative
cl.	=	noun class (gender)
comit.	=	comitative
cvb.	=	converb
dat.	=	dative
deic.	=	deictic
dem.	=	demonstrative
det.	=	determined
dir.	=	directional
du.	=	dual
erg.	=	ergative
evid.	=	evidential marker
excl.	=	exclusive
fem.	=	feminine
fut.	=	future

gen.	=	genitive
hon.	=	honorific
hum.	=	human
imp.	=	imperative
iness.	=	inessive
inf.	=	infinitive
ins.	=	instrumental
interr.	=	interrogative
intrans.	=	intransitive
ipf.	=	imperfective
irr.	=	irrealis
loc.	=	locative
local	=	local case
m.	=	masculine
m.abl.	=	modal ablative
nar.	=	narrative
nmsr.	=	nominalizer
nom.	=	nominative
obj.	=	object
obl.	=	oblique
part.	=	participle
pauc.	=	paucal
perf.	=	perfect
pf.	=	perfective
pl.	=	plural
poss.	=	possessive
pres.	=	present
pret.	=	preterite
pst.	=	past
ptc.	=	particle
real.	=	realis
refl.	=	reflexive
sg.	=	singular
subj.	=	subject
top.	=	topic
trans.	=	transitive
v.dat.	=	verbal dative

Part I

Theoretical Prerequisites

1   Introduction

1.1   The Topic of This Book

Languages differ in a vast number of features,[1] but linguistic diversity is unevenly distributed in space. This is the insight behind *areal typology*, the linguistic discipline that seeks to discover areal patterns in the distribution of linguistic features in the world's languages. Some asymmetries in the distribution of particular linguistic features are easily discovered, especially on small-scale levels. This can be done when an area of long-established language contact in which a set of features is present is contrasted with its surroundings in which that set is absent. For example, it has long been known that languages of Mainland Southeast Asia share a number of features, irrespective of the language family they belong to: Some are Sino-Tibetan (e.g. Burmese and Cantonese), some belong to the Austro-Asiatic family (e.g. Vietnamese and Khmer), and others to Tai-Kadai (e.g. Thai and Lao). The shared features include pitch accent, isolating structure, the presence of honorifics and the SVO order of syntactic constituents, and this clustering of features is explained by well-documented and long-lasting contacts between speakers of languages in that area. In a similar manner, we know that languages of the Balkans share a number of characteristics, including the lack of infinitive, the presence of the vowel "schwa" (ə), the syncretism of the genitive and dative cases, the postposed definite article and the analytical future tense construction (usually formed with the auxiliary verb meaning "to want" and the present (subjunctive) of the lexical verb). Historical grammars of individual Balkan languages (Albanian, Romanian, Greek, Bulgarian and Macedonian) explain how and even when such features spread in the area and show that they cannot be inherited from the common proto-language (Proto-Indo-European). All of this is the subject of *contact linguistics*, which seeks to explain how languages borrow

---

[1] In this book, we will use the term *feature* to refer to any characteristic of languages that, for whatever reason, a typologist may find relevant. The term is also used to refer to a special subset of morphosyntactic features, such as number, gender, case, singular, dual, masculine, feminine, etc. (Corbett 2012). For these features we will also use the terms *categories* and *subcategories*.

structural features in situations of intensive contact (see, e.g., Thomason and Kaufman 1988). However, we can also look at the distribution of individual linguistic features (or of clusters of features) from the global point of view. For example, we can ask how languages with pitch accent (or without infinitives, or with "schwa"...) are distributed over large areas where no historical contacts are documented. We can also try to determine whether the presence or absence of certain features in particular areas are correlated, and whether the presence (or absence) of individual features in an area predicts (or implies) the presence or absence of other features in that area. Of particular interest is determining whether the areal distribution of particular linguistic features is correlated with the distribution of languages belonging to certain language families, i.e., whether genetic factors play a role in the explanation of the attested distribution of features. Such investigations are the proper domain of areal typology.[2]

This book is about the areal distribution of various patterns of *agreement*, which is a type of grammatical rule that some languages have, while others lack it, and those languages that have it may have it in different domains and for different grammatical categories.[3] In the following chapters, we shall mostly limit ourselves to two syntactic domains of agreement: (1) the noun phrase (NP), in which modifiers agree with the head noun; for example, in English there is number agreement shown in the opposition between the NPs *this book* and *these books*; and (2) the clause, in which the verb usually agrees with one or more of its arguments; for example, in English the verb agrees with its subject in number and person, as shown in the opposition between *The man sings* and *We sing*. In the NP domain, we shall systematically investigate the areal distribution of agreement patterns for the categories of gender, number, case and (in possessive NPs) person. In the domain of the clause, we shall be looking at the areal distribution of agreement patterns for the categories of person, number and gender. Our conclusions will be drawn from a systematic investigation of a sample of 300 languages, constructed so as to be representative both genetically (by including languages from many different families) and areally (by including languages from many different parts of the world). However, examples will occasionally be presented from languages not in that sample, since some typologically relevant data were collected also from languages that could not be included in the sample in order not to make it areally or genetically biased.

---

[2] As Balthasar Bickel, who considers this type of enterprise as "twenty-first-century typology," succinctly put it (2007: 239): "Instead of asking 'what's possible?', more and more typologists ask 'what's where why?'. Asking 'what's where' targets universal preferences as much as geographical or genealogical skewings, and results in probabilistic theories stated over properly sampled distributions."

[3] For a definition of agreement used in this book see Chapter 2.

To the best of our knowledge, this is the first monograph devoted exclusively to this topic, which is not to say that it is the first attempt to answer the questions which it raises. Global asymmetries in the distribution of particular categories and patterns associated with agreement have long been noted in linguistic literature. Since the inception of linguistic typology as a discipline it has been known that isolating languages of Mainland Southeast Asia and parts of Western Africa have uninflected verbs and, consequently, no verbal agreement.[4] Gerlach Royen, in his 1030-page monograph on the nominal classification systems in the languages of the world (Royen 1929) noted that gender, as a category, has a very uneven distribution in the world's languages, that it is quite common in some parts of the world while being absent (or nearly so) in others. Unfortunately, Royen's work was largely neglected,[5] but after the Second World War, with the development of contact linguistics and the notion of language areas or *Sprachbünde*, patterns in the worldwide areal distribution of certain agreement features were noted, especially with respect to gender and person agreement; studies on large language areas include Emenau (1956) for the Indian Subcontinent, Campbell, Kaufman and Smith-Stark (1986) for Mesoamerica, and Sherzer (1973) for a number of areas in North America (especially for the languages of the Northwest Coast). In these works the presence or absence of specific agreement patterns plays a role in the definition of individual language areas.

By the late 1980s, most large linguistic areas had become recognized, as well as the global skewings in the distribution of many typologically prominent linguistic features (Dryer 1989). "It has become clear... that hardly any typological variable, and only some combinations thereof, is evenly distributed in the world" (Bickel 2007: 243). The time was ripe for a new synthesis of areal typology, and this came in the form of Johanna Nichols' award-winning book *Linguistic Diversity in Space and Time* (Nichols 1992). In that book, Nichols examined the distribution of many linguistic features among language areas and linguistic families, with the specific purpose of determining their areal and genetic stability. Among the surveyed features were, e.g., the presence of inclusive/exclusive opposition in pronouns, word order, the alienability contrast in possessive constructions, but also some grammatical categories, including

---

[4] Wilhelm von Humboldt, in a talk given to the Prussian Academy of Sciences in 1827 (reprinted in von Humboldt 1963), had already noted that the dual (as a subcategory of the category of number) has a limited distribution in the world's languages. Moreover, he was aware that in some languages (especially in the languages of Polynesia and the Philippines), the dual is expressed only in pronouns, in others it is found only in nouns (e.g. in Totonac), while only in some languages and areas it characterizes several parts of speech, thus participating in agreement (in this group he rightly included Indo-European and Semitic languages as well as Greenlandic).

[5] For a general history of nominal classification in languages of the world, see Kilarski 2013.

number and gender. Number oppositions and their neutralizations were examined without considering whether languages exhibit number agreement or not, but the distribution of gender agreement was very carefully investigated, and it was concluded that gender is one of the genetically most stable categories in language. That is, gender characterizes whole language families, and languages that belong to gendered families are unlikely to lose gender agreement, while those that belong to genderless families are unlikely to acquire it. This insight is, as we shall see further below, very important for our more general investigation into the areal distribution of agreement systems, and Nichols' findings are fully confirmed by our data.

The areal distribution of some of the features discussed by Nichols, although those features are not involved in agreement themselves, has a direct bearing on the areal distribution of agreement systems. For example, Nichols has shown that head-marking languages (those in which the head of a syntactic construction is morphologically marked rather than the dependent element) tend to cluster in areas she calls "hotbeds," and that they are unexpectedly more common in the New World (Australia, New Guinea, Oceania and the Americas) than in the Old World (Africa and Eurasia). On the clause level, head-marking languages do not have case, but rather indicate grammatical relations by cross-referencing on the verb. This means that case agreement cannot be found in head-marking languages because, trivially, there cannot be case agreement where there is no case. In a similar manner, modifiers of the noun (adjectives, demonstratives, numerals and articles) are dependent elements of the NP, while the noun is its head. In a head-marking language the modifiers of the noun will not agree with it in categories such as number and gender (although verbs may agree with one or more arguments on the clause level), so languages with extensive adnominal agreement will typically not be head-marking languages, and the areal distributions of the two types will greatly differ. Therefore, although agreement as a grammatical phenomenon was not in the focus of Nichols' investigation, her work contains many insights into the areal typology of agreement systems.

Considering that many patterns in the areal distribution of agreement systems were already noted in the literature, the question arises whether a monograph about areal typology of agreement is really necessary, or even useful. Why should one read a book on the areal typology of agreement written by a general typologist, when one can read about patterns of agreement in works written by specialists on various languages and families spoken in different parts of the world? Indeed, information about the distribution of individual categories involved in agreement, such as number, gender, person and (less often) case, can be found in several specialized monographs dealing with large, often continent-sized macro-areas. We can mention Adelaar (2004) for languages of the Andes (and some neighboring areas), Dixon and Aikhenvald (1999) for languages of the Amazon, Dixon (2002) for Australian languages, Crowley (1998) for languages of the Pacific, Welmers (1973), Gregersen (1977) and Heine and Nurse (2000) for African languages, Van Driem (2001) for languages of the Himalayas, Foley (1986) for Papuan languages, Mithun (1999) for languages of North America and Suárez (1983) for Mesoamerican languages. The series of monographs on the "languages of the Soviet Union" (e.g. Vinogradov 1967) is still very useful for the languages of Siberia and the Caucasus, and for the latter there are also monographs by Klimov (1986) and Hewitt (2004). Comrie (1981) covers all of the languages of the former Soviet Union. However, data from such sources is often difficult to use, since the categories involved in agreement are not defined consistently by different authors. For example, in some sources the term "gender" is reserved for languages in which nominal classification is based on sex-based oppositions, while in others it refers to any system of nominal classification which manifests itself in agreement. Likewise, in some sources (especially in the Africanist tradition, see Creissels 2006), morphemes that would otherwise be called person agreement markers are treated as independent pronouns, which makes it difficult to establish the distribution of languages with verbal person agreement using the same standards in all languages. To be able to tell whether a particular agreement pattern is common in a given area, one first has to make sure that the source one is consulting for the languages of that area uses the same definition of the relevant agreement pattern, and uses it consistently. However, that is very often not the case.

Surveys of areal distribution of individual agreement patterns are rare in the existing literature. Nevertheless, Hurskainen (2000) gives a useful overview of gender systems in African languages, and for gender systems in Eurasia there is a paper by Juha Janhunen (2000) and a chapter of my book on gender in Indo-European (Matasović 2004: 191–211). Michael Rießler's PhD thesis (2011, published in 2016) showed areal patterns in adjective attribution in the languages of Northern Eurasia. It basically confirmed that agreement in the NP is rare in that area and virtually limited to Indo-European languages. Balthasar Bickel and Johanna Nichols (2009) looked at the global distribution of various aspects of case systems, and one of the features they surveyed was case agreement, which they call "case spreading" (i.e. the spreading of case marking from the head noun to other elements of the NP). They did not find any areal biases in the distribution of languages with case agreement, "perhaps because the datasets for these variables are so small" (Bickel and Nichols 2009: 489; they examined only 63 languages). To the best of our knowledge, there are no areal–typological studies about the distribution of languages with number agreement in either the NP or the verb. This is perhaps surprising, since the last few decades have seen a growth of interest in the areal typology of languages, and the distribution of many linguistic features has been investigated and plotted on language maps.

With the publication of the "World Atlas of Linguistic Structures" (or WALS) in 2005 areal typology received a big boost as a linguistic discipline. Some of the maps in WALS bear directly on the questions we are dealing with in this book. Greville Corbett's Map 30A (Corbett 2013a) shows the distribution of languages with gender worldwide. It demonstrates that there are areas in which this category is rare (e.g. Northern Eurasia, the Andes, Southern Australia, etc.), as well as those where it is common (e.g. Southeast Eurasia, most of sub-Saharan Africa). However, it does not show the syntactic domains in which the represented languages have gender agreement (some have it in the NP, some on the verb, and some in both domains), and the same holds for the other maps dealing with gender (Maps 31A and 32A, see Corbett 2013b and Corbett 2013c). Map 29A "Syncretism in Verbal Person/Number Marking" by Matthew Baerman and Dunstan Brown (Baerman and Brown 2013) can be used to show the areal distribution of languages without person marking (these are common in Mainland Southeast Asia, parts of sub-Saharan Africa and Southern Australia), but only languages where the subject person is marked on the verb are included in the category of languages with verbal person marking. Languages in which the verb agrees with its object, but not its subject, although they are rare, were not recorded. Moreover, that map cannot be used to find languages that have verbal agreement in gender and number, but not in person. Map 58A (Bickel and Nichols 2013) shows the distribution of languages with obligatory possessive inflection, and while this map shows an indication of the distribution of languages with person agreement in the NP, the two sets cannot be equated, since not all the languages with obligatory possessive inflection have person agreement with the possessors (see our discussion in Section 4.6).

The maps contained in WALS do show us the distribution of languages that have case marking (e.g. Map 49A "Number of Cases," Iggesen 2013), but they do not show us the distribution of languages with case agreement, and those are, obviously, a subset of languages that have the category of case. There are also maps from which the reader can gather the distribution of languages with number marking in the NP, but not the distribution of languages with number agreement, and it is impossible to get the information on the areal distribution of languages in which number is marked on the verb (separately from person/gender). On the whole, the features surveyed in WALS are strictly defined so as to assure that identical phenomena are compared across languages, but theoretical approaches to different features may and often do differ: for example, morphological marking for some categories surveyed in WALS was limited to affixes, while for others it also included clitics. Finally, it must be mentioned that the sizes of the samples of languages used for different features differ dramatically. Thus, we know more about the distribution of languages with nominal plurality (Map 33A, "Coding of Nominal Plurality" (Dryer 2013), with 1066 languages) than about the distribution of languages in which the coding of nominal plurality is optional (Map 34A, "Occurrence of Nominal Plurality" (Haspelmath 2013b), with 291 languages). Therefore, although WALS is a major step in the development of areal typology as a discipline, the data contained in it cannot be directly used to answer the questions raised in this book.

Having seen that answers to questions we would like to ask cannot be found in the literature, it remains to be seen if those answers are interesting and deserve the effort of looking for them. This is what the rest of this book is dedicated to.

1.2   Outline of the Book

After a brief introduction to the topic of our investigation, let us present the outline of the remainder of this book by chapters.

Chapter 2 ("What Is Agreement?") starts with the general definition of agreement mostly found in textbooks and reference works ("systematic covariance between a semantic or formal property of one element and a formal property of another" [cf. Corbett 2006: 4; Wechsler 2015: 309]). After discussing this definition, we attempt to make it more operational for typological sampling, especially for determining whether a language has agreement or not, as well as for determining the typological parameters according to which languages with agreement differ.

Chapter 3 ("Domains of Agreement and Categories Involved") systematically discusses the syntactic domains in which agreement is found (chiefly the NP and the clause, although the instances of agreement within the domain of the sentence and the discourse are also briefly analyzed). It is argued that the most common agreement pattern within the domain of clause is verbal agreement (i.e. the pattern where verbs are targets of agreement), but several typologically unusual cases show that this is not the universal rule. There follows a discussion of grammatical categories involved in agreement, and we focus on the cross-linguistically most common patterns, including agreement in gender, number, person and case. Correlations between different agreement categories are also discussed, such as the universal claim that languages with gender agreement always have number agreement, and some counter-examples to such universals are presented.

Chapter 4 ("Problems with Agreement") deals with a number of phenomena that are sometimes not considered to instantiate agreement (case agreement and person agreement in possessive constructions), as well as with some constructions that are not universally accepted as agreement (constructions with omissible controllers and those with referential targets). This is important, as it is necessary to determine in advance which types of constructions will be counted as instantiating agreement for any areal typology to make sense. This can only be achieved if we make sure that strictly defined and identical phenomena are compared across languages.

Chapter 5 ("Grammatical, Ambiguous and Anaphoric Agreement") attempts to extend Siewierska's (1999, 2004) typology of verbal agreement (in person) to adnominal agreement as well. This is important, as we wanted to make sure that verbal and adnominal agreement are truly comparable phenomena. We argue that comparing types of agreement patterns in both domains (the clause for verbal, the NP for adnominal agreement) makes cross-linguistic sense only if we limit our investigation to ambiguous agreement, and this is generally done in the rest of the book. However, since grammatical verbal agreement is a well-defined notion, and it is clearly relevant in any discussion of the typology of agreement systems, we have decided to examine its areal distribution as well.

Chapter 6 ("Marginal Agreement") discusses instances where a language has only a few lexical items that show agreement in some particular domain. It is clear that, in a typological investigation that aims to show some general patterns in the distribution of agreement features, one needs to identify languages where a particular type of agreement is marginal (e.g. adnominal number agreement in Hungarian, which is limited to a couple of lexical items), and treat them differently from those in which agreement is a pervasive phenomenon, as in Italian, where nearly all adnominal modifiers agree in gender and number with the head noun. In our study, we tried to consistently identify marginal agreement patterns in all languages included in our sample, and to test whether the statistical generalizations we found depend on the inclusion or exclusion of such languages.

Chapter 7 ("The Sample of Languages") explains in some detail the principles that guided us in the selection of languages in the 300-language sample on which the present investigation is based. Since the aim of our study was to show that certain patterns of agreement were unexpectedly rare in some macro-areas, we wanted to make sure, first, that areas were defined independently, before the sample of languages was determined, and, secondly, that the language sample was representative, in the sense that every macro-area should contain a number of languages proportional to its overall linguistic diversity.

Chapter 8 ("Areal and Genetic Patterns in Agreement Systems") looks at the areal and genetic distribution of different agreement patterns. The chapter is subdivided into sections, and each section deals with the distribution of agreement patterns in one macro-area (Eurasia, Africa and the Middle East, North America, South America, Australia and Oceania). Each section is recapitulated by a table showing which language families in a particular macro-area can be characterized as either having or lacking a particular agreement pattern. The results presented in this chapter are not based just on the analysis of the 300 languages in our sample, but also on a comprehensive survey of the relevant typological and areal linguistic literature.

Chapter 9 ("Typological Correlations in Agreement Systems") applies statistical analyses to establish which agreement patterns are correlated, irrespective of the areas in which they are found. For example, we show that the rareness of languages with adnominal agreement without verbal agreement is statistically unexpected, and that languages with grammatical verbal agreement (i.e. where the controller of verbal agreement is obligatorily present in all clauses) regularly also have some adnominal agreement. On the other hand, we were unable to show any clear correlation between the presence or absence of agreement and word order patterns.

Chapter 10 ("Diachronic Patterns in the Development of Agreement") is, understandably, rather speculative, as the history of the majority of the world's languages remains unknown. However, we have attempted to offer a number of historical hypotheses that could explain why the geographical distribution of certain agreement patterns appears to be a priori unexpected. Since verbal agreement has been shown to be very common and evenly distributed among the world's languages, the crucial fact in need of an explanation is the distribution of languages with adnominal agreement, which is areally rather limited. We look at a number of well-documented or reasonably well-reconstructed cases, including Zande (a Ubangian language), Nilo-Saharan, Daly languages of North Australia, Proto-Indo-European, etc., and discuss the attested and probable paths in the development of adnominal agreement. It is argued that agreement often spreads from the clausal domain, where it is pragmatically motivated, to the domain of the NP, where it is largely redundant. However, adnominal agreement quite often also arises in situations of intensive language contact, e.g. in the case of Baltic Finnic languages which borrowed case agreement from neighboring Indo-European languages, or in the case of some Mande languages in West Africa, which borrowed number agreement from neighboring Gur languages. On the other hand, since all agreement patterns can be lost at any time, due to phonological erosion of agreement markers, or due to syntactic changes in a language, the rare language type with adnominal agreement and without verbal agreement is bound to develop occasionally and unpredictably.

Finally, Chapter 11 ("Conclusions") summarizes our results.

2   What Is Agreement?

The notion of *agreement*, or *concord*, as it also used to be called, is inherited from the grammar of classical languages. In their grammar of Latin, Gildersleeve and Lodge (1895: 148) say that Latin has "three great concords" and they specify the agreement patterns in Latin as follows: "1. The agreement of the predicate with the subject; 2. The agreement of attributive or appositive with the substantive; 3. The agreement of the relative with the antecedent." Then they go on to the first of these types of agreement, saying that "the verbal predicate agrees with its subject in number and person. The adjective predicate agrees with its subject in number, gender, and case. The substantive predicate agrees with its subject in case." Basically, what they do in defining agreement is that they first identify the *domains* of a syntactic process, or a syntactic rule, and then the *morphosyntactic features*, or *categories* involved in it. Syntactic domains are best seen as constituents in which certain syntactic rules apply (see, e.g., Van Valin and LaPolla 1997: 31ff.). In some languages (such as Latin) constituents need not be continuous, but they can still be identified by using standard syntactic tests such as permutation, substitution and coordination. Morphosyntactic categories, on the other hand, are usually defined as sets of word-forms having the same syntactic and/or semantic function.

Let us illustrate these notions with an example from Gildersleeve and Lodge's grammar (1895: 148):

(1) *Ego reg-es   eiec-i,   vos   tyrann-os   introduc-itis*
 I   king-ACC.PL throw.out-1SG.PF you(PL) tyrant-ACC.PL introduce-2PL.PRES
 'I threw out the kings, you are introducing tyrants' (Cicero, *Ad Herennium*, 4.53)

In (1), the verb *eieci* 'threw out' agrees with the subject of the first clause *ego* 'I' in number (singular) and person (1st person), while the verb *introducitis* 'introduce' agrees with the subject of the second clause *vos* 'you all' in the same categories. In another syntactic domain, the NP, Latin demonstratives and adjectives agree in number, gender and case with the head noun, which is illustrated in (2a–b):

(2a) *haec*   *puella*   *pulchra*
      this.NOM.SG.F   girl.NOM.SG   beautiful.NOM.SG.F
      'this beautiful girl'

(2b) *horum*   *virorum*   *bonorum*
      this.GEN.PL.M man.GEN.PL   good.GEN.PL.M
      'of these good men'

Both (2a) and (2b) contain NPs in which the head noun is modified with an adjective following and a demonstrative preceding it. In (2a), the demonstrative *haec* 'this' and the adjective *pulchra* 'beautiful' agree with the head noun *puella* in gender (feminine), number (singular) and case (nominative), while in (2b) the demonstrative *horum* 'these' and the adjective *bonorum* 'good' agree with the head noun *virorum* in the same categories (masculine, plural, genitive). We see, then, that Latin has agreement in at least two syntactic domains (the clause and the NP) and in at least four categories (number, gender, case and person).

Now, languages with agreement need not have any of the just-mentioned categories, or they may have any subset of them. Moreover, languages need not have agreement in the same domains as Latin, so their agreement patterns may be very unlike the ones we have just discussed. Therefore, clearly a more general definition of agreement is needed if we want to be able to compare this phenomenon across languages.

In contemporary linguistics, agreement is often defined as "systematic covariance between a semantic or formal property of one element and a formal property of another" (Corbett 2006: 4, cf. also Moravcsik 1978, 1988; Wechsler 2015: 309). This definition is basically in accordance with the one used in this book, but as it stands, it does not tell us what agreement actually is, and how it is related to other linguistic phenomena. Is "covariance" something agreement shares with other syntactic processes, and which? Moreover, which kinds of elements are involved in agreement – can they be syntactic, lexical, or both? Hence, the operational definition of agreement used in this book will need to be somewhat more specific.

We see agreement as a type of grammatical rule that a language may, but need not, have. It is a rule that says, basically, that the presence of the feature A (out of a limited number of features) on the lexical unit X (the *controller*) requires the presence of A on the lexical unit Y (the *target*), within a syntactic domain D.[1] The units X and Y can, in principle, belong to any lexical

---

[1] This does not necessarily mean that we are taking a "feature-copying" approach to agreement, which is burdened with theoretical problems, including mismatches in features between controllers and targets; for a different, "unification-based" approach to agreement see, e.g., Barlow

class that the language in question distinguishes (e.g. nouns, verbs, adjectives and articles). The feature A can, in principle, be any grammatical category the language has (e.g. number, person, case, tense), and D can be any well-defined syntactic domain (e.g. NP, clause, sentence). It is a matter of empirical investigation to determine which categories are actually attested in agreement, and in which syntactic domains it applies cross-linguistically. This cannot be simply posited a priori. If required, our definition of agreement can be stated more formally:

> *The target Y agrees with the controller X in the syntactic domain D if and only if the presence of the feature A on X triggers the presence of A on Y if both X and Y are in the domain D.*

Agreement should be distinguished from *government*, which is a different kind of rule. An element X (*governor*), which may in principle be any lexical unit, governs a lexical or syntactic unit Y (*governee*), if the mere presence of X triggers a particular choice of a feature on Y (the feature that the governor itself lacks). Hence we say that the preposition *ad* 'to' in Latin governs the following NP, which has to take the accusative case (e.g. *ad hominem* 'to the man', where *hominem* 'man' is in the accusative singular), or that the Latin verb *medeor* 'to heal' governs its oblique argument, which has to be in the dative case (*medeor tibi* "I heal you," where *tibi* 'you (sg.)' is in the dative). Neither the verb *medeor* nor the preposition *ad* are specified for case, but they assign case to the nouns they govern. On the other hand, the demonstrative *illa* 'that' and the adjective *pulchra* 'beautiful' agree in case (and number and gender) with the noun *puella* 'girl' in the NP *illa puella pulchra* 'that beautiful girl'. All of the words in the NP share the features they agree in, and the agreeing words (the targets) all have more than one form to agree with the controller: The demonstrative pronoun also has the neuter form *illud* and the masculine form *ille*, and the adjective has the neuter form *pulchrum* and the masculine *pulcher*. If a masculine noun is selected as the head of the NP, a different form of the agreeing modifiers has to be selected as well, and 'that beautiful man' would be rendered as *ille vir pulcher*. This means that nominal heads of NPs can have different features (genders, numbers and cases) and their modifiers have to share those features with their heads. In contrast to that, prepositions which govern nouns in prepositional phrases do not have different features which the governed nouns have to share. Likewise, verbs governing their objects do not have the feature they assign to their governees (although they may have different features irrelevant for government, such as person, number, tense, and others).

(1992) and Corbett (1997). As we will show below, our definition allows the controllers to be underspecified for certain features assigned to targets.

There is no principled reason why both agreement and government should not be subsumed under a single concept, since from our definition above it follows that the difference between the two types of grammatical rules lies in the difference between controllers (which distinguish features in which they agree with the targets) and governors (which do not distinguish features assigned to their governees). Government is, in this respect, a special type of agreement, in which the controller assigns only one feature to the target, but lacks the feature itself.[2]

However, distinguishing agreement and government still makes sense because it allows us to make empirical generalizations, claims that hold for languages that have one type of grammatical rule but lack the other. Thus, while all languages with grammatical case systems can be said to have some form of government, this does not mean that such languages have agreement. In a language such as Turkish, we have government within the NP (3), but no agreement, as there is no gender, and case and number suffixes are added only to the last element of the NP, which is the head noun (3–4):

(3) *o*   *zaman-a kadar*
     that   time-DAT until
     'until that time'

(4) *bu büyük ev-ler-de*
     this big house-PL-LOC
     'in these big houses'

In (3), the postposition *kadar* 'until' governs the dative case of the noun phrase *o zaman* 'that time' (with a different postposition, e.g. *sonra* 'after', the noun in the governed NP would have to be in a different case, the ablative). In (4), the head noun *ev* is in the locative plural, but the modifiers *bu* 'this' and *büyük* 'big' do not bear any case or number marking. A choice of a different head, say *at* 'horse' or *kadın* 'woman' would not trigger any change in the modifiers either: 'in these big horses' would be *bu büyük at-lar-da* (the suffixes for the plural and the locative case are *-lar-* and *-da-*, respectively, because of the vowel harmony).

In contrast to Turkish, a caseless language in which all elements of the NP show gender/number distinctions, such as Swahili (5), can be said to have agreement but lack government:

---

[2] Evans (2003b) also challenges the notion that government and agreement are fundamentally different and discusses a number of constructions from Kayardild (an Australian language of the Tangkic family) with features of both. Note that government and agreement are treated as essentially the same phenomenon in at least some approaches to minimalist syntax (see, e.g., Chomsky 2000; Polinsky 2003).

(5) *kwa kisu*
    with knife
    'with a knife'

(6) *m-tu   m-kubwa m-moja*
    SG-person CL.1-one CL.1-big
    'one big person'

In (5), the preposition *kwa* 'with' does not require its dependent noun, the noun *kisu*, to be in any particular form, and the choice of a different preposition, or prepositional phrase (say *mbele ya* 'in front of'), would not involve a change of the form of the noun. In (6), the modifiers *-kubwa* 'one' and *-moja* 'big' get gender/number prefixes to agree with the head noun *-tu* 'person' (which also bears the gender/number prefix *m-*).

At this point the reader should note that our definition of agreement is stated in terms of sufficient and necessary conditions, which some linguists may find objectionable. This is because there certainly exist more and less canonical, or prototypical instances of agreement (see, e.g., Corbett 2006; Brown and Chumakina 2013 and Chapter 6), and the more canonical instances do not necessarily have all the properties of the less canonical ones. For example, the Swahili type of gender agreement, in which all verbs agree in gender with their subject, is more canonical than the system found in Chechen, where only some 30 percent of verbs agree in gender with the absolutive argument, or in Khwarshi, where only verbs beginning with a vowel agree in gender (Khalilova 2009: 42–3):

(7) *B-eč-un-ło*   *bercina-b*   *kandaba*
    HUM.PL-be-PRET-NAR   beautiful–HUM.PL   girl.PL.ABS
    '(Once) there were three beautiful girls'

(8) *Miłʲ łʲo*   *b-ołoťo*   *heⁿše*   *gul-o*
    2PL.GEN2   III-middle   book   put-IMP
    'Put the book between you'

In (7), the verb agrees with its subject (*kandaba*) in gender and number, but in (8) the verb begins in a consonant, and shows no agreement. Canonical types are not necessarily more common in languages of the world than less canonical ones. Rather, they are a practical tool defined by the analyst in order to compare similar phenomena across different languages. Thus, Corbett (2006) explicitly lists the criteria for distinguishing between more and less canonical types of agreement, which helps him draw a fuller picture of the actually attested diversity of agreement systems.[3] To state but a few of those criteria, agreement patterns

---

[3] The consequence of the canonical approach is that it tends to blend agreement with other similar grammatical phenomena, such as systems of nominal classifiers, which may be viewed

in which controllers are present are more canonical than those in which controllers are absent, those in which controllers have overt expression of agreement
features are more canonical than those in which the expression of agreement features is covert, obligatory agreement is more canonical than optional agreement,
etc. (for a discussion of some of these concepts, see Chapter 4).

We believe that this approach is laudable for its empirical adequacy, but that
it runs the risk of missing a number of important empirical generalizations
about agreement systems. If we are seeking to discover whether a particular
agreement pattern P is correlated with some other phenomenon in a language
L, we want to be able to say unambiguously whether L has P or not, rather
than that in L, the agreement pattern P is less canonical than the pattern R in
the language X, but more canonical than the pattern Q in language Y. In a book
that explicitly seeks to capture empirical generalizations about areal distribution of particular types of agreement systems, taking the canonical approach
to agreement is not really an option. Adopting it would not allow us to decide
whether to treat more and less canonical types of agreement in the same manner, and how to quantify the "canonicity" of particular types in order to be able
to do statistical analysis of the data.

A comparison with the methods in another field of research might help us
in explaining why, while not criticizing the canonical approach as a method
in language typology, we do not see it as applicable to our project. Suppose
an anthropologist wanted to show that blond hair is much more common in
northern Europe than in other parts of Eurasia. In order to do that, he or she
would need to be able to classify each person's hair as either blond or not
blond, disregarding the fact that "blondness" is actually a scalar phenomenon,
i.e. that people's hair can be either light blond or dark blond, or anywhere in
between the two polar points on the scale.[4] One can say that people's hair tends
to be more blond as one moves to the north of Europe, or that "canonical"
blondes are more common there, and such statements are true, but impression-
istically vague. Surely, if "blondness" were not such a common and visible
feature of individuals, stating the argument in these terms would fail to per-
suade anyone that the observation has been empirically tested, or that it is even
testable. It is much more objective and precise to say that over 80 percent of
people are blond in parts of Sweden, while under 20 percent are blond in most
of Italy,[5] although one runs the risk that the hair of some people who were

as very non-canonical agreement systems (Fedden and Corbett 2017). Thus, when taking the
canonical approach it is difficult, or even inappropriate to classify languages into those that
have or do not have agreement. Rather, languages must, somewhat subjectively, be evaluated as
having more or less canonical agreement patterns.

[4] Actually, physical anthropologists use the so-called "Fischer-Saller" scale in determining the
shades of hair color. The designations from A to O may be called "blond."

[5] Data are taken from http://bigthink.com/strange-maps/214-the-blonde-map-of-europe
(accessed June 13, 2017).

classified as blond in Sweden is actually chatain or light brown, while some of the red-haired people in Italy could have been classified as blondes. While some subjectivity cannot be excluded, using the categorical rather than scalar classification allows us to make testable empirical generalizations, and the same goes for language typology as applied to agreement systems, whereby the areal distribution of linguistic types is not as commonly known as the distribution of hair-color types in Europe. We might make a few mistakes in classifying certain languages as having or lacking agreement, but if a sufficiently large sample is used those mistakes will cancel each other or be negligible, and we will be able to show statistical patterns of areal distribution, if they exist.

To go one step further with this analogy, one may say that "blondness" is an epiphenomenon caused by the presence of a particular variant of the hair-color gene (MC1R), and that the "real" question for an anthropologist is not how blondness is distributed among the peoples in Eurasia, but how different variants of the hair-color gene – each of which has been identified by geneticists – are distributed in the populations of Eurasia. The same could be said about agreement in linguistic typology: that it is not a notion that can be defined objectively and cross-linguistically, and that we rather need to look at the areal distribution of individual constructions that are traditionally subsumed under the notion of agreement, e.g. obligatory co-occurrence of personal pronouns with non-referring subject and object affixes on verbs, or obligatory repetition of information expressing different types of quantification in the NP.[6] Indeed, this approach may be correct, but it is probably premature in linguistics: We still do not know what the true "genes" of language are and how large-scale notions such as agreement should be decomposed. Moreover, even if we could be sure about the true linguistic elements determining the syntactic patterns that are traditionally called "agreement," we would still face the problem of data availability: Descriptive grammars are seldom exhaustive enough to offer answers to all the questions about the presence or absence of each construction or element chosen in this manner. We could, in principle, construct matrices with the selected features for a small number of well-described languages, but not for a sample large enough to be representative of the world's languages. Therefore, for the time being, linguistic typology must be prepared to strike a balance between empirical adequacy, theoretical precision and availability of data.

It is for these reasons that our definition of agreement is formulated in terms of sufficient and necessary conditions. It is assumed in this book that a language either has or does not have syntactic patterns that can be subsumed under the notion of agreement.

---

[6] This would be in line with Balthasar Bickel's approach to typology (2007) in which one compares only specific constructions and features across languages, rather than large-scale notions such as agreement.

However, the question can still be raised whether our definition of agreement is too broad and whether it includes a range of essentially different phenomena. As it stands, our definition is formulated in a way that also includes the following syntactic patterns, which are often seen as problematic in theories of agreement (see Chapter 4):

a. agreement in person/number (in some languages also gender) in languages where arguments of the verb can be omitted (but their reference can be retrieved from the context), as in the Italian example (9), in which the 1st plural subject pronoun (*noi*) need not be expressed:

(9) *Vogli-amo   partire*
     want-1PL.PRES   to.leave
     'We want to leave'

b. agreement in person/number(/gender) in languages in which person/number(/gender) markers on verbs are referential, i.e. where they are arguments of verbs rather than just morphemes that agree in the formal feature of person/number(/gender) with the independent NPs that are the arguments[7]

c. case agreement in the NP (as in the Latin examples (2a–b) above)

d. person(/number) agreement in the NP (in possessive phrases where the possessive affix or clitic on the head noun agrees with the possessor NP), as in Kabardian (NW Caucasian) example (10), where the possessed noun *-gᵂ* 'heart' must agree in person/number with the 1st person singular possessor *sa* 'I':

(10) *sa sə-gᵂ*
      I 1SG.POSS-heart
      'My heart'

In Chapter 4 we will look at all of these phenomena in turn, but before that we must clarify two other elements of our definition: Where (in which domains) does agreement take place and which features are involved in this phenomenon.

---

[7] Of course, what is "referential" is also subject to some controversy. Demonstrative and personal pronouns are always referential in the sense that they refer to concrete, individual objects, and in many languages argument indices/agreement markers on verbs need not be referential in that sense, because they can represent generic and indefinite objects, which true pronouns generally do not refer to (see below on Bininj Gun-wok).

3 Domains of Agreement and Categories Involved

3.1 Domains

We have defined domains (at the beginning of Chapter 2) as constituents in which grammatical rules apply. In order to be able to identify various domains across languages, and without committing to any particular syntactic theory, we will distinguish the following domains: (1) the noun phrase (NP),[1] consisting of the referring expression and its modifiers; (2) the clause, consisting of the predicating element (usually the verb) and its arguments, as well as verbal modifiers (usually adverbial expressions); (3) the sentence, consisting of one or several clauses. In most syntactic theories a more fine-grained catalog of domains is usually proposed,[2] but adopting any such proposal would make large-scale typological comparison of languages more difficult, since descriptive grammars are written in very different theoretical frameworks.

As already mentioned in Chapter 1, the two chief domains of agreement are the NP and the clause. In both domains, agreement takes place between the head and its dependents. The head is the element which determines the type of construction in question (Zwicky 1985). In the NP, the nominal head is the controller, whereas in the clause, the controller is one of the arguments of the verb, and the verb is the head of the clause. Thus, we see that the clause and the NP are not wholly symmetrical, since the relationships between the head of the respective syntactic domain and the controller and agreement are different (Table 1).

With respect to the domains of agreement, we can distinguish two types of agreement. In the clause, *verbal agreement* is the pattern in which the verb

---

[1] Since the noun does not have to be the referring expression (pronouns and other elements can head NPs as well), it has been proposed that the term NP be replaced with RP or *referential phrase* (Van Valin 2008). Although this is, indeed, a reasonable proposal, we shall stick to the traditional terminology and use the abbreviation NP.

[2] For example, Role and Reference Grammar (Van Valin 2005) assumes that the clause has a layered structure consisting of the *nucleus* (the predicating element), the *core* (including the nucleus and its arguments), the non-argument NPs, various modifiers of the core and the so-called *pre-core slot* (or *postcore slot* in some languages), usually reserved for fronted question words.

Table 1 *Asymmetries in agreement domains*

	Controller of agreement	Head of the domain
NP	Noun (= Head)	Noun
Clause	Argument (≠ Head)	Verb

is – under syntactically or phonologically specifiable conditions – obligatorily modified by a morpheme (affix or clitic) expressing the agreeing category. The most common agreeing categories in verbal agreement are person, number and gender, although other categories are also attested. *Adnominal agreement* is the pattern in which all or some adnominal modifiers within the NP are – under syntactically or phonologically specifiable conditions – obligatorily modified by a dependent morpheme (affix or clitic) expressing the agreeing category. The most common categories in this agreement pattern are gender, number and case,[3] though others are also attested. The definitions of different agreement patterns presented here are deliberately general and theory-neutral, because only such definitions make it possible to compare agreement phenomena across languages, while using data from sources often written in different theoretical frameworks.

Together, verbal and adnominal agreement represent the two main types of agreement domains cross-linguistically: Since the verb is the head of the clause, verbal agreement is for practical purposes equivalent to agreement in the domain of the clause, while adnominal agreement represents agreement in the domain of the NP (Corbett 2006: 40–1). In this book we will mostly disregard other domains of agreement and focus on the NP and the clause, but this is not to deny that sentences and even stretches of discourses can be domains of agreement, and that the correlation between verbal and adnominal agreement with the clause and the NP, respectively, is not perfect. A few examples will have to suffice to illustrate this claim.

One interesting pattern of agreement that can be considered neither adnominal nor verbal is found in Coahuilteco (or Pajalate), an extinct language

[3] Throughout this book, we will be using the terms "person," "gender," "case" and "number" in the same sense as in the standard functional-typological handbooks (e.g. Siewierska 2004 for person, Corbett 1991 for gender, Blake 1994 for case, Corbett 2000 for number). This means that we will not distinguish between "gender" and "noun classes" (the latter term is often used to refer to gender in some language families, such as Niger-Kordofanian and Northeast Caucasian, see, e.g., Topuria 1994). Also, on this general level, we will not distinguish between "person agreement markers," "person indexes," and "incorporated pronouns" (but see below about the different types of person agreement). Finally, note that languages can have the grammatical categories of person, case and number without having agreement in these categories, if they are expressed by independent words rather than morphologically (gender is intentionally not mentioned here, as this category necessarily involves agreement, see Section 3.2.3).

isolate that was spoken in Texas (see Troike 1981, 1996; Mithun 1999). In that language, objects apparently agree with subjects in person. In Coahuilteco the grammatical object takes the ending *-n* if the subject of the clause is in the 1st person, *-m* if it is in the 2nd person, and *-x* or *-t* if the subject is in the 3rd person. Thus, the choice of the object marker depends on the person of the subject of the clause. It is as if there were three endings for the accusative, and their use depended on the person of the subject. This unusual agreement pattern is illustrated in (11) and (12):

(11)   *Dios tupo-n*   *naxo-xt'e:wal wako*
      god ART-ACC.1SG.SUBJ   1SG.SUBJ-offend CAUS
      'I offended God'

but:

(12)   *Dios tupo-m*   *xa-ka:wa*   *xo*   *e?*
      god ART-ACC.2SG.SUBJ   2SG.SUBJ-love   AUX   INTERR
      'Do you love God?'

In both examples the phrase *Dios tupo* 'god' is in the accusative, but the endings are different because the person of the subjects (as expressed in the verb) differs. The domain of this agreement pattern is clearly the clause, but we would not call it verbal agreement, since it takes place between arguments, and the verb is not the target of agreement. As the agreeing category is person, we have to say that the object of the verb agrees with the subject in person. Thus, while verbal agreement usually has the clause as its domain (but see below), Coahuilteco shows us that there are agreement patterns within the clause that cannot be called "verbal agreement." This curious agreement system appears to be unique on first sight, but, as with other similar typological rarities, it deserves to be mentioned in a comprehensive study of agreement systems and their areal distribution.

Instances of arguments agreeing with each other do occur elsewhere: The Italian dialect of Ripatransone (Lüdtke 1974) is reported as having gender agreement between subject and object of the clause, e.g. *l-u fra'ki ča 'fam-u* 'the boy is hungry' (lit. 'the boy has hunger', where *fam-u* 'hunger' agrees with the masculine subject *l-u fra'ki* 'the boy') vs. *l-e fra'kine ča 'fam-e* 'the girl is hungry', where *fam-e* 'hunger' agrees with the feminine subject *l-e fra'kine* 'the girl'. From Lüdtke's discussion it is not clear whether this pattern of agreement applies across the verbal lexicon, or whether the number of verbs that show it is limited, but the examples he presents have to be interpreted as exhibiting agreement in gender between the arguments of the verb. As in Coahuilteco, the domain of agreement is the clause, but the pattern cannot be called verbal agreement.

A somewhat similar system, in which arguments agree in gender with other arguments of the verb, is found in Archi (Corbett 1991: 114–15, 2006: 67) and in some other NE Caucasian languages.[4] In Tsakhur, a focused dative argument agrees with the absolutive argument of the verb in gender (Ibragimov 1990: 72):

(13) *duxajs-yd* *mašin* *ališšu*
   for.son-also.CL.2 car he.bought(CL.2)
   'He bought a car also for the son'

(14) *duxajs-yb* *parče* *aliwšu*
   for.son-also.CL.1 cloth he.bought(CL.1)
   'He bought cloth also for the son'

In the examples above, not only does the verb (*ališšu* viz. *aliwšu* 'buy') agree with the absolutive argument (*mašin* 'car' in (13), *parče* 'cloth' in (14)), but the oblique argument (*duxajs* 'son') also agrees with the absolutive argument, provided it is focused with the suffix glossed as 'also' (-*yd* for gender 2, agreeing with *mašin* 'car', -*yb* for gender 1, agreeing with *parče* 'cloth').

In all of the preceding examples, the domain of agreement is the clause, although agreement is not between the verb and its arguments but rather between different arguments of the verb. However, elements that are structurally not in the clause, but rather in the sentence, can also agree with the verb's arguments. For example, in Mosetén (a Mosetenan language spoken in Bolivia) interrogative particles have different masculine (*ika?*) and feminine forms (*öka?*) and agree with the topic of the clause (Sakel 2002: 348):[5]

(15) *Tyi-ra?* *ö-ka?* *mö?* *ti?-i-?*
   person-IRR FEM-INTERR 3.FEM.SG name-STEM.MARKER-FEM.SG
   'What was her name?'

In Archi, a NE Caucasian language, some adverbs (around 18 percent of them) agree with the absolutive argument of the verb in gender and number. For those adverbs that are clearly modifiers of the verb (e.g. 'quickly', 'freely'), this is not a problem, because they are structurally within the clause, and, syntactically,

---

[4] See Haspelmath (1999: 133) for a similar agreement pattern in Lak. Lak, Tsakhur and Archi all belong to the Daghestanian branch of NE Caucasian, but they are not very closely related, so their unusual agreement patterns might be the results of independent development.

[5] The data provided by Sakel (2002) leave some place for doubting whether the interrogative particle *-ka?* has scope over the whole sentence (in which case the domain of agreement is the sentence), or only over the clause (in which case the domain of agreement is the clause).

they are always placed next to the verb (Bond et al. 2016: 70–1). However, there are a few sentence adverbs (modifying the whole sentence, rather than just the verb) that also agree in gender and number with the absolutive argument of the verb, e.g. *no:sut'u* 'a long time ago' and *horo:keij-u* 'a very long time ago'. In (16), the adverb *horo:keij<t'>u* agrees in gender 4 with the absolutive argument *č'at* 'word' (Bond et al. 2016: 71):

(16)   *godo-r*   *laha-n*   ***ummi***   *ez*
       that-CL.2.SG child(2).SG.OBL-GEN father(2).SG.ERG [CL.4]1SG.DAT

       horo:keij<t'>u   *č'at*   *kło-li*   *edi*
       long.time.ago<CL.4.SG> word(4)[SG.ABS] [4.SG]give.PF-CVB [4.SG]be.PST
       'The father of that girl gave me his word a very long time ago'

From such examples it appears that in Archi the domain of gender/number agreement can be not only the clause but the sentence as well.

The final agreement pattern to be mentioned here is called "long-distance agreement." In this pattern, which is observed chiefly in NE Caucasian languages (see Haspelmath 1999 on Godoberi, Polinsky and Potsdam 2001 on Tsez), as well as in some Algonquian languages (e.g. in Passamaquoddy, see Polinsky 2003), the verb in the main clause can agree with one of the arguments of the verb in the complement clause. Here is an example from Tsez (Corbett 2006: 66):

(17)   *eni-r*   *[už-ā*   *magalu*   *b-āc'-ru-łi]*
       mother(CL.2)-DAT boy(CL.1)-ERG bread(CL.3.ABS) CL.3-eat-PART-NOMINALIZER(ABS)

       b-iy-xo
       CL.3-know-PRES
       'The mother knows that the boy ate the bread'

In (17), the matrix verb *biyxo* 'knows' shows gender 3 agreement and thus agrees with *magalu* 'bread', which is within the complement clause. This pattern of agreement can certainly be called "verbal," as it is shown on the verb. Polinsky (2003) uses several arguments to show conclusively that the controller and the target are in different clauses in such constructions in Tsez. For example, both verbs can be negated separately (i.e. one can say both "The mother knows that the boy did not eat the bread" and "The mother does not know that the boy ate the bread" by using the same construction as in (17)); moreover, the position of the verb (*biyxo*) is not fixed with respect to its complement, and both features are indicative of a bi-clausal, rather than a monoclausal, structure. Therefore, it appears reasonable to conclude that the domain of agreement in such constructions is larger than the clause, i.e. that it is the sentence.[6] However, languages like Tsez, in which such long-distance agreement exists, appear to be rare: Polinsky (2003: 301) claims that, apart from NE Caucasian and Algonquian, this phenomenon might be attested only in some Austronesian languages (e.g. Fijian, Samoan) and possibly in Hindi. Consequently, the generalization that verbal agreement chiefly occurs within the clause remains valid, and long-distance agreement will be largely ignored in the rest of this book.

3.2   Categories

The number of grammatical categories a language may have is much larger than the number of syntactic domains in which syntactic processes occur and, a priori, any category might be involved in agreement in just about any domain. We could imagine a language in which numerals modifying the subject of the clause agree in aspect, or evidentiality, with the verb, and a language in which nominal heads of NPs agree in grade (positive, comparative and superlative) with the modifying adjectives, but such languages have not been discovered. The actual number of categories involved in agreement systems in attested languages is rather limited, and this section will give an overview of those categories.

Person, number and gender are the categories most commonly involved in agreement. Together, these are usually called *Phi-features*. We mentioned earlier that it is also possible to consider case as a category involved in agreement (within the NP), although it is also consistent to consider case as always instantiating government, whereby case is assigned independently to all the elements of the NP by the governor (a verb or an adposition). The decision essentially depends on the theoretical stance of the analyst (see Section 4.5).

3.2.1   Number and Gender Agreement in the NP

When it comes to number and gender agreement in the NP, these categories are rarely independent, in two senses.

Firstly, a language that has gender agreement in the NP almost always has number agreement.[7] In our 300-languages sample, the following languages have gender, but lack number agreement: Baure, Gaagudju, Dyirbal, Khasi,

---

[6] There is a way around that conclusion, if one adopts, as Polinsky (2003) does, a somewhat different conception of agreement within the Minimalist framework. However, this is a question for syntactic theoreticians rather than for typologists.

[7] This claim is more restricted than the universal no. 179 in the University of Konstanz's universals archive (see UnivArch no.179): "If a target agrees in gender, then it also agrees in number." Likewise, our formulation is similar, but not identical, to Greenberg's Universal no. 36, stating that if a language has the category of gender, it always also has the category of number.

Kwaza and Warekena (Mocovi has obligatory gender and optional number agreement in the NP). This number has to be considered against the fact that 114 languages in the sample have number agreement (in the NP), and 126 have gender agreement. Therefore, although we have found exceptions, their rareness is certainly unexpected a priori and has to be taken into account in any typological and areal investigation. This rare pattern is exemplified by Gaagudju (an extinct Aboriginal language, Harvey 2002: 292):

(18)   *na*   *ya-gaama-y=mba*   *magaarrra=mba*   *njinggooduwa*
       what   CL.3.CL.1-do-PRES=PL   that.CL.1=PL   woman
       'What are those women doing?'

In (18), in the NP *magaarrra=mba njinggooduwa* 'those women', only the demonstrative is marked with the plural clitic, while the head noun remains unmarked. Hence, there is no number agreement, but the demonstrative agrees in gender 1 with the noun.

Secondly, morphemes expressing number and gender agreement are quite often fused; the situation where these two categories are expressed by different agreeing morphemes is much less common (Renault 1987). Tamashek (Berber branch of Afro-Asiatic) has separate number and gender morphemes in some constructions (Heath 2005), and Gaagudju, as we saw above, has different number and gender markers in the NP, but only gender agreement (number is marked only on one word in the NP).

It has been claimed (Plank 1994 and UnivArch no. 119) that the most common combinations of agreement patterns in the NP are gender and number and number and person (in possessive agreement); the first pattern is attested, e.g. in Swahili (Niger-Kordofanian), and the second one in Navajo (Athabaskan-Eyak). Further, it has been stated that agreement in number and case is rarer, but still attested (e.g. in Finnish), and that the only other possibility is agreement in gender and case (e.g. in Dyirbal, a Pama-Nyungan language). This would mean that there are no languages showing agreement in gender and person, but this claim is problematic. Exactly this pattern of agreement appears to be found in some Khoisan languages, such as Nama (Vossen 2012: 326). In that language, a noun must be marked with a "person-gender-number marker," which can be said to agree with the noun in gender and person (since the number is unexpressed on the noun itself, there is no number agreement). This is illustrated in (19a–b):

(19a)   *tara-s* woman-3SG.FEM 'woman'

(19b)   *tara-ta* woman-1SG.FEM) 'I a/the woman'

It is somewhat awkward to say that "person-gender-number" markers -*s* and -*ta* agree with the noun they are attached to, since they are not independent words,

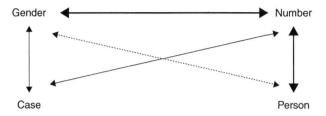

Figure 1 Combinations of categories involved in adnominal agreement

but suffixes. However, if we acknowledge this as an instance of agreement, then it represents a rare instance of agreement in gender and person in the NP (this will be discussed further in Section 4.4). In any case, it remains probable that different combinations of agreeing categories are not equally common, and their relative frequencies are represented in Figure 1.

From Figure 1 we can also infer the universal claim that was made by Lapointe (1988), to the effect that no target can agree in case and person simultaneously (see also UnivArch no. 52). This is a consequence of the different mechanisms involved in these two patterns of agreement: In the NP, the head nouns may agree in person (in possessive phrases), while case agreement is always found on modifiers, which agree with the head noun *per definitionem*. We could logically conceive of a language in which modifiers would have to agree with the head nominal (a noun or a pronoun) in person (as in the above-mentioned examples from Nama), while also agreeing in case, but there are no such languages in our sample and we have no indication that they exist.[8]

3.2.2   Categories in Verbal Agreement

As for verbal agreement, it can also be stated that gender and number are rarely independent. Greenberg's Universal 32 states that if the verb agrees in gender, it also agrees in number (cf. also UnivArch no. 509), but there are counter-examples, e.g. Andi (Corbett 1991: 198ff.), some Arawak and Jê languages in South America, as well as several Ndu languages in New Guinea.

In a similar manner, person and number are rarely independent in verbal agreement. If a language has verbal agreement in number, it usually also has verbal agreement in person, and vice versa:[9] the only languages in our

---

[8] Frans Plank (1991 and UnivArch no. 50) adduces Nenets (Samoyedic branch of Uralic) as a counter-example, claiming that in that language, in possessive NPs, there is agreement in person/number, and that modifiers can also agree in case with the head noun. He relies on personal communication by Irina Nikolaeva for this claim, but from our sources it appears that in Nenets case agreement in the NP is optional at best (Almazova 1961; Salminen 2012).

[9] These universals were also proposed by Frans Plank (UnivArch no. 1054, 1055). Plank notes that there are exceptions, e.g. Archi (NE Caucasian), Hopi (Uto-Aztecan) and Nivkh (isolate)

sample with person, but not number agreement on verbs are Panare (Cariban), Dime (South Omotic branch of Afro-Asiatic), Ma'di (Central Sudanic branch of Nilo-Saharan) and Bengali (Indo-Aryan branch of Indo-European); there are also a few languages with number, but without person agreement on the verb (Eastern Pomo, Warao and Makalero and !Kung in our sample). In some languages, there is marginal number agreement on verbs, e.g. in Eastern Pomo (Pomoan) and in !Kung (Northern Khoisan, Snyman 1970: 24–6), where only a few irregular transitive verbs agree in number with their objects (20a–b), while regular verbs do not show agreement (21a–b):

(20a)   *Mi gu n!ao*
         I take bow
         'I take the bow'

(20b)   *Mi   nl'hwi   n!aosi*
         I   take.PL   bows
         'I take the bows'

(21a)   *Dz'heu !xom da'ama*
         woman dress child
         'The woman dresses the child'

(21b)   *Dz'heu !xom de'ebi*
         woman dress children
         'The woman dresses the children'

Note that the verb *nl'hwi* in (20b) "agrees" with the object *n!aosi* 'bows' by suppletion rather than affixation, so this is a truly atypical case of agreement.

If a language has verbal agreement in gender, this is almost always dependent on person/number agreement. Again, person and number morphemes are usually fused, as are the gender and number morphemes. In Sesotho (Bantu group of Niger-Kordofanian, Rijkhoff 2002: 82), there is extensive gender/number agreement, where prefixes expressing genders also express the plural number:

(22a)   *mǫ-thǫ   é-mǫ-hǫlǫ   ǫ-rata   0-ntjá   é-ntlɛ   eá-haǫ*
         CL.1-person CL.1-CL.1-big CL.1-like CL.9-dog CL.9-beautiful CL.9-CL1.POSS
         'The old man/woman likes his/her beautiful dog'

---

have verbal agreement in number, but not in person, while Buginese (Austronesian) and Classical Arabic are mentioned as languages in which there is verbal agreement in person but not in number. For Classical Arabic this holds only in some verbal paradigms.

(22b)   *ba-thǫ*   *bá-ba-hǫlǫ*   *ba-rata*   *li-ntjá*   *tsé-ntlɛ*   *tsá-bona*
          CL.2-person CL.2-CL.2-big CL.2-like   CL.10-dog CL.10-beautiful CL.10-CL2.POSS
          'The old people like their beautiful dogs'

In (22b), the gender (class) markers *ba-* (for gender 2) and *tsV-/li-* (for gender 10) also express plurality; conventionally, gender markers in the plural are differently labeled from the ones in the singular. Similar systems of gender/ number agreement exist in most other Bantu languages.

There are, of course, exceptions to the claim that number markers tend to be fused with person and/or gender markers. For example, in Aymara (Pichacani), the verb has a special plural marker (*-px-*) which is independent of person markers (Adelaar 2004: 269):

(23)   *laru-si-px-tʰ-wa*
       laugh-REFL-PL-1SUBJ-AFF
       'We (excl.) laugh at him'

With respect to gender and number, it can be stated that a language is unlikely to have gender agreement on the verb if it does not also have number agreement on the verb. The exceptions to this claim are rare, if they exist at all.[10]

Likewise, languages almost always have person agreement on the verb if they also have verbal agreement in gender (but not vice versa). The exceptions to this claim are found only in NE Caucasian languages, of which Chechen, Ingush, Kryz and Khwarshi are in the sample,[11] and perhaps in some Tucanoan languages (Baerman and Corbett 2013).

Here are some examples from Chechen to illustrate this pattern (Nichols 1989b: 59):

(24a)   *suona*   *v-ieza*   *sej*   *vaša*
       1SG.DAT CL.1-like my brother (CL.1.ABS)
       'I like my brother'

---

[10] Noon (Atlantic branch of Niger-Kordofanian, Soukka 2000: 177) has number agreement expressed by suffixes on the verb for animate, but not for inanimate subjects. The language does have clitic person/number markers, and it also has extensive gender agreement in the NP. Iraqw (Cushitic branch of Afro-Asiatic, Mous 1993) appears to have gender (but not number) agreement on verbs, but the analysis provided by Mous' grammar is not completely clear. Plank (UnivArch no. 1056) claims that Burushaski has gender agreement, but not number agreement for direct objects (although the language has both types of agreement for subjects). He also includes Classical Arabic as a counter-example to this universal, but this should not be taken to mean that Classical Arabic does not have any verbal agreement in number at all: in the past indicative the language distinguishes between *kataba* (3sg. m.) 'he wrote', *katabat* (3sg. f.) 'she wrote', *katabā* (3du. m.) 'they two wrote', *katabatā* (3du. f.) 'they two wrote', *katabū* (3pl. m.) 'they wrote' and *katabna* (3pl. f.) 'they wrote'.

[11] In Batsbi (or Tsova-Tush, Dešeriev 1953), some verbs have only gender/number agreement, while some verbs also show person agreement.

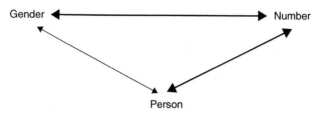

Figure 2 Combinations of categories involved in verbal agreement

(24b)   *suona   j-ieza   sej jiša*
         1SG.DAT CL.2-like my sister(CL.2.ABS)
         'I like my sister'

(24c)   *suona d-ieza yz   bier*
         1SG.DAT CL.3-like this child(CL.3.ABS)
         'I like this child'

In these examples the verb agrees with the absolutive argument only in gender, not in person. Aghem (Bantu branch of Niger-Kordofanian) is similar in that verbs do not have agreement markers for the first and second persons, but in the third person a clitic must be used to show gender agreement with the subject (Hyman 1979: 48). In that language one could say that it has no person agreement at all, only gender agreement with non-pronominal subjects, but the system is different from the one found in NE Caucasian, where the verb agrees with the gender of all subjects, including pronominals.

   Figure 2 summarizes the relative frequencies of the combinations of categories in verbal agreement.

3.2.3   *Gender and Other Systems of Classification*

Of all the Phi-features, gender is the only one that does not exist independently of agreement. Languages can have number marking in the NP and on verbs, but no number agreement, and it can be argued that there are languages with verbal (and nominal) person marking, but no person agreement (see Section 4.2). In contrast to that, gender is by definition a system of nominal classification which is expressed in agreement, so a language with gender, but without gender agreement, is impossible. There are, of course, many systems of nominal classification that do not involve agreement. The examples include the classification of nouns into inflectional classes (e.g. in Latin declensions), or the classification of nouns into animate and inanimate classes (in languages where this is reflected in case marking rather than gender agreement), or into countable and non-countable classes, etc. All of these classifications can be reflected in grammar, but if there is no agreement, we are not dealing with gender. In this sense, gender is the only category which is *defined* by agreement.

Gender systems should, in principle, be distinguished from systems of classifiers (Allen 1977; Aikhenvald 2000); like genders, classifiers are a nominal classification device, but unlike genders, classifiers are usually independent words used with nouns in certain constructions, most commonly with numerals (in numeral classifier systems) and in possessive constructions (in possessive classifier systems). As they are independent words, or (less commonly) monomorphemic clitics, they cannot be said to *agree* with the head of the NP in which they occur. Moreover, unlike in gender systems which seldom have more than four classes, there are usually dozens of classifiers, sometimes even more than a hundred. Although gender and classifier systems are different, there are intermediary types of systems, having properties of both classifiers and genders (Corbett 2007; Fedden and Corbett 2017). A good example is Kilivila (an Austronesian language spoken on the Trobriand Islands). This language has at least 177 "classifiers," prefixes that have to be used in quantified NPs and in some other constructions (Fedden and Corbett 2017: 21f., quoting from Senft 1986: 16):

(25)   *mi-na-si-na*   *na-yu*   *na-manabweta*   *vivila*
       this-FEM-PL-this   FEM-two   FEM-beautiful   girl
       'these two beautiful girls'

Although the number of prefixes that pattern like *na-* is much larger than the one usually found in gender systems, and quite comparable to some typical classifier systems, the fact that the prefix *na-* must be repeated before each modifier of the noun in the NP makes the system of Kilivila quite like many other gender agreement systems. Moreover, sex plays a role in the choice of the prefix that has to be used, and this is again typical of gender systems. For our purposes, it is largely irrelevant whether Kilivila is considered as a language with gender or a language with classifiers. What is important is that it clearly exhibits agreement in the NP, and if we had to specify which category is involved in this agreement pattern, we would not hesitate to say that it is gender agreement.

Another grammatical phenomenon that has certain characteristics of gender systems is the classificatory verb, typical of the Athabaskan languages. Although the choice of the verb stem is determined by the class to which an argument of the verb belongs, it would not be correct to say that a classificatory verb *agrees* with its argument. Unlike in a true gender system, the same argument can trigger different forms of a classificatory verb, but it changes its meaning accordingly, while in a gender system, the controller of the agreement always has the same meaning. For example, in Navajo, the noun *béésò* 'money' can mean 'a coin' in *béésò sì-ʔą́* 'A coin is lying (there)', but it means 'a note (bill)' with a different choice of the classificatory verb stem: *béésò sì-ltsòòz* 'A note is lying (there)' (Allen 1977: 287). A noun like *bilasaana* 'apple' denotes a round, concrete object and consequently requires the same stem of the verb as *béésò* in the sense of 'coin', so 'The apple is lying there' is *bilasaana sì-ʔą́* (Fedden and Corbett 2017: 47). Similar phenomena are attested in some other languages of North America, e.g. in Caddo (Caddoan, Mithun 1986: 386), Klamath (Klamath-Modoc, Barker 1964), as well as in some Papuan languages (e.g. Waris, Foley 1986: 90–1, and Mian, cf. Fedden 2011).

It should be noted that classificatory verbs have different forms only in some semantic fields, including verbs of motion, position and state, and they classify only a subset of the referents of nouns in terms of shape, consistency and position. A gender system typically classifies all of the nouns in a language. Therefore, it would be inappropriate to say that a classificatory verb agrees with its argument(s). Rather, classificatory verbs show certain properties of their arguments, such as shape or consistency, which may be subject to change or depend on the extralinguistic context.

The same goes for other grammatical devices that classify referents of nouns in terms of their contingent properties, rather than nouns themselves in terms of the inherent properties of their referents, e.g. the demonstrative pronouns that differ in form when referring to visible or invisible entities. In languages with such demonstratives we certainly have a choice of grammatical form determined by a certain property of the referent, but we do not have agreement. That is, we would not say that in a language such as Panare (Cariban), which has visibility opposition in pronouns, these pronouns *agree* with the noun in visibility, but rather that the demonstratives show whether the referent is visible or not.[12]

3.2.4   Person

Let us now turn to the category of person. Like gender, person is not unproblematic for typological comparison, and we should state clearly which phenomena will be taken as instantiating this category. We are accustomed to take it for granted that there are three persons, corresponding to the speaker, the addressee, and to other(s), i.e. to non-speech-act participant(s). However, in some languages there is a "fourth person," usually sharing the same type of morphological marking as the more common three persons, but denoting an

---

[12] In certain languages, such as Kwak'wala (Boas 1947: 261), verbal person/number endings differ also in terms of visibility of referents. Here, again, we would not say that the verb agrees with its argument in visibility; rather, we would say that it agrees in person and number, but that it also codes the visibility of the referents of arguments.

"indeterminate speech-act participant," usually translatable as "someone." This type of system is found in Eskimo-Aleut languages as well as in several other languages of the New World. In Chamorro (Austronesian), the verb has special agreement markers if it agrees with the interrogative pronoun (Chung 1994); although this has been called "wh-agreement," for our purposes it seems more appropriate to treat it as instantiating person agreement, with the interrogative pronoun behaving like a "fourth person."

A similar analysis can be applied to the so-called "obviation agreement" that exists in Algonquian languages, as well as in some other languages of North America (e.g. Kutenai and Keres).[13] In such languages, one third person[14] is characterized as proximate, and all others as obviatives. The proximate third person is usually topical and animate, and the referent initially characterized as proximate remains proximate over a large stretch of discourse (although in some languages the proximate person must be identified in each sentence). A verb agreeing in person has different markers for obviative and proximate arguments. So far there is no reason why we should not treat agreement in obviation as a type of person agreement, but in some Algonquian languages, nouns are also marked for obviation (proximates are usually unmarked and obviatives are marked with affixes). This may be understood as a kind of overt person marking, parallel to overt gender marking in Bantu languages and NE Caucasian languages, where nouns which trigger gender agreement also bear affixes for gender. However, in some languages, such as Ojibwa (Mithun 1999: 76), modifiers of nouns are also marked for obviation:

(26) *Ogii-biindoomon-an   iniw   anishnaabe-n ahaw Misaabe*
       3-carry.in.garment-3.OBV those(OBV) people-OBV   that giant
       'Giant (proximate) carried people (obviative) in the fold of his garment'

In (26) the demonstrative *iniw* agrees in obviation with the noun *anishnaaben* 'people'. This seems rather like case agreement, which "spreads" from the controller (the head noun) to its modifiers in the NP (see Section 4.5). It is an interesting instance of adnominal person agreement, similar to the system of "person/gender/number" markers in Khoisan languages, which will be mentioned below.

Another complication with the traditional values of the category person is found in a number of languages that oppose the first person ("the speaker") to all other persons that can be subsumed under the label "non-speaker(s)." This is

---

[13] It is also reported for Ingush, a NE Caucasian language (Nichols 2011), and in some African languages, e.g. Ma'di (Blackings and Fabb 2003).

[14] It is claimed that some African languages (e.g. Logbara, a Nilo-Saharan language of the Central Sudanic branch) have different proximate and obviative forms for the second person (Gregersen 1977: 51).

attested in the Barbacoan family in Ecuador and Colombia, e.g. in Guambiano (Adelaar 2004: 146):

(27) *na-m misák k-er*
  1-PL people be-SPEAKER.PL
  'We are Guambianos'

In (27) above, the verb shows the suffix *-er* only in the 1st person (singular or plural), as if agreeing in "speakerhood" with the subject. Of course, we could assume that Guambiano has a full person/number verbal paradigm, but that the verbal endings are *-0* except in the first person plural and singular, where the ending is *-er*. Although possible, such an analysis is clearly less economical than saying that Guambiano opposes "speaker" (expressed by *-er*) to "non-speaker" (expressed by *-0*). Thus, the pattern of agreement found in Guambiano forces us to either define the category of "person" in broader terms, or to say that there is a category of "speakerhood," different from "person," and that Guambiano has agreement in "speakerhood." Since Guambiano and languages with this kind of system are not in our sample, we did not have to make that theoretical choice, but in a larger sample the question whether Guambiano has person agreement would have to be answered unambiguously.

3.2.5 Number

Finally, the category of number is usually defined in terms of the values singular, dual, and plural (in some languages also trial and/or paucal, etc.). These are, indeed, the most common values, but expressions of number in languages can differ in so many ways that it is difficult to describe them only in these terms. For instance, it has been claimed that many Australian languages are better analyzed as having number systems that distinguish between minimal and augmented forms (sometimes also "unit augmented") forms. Minimal forms refer only to the speaker (1st person), only to the addressee (2nd person), only to both of them (1+2) and only to a person who is neither the speaker nor the addressee. Augmented forms, on the other hand, include other referents besides those referred to by the minimal forms. This type of system is found in Baardi, a Nyulnyulan language of NW Australia (Dixon 2002: 69):

(28) Minimal   Augmented
  1 *ngayu*   *arrudu* (+speaker −addressee)
  2 *dyu*   *gurr* (−sp. +adr.)
  1+2 *ayu*   *arridil* (+sp. +adr.)
  3 *ginjinngi* *irr* (−sp. −adr.)

The analysis of these forms in terms of singular, dual and plural is certainly possible, but uneconomical, as it involves ad hoc interpreting many forms as results of number/person neutralization. For example, the form *irr* would be used for the 3rd person plural and dual, *gurr* would be the 2nd person dual exclusive, and we would also have to say that the exclusive/inclusive opposition exists only in the dual, but not in the plural. On the other hand, the analysis that is more economical for one language may make its system less comparable with other languages. If we say that the category number always includes the values specifiable as singular, dual, plural, etc., then, provided that we accept the above analysis, we would have to claim that Baardi, and many other Australian languages, do not have number. If, however, we say that Baardi has number (and number agreement),[15] this means that we have to "translate" the Baardi system into one with more familiar number values, i.e. we have to analyze it less economically. Since the focus of this book is on cross-linguistic comparison, this was generally the approach we took when faced with problems such as the one sketched above for Baardi.

Kiowa-Tanoan languages, with their typologically unusual "inverse number" system, can be approached in an analogous way. In those languages, e.g. in Kiowa (Mithun 1999: 445, cf. also Watkins and McKenzie 1984), certain nouns are inherently singular/dual, and receive the suffix *-gɔ* only when they are not, e.g. *cę-gɔ* refers to three or more horses, since *cę* 'horse' can refer to either a single horse or a pair of them. On the other hand, nouns such as *alɔ* 'apple' are inherently dual, so *alɔ-gɔ* must be translated as 'one or many apples (but not two)'. There are also nouns that are inherently plural (e.g. *tʰǫ-se* 'bones'), and they receive *-gɔ* only when they refer to a single entity, so *tʰǫ-se-gɔ* means 'bone'. The suffix *-gɔ*, then, cannot be interpreted as expressing any particular "number," but it rather expresses "inverse number," i.e. the non-default number of referents, depending on the class of nouns to which it is added. However, the verb in Kiowa has different prefixes for (some) singular and dual arguments, so that we can say that it agrees in number after all, rather than in "inverse number" (Mithun 1999: 445):

(29a)　　*cę*　　　*gya-tʰɔn*
　　　　horse　1SG.SUBJ/SG.OBJ-find.PF
　　　　'I found a horse'

(29b)　　*cę*　　　*nen-tʰɔn*
　　　　horse　1SG.SUBJ/DU.OBJ-find.PF
　　　　'I found two horses'

---

[15] In many languages the opposition of minimal and augmented forms applies not just to independent pronouns but to bound pronouns (verbal agreement markers) as well.

Although *cǫ* can mean either 'a horse' or 'a pair of horses', the singular object/ 1sg. subject prefix *gya-* specifies that 'a horse' is the intended reading of (29a), while the prefix *nen-* specifies that 'two horses' are meant in (29b). Unlike the nominal suffixes expressing inverse number, the verbal prefixes clearly express either the number singular or the number plural (for objects).

Number systems also differ in the way the morphemes for non-singular values express the plurality of denoted objects. In many languages, nouns construed with a numeral do not get plural marking, but rather remain unmarked, as in example (30) from Oromo (Cushitic branch of Afro-Asiatic). It has been stated that such languages actually have *set nouns* rather than *individual object nouns*, which are found in languages such as Dutch (31), cf. Rijkhoff (2002: 46):

(30) *gaala   lamaani*
      two   camel
      'two camels'

(31) *twee   boek-en*
      two   book-PL
      'two books'

Rijkhoff notes that in languages with set nouns, such as Oromo, the unmarked noun is inherently neither singular nor plural, and the plural marking only resolves the ambiguity. In languages with individual object nouns, such as Dutch, the unmarked noun is inherently singular, and cannot be used to refer to more than one object. Thus, in Oromo *farda* can mean both 'horse' and 'horses', *nad'eeni* is both 'woman' and 'women', while in Dutch *auto* means only 'car', while *autos* is 'cars', and *boek* is 'book' while *boeken* must mean 'books'. Oromo nouns apparently denote sets rather than individual objects, and the context shows when the set contains just one individual. Alternatively, individual reference can also be specified by adding a singulative suffix, *-ca* (masculine) and *-ttii* (feminine), cf. Oromo *nama* 'man/men' vs. *namica* 'man', *nad'eeni* 'woman/women' vs. *nad'ittii* 'woman'.

Consequently, the opposition between singular and plural in Dutch and Oromo does not mean the same thing, and one could question whether both can be subsumed under the category of "number." Indeed, Rijkhoff (2002: 103) argues that so-called "number markers" in languages like Oromo are actually "grammatical elements indicating that the noun designates a property of a set which consists of one individual (singleton set) or signalling that the set consists of multiple individual entities which together form a collective (collective set)." This typology of ways that singular and plural reference is grammaticalized has consequences for agreement systems, because number agreement (agreement involving morphemes signaling singular or multiple entities) is found in both types of languages. Of languages with set nouns mentioned by Rijkhoff (2002: 38–41) and included in our sample, adnominal number agreement is lacking in Hixkaryana, Berbice Dutch Creole, Guarani, Miao (Blue) and Kayardild, but it exists in Chukchi, Georgian and (marginally) in Hungarian. Of languages with individual object nouns (Rijkhoff 2002: 34–6), adnominal number agreement is lacking in Abkhaz, and it exists in Babungo, Burushaski, Kisi, Ngiti, Tamil (for nouns belonging to the 'rational' class) and West Greenlandic.[16] This means that our conception of "number" must be broad enough to subsume agreement phenomena in both languages with set nouns and in languages with individual object nouns. Therefore, "number" for us involves the grammatical opposition between reference to individual entities (be they objects or sets) and multiple entities.

3.2.6   Minor Agreement Patterns

Finally, we come to the problem of typologically rare agreement patterns. Besides agreement in Phi-features and case, some other minor patterns are known. There is, for example, adnominal agreement in definiteness, found in Hebrew, Norwegian and some other languages. Here are examples showing definiteness agreement in Hebrew (Wintner 2000):

(32a)   *sefer gadol*
        book big
        'a big book'

(32b)   *ha-sefer ha-gadol*
        DEF-book DEF-big
        'the big book'

When a definite noun is modified by an adjective, both the noun and the adjective must have the definiteness marker (the preposed article) *ha-*. On the other hand, in some NPs, definiteness agreement is apparently optional:

(33a)   *sefer ze*
        book this
        'this book'

---

[16] It is probably not accidental that there are more individual object languages with number agreement than set languages with number agreement in this little sample. Note also that number agreement in Hungarian is limited to a pair of lexical items and that it is rather limited in Chukchi and Georgian. It may well be that there is a statistical implicational universal stating that languages with individual object nouns are more likely to have number agreement than languages with set nouns, but the collected data do not allow us to check this for all 300 languages in our sample.

(33b)   *ha-sefer   ha-ze*
        DEF-book DEF-this
        'this book'

In the preceding examples the definiteness marker must be on both the noun and the demonstrative, or on neither, and, apparently, the meaning is not affected. Again, Corbett (2006: 136–7) argues that the patterns found in Hebrew should not be counted as agreement, but that definiteness is independently assigned to both the noun and its modifiers (from where?). However, we do not see any reason why this should be so. We think that it is preferable to accept that some agreement patterns exist, but are typologically extremely rare (or areally and genetically restricted), just as there are some extremely rare consonants (e.g. clicks in Khoisan languages), which are nevertheless to be counted as consonants in the general typology of speech sounds. And even the Hebrew system of definiteness agreement is not without typological parallels. In Guató, a Macro-Jê language of Brazil, adjectives must take the same marker expressing determination as the head nouns of the NP (Rodrigues 1999: 193):

(34)   *gó-dá   g-ítavi*
        DET-basket   DET-heavy
        'the heavy basket'

In Albanian, adjectives following a definite form of the noun must be preceded by a definite article, which thus agrees in definiteness with the noun (at least for some case forms):

(35)   *gur-in   e   bardhë*
        stone-DEF.ACC.SG   ART.DEF.ACC.SG.   white
        'the white stone'

If the noun is indefinite, the indefinite accusative form of the article must be used (*gur të bardhë* 'a white stone'). Note that both **gurin bardhë* and **gur bardhë*, without the definite article before the adjective, are ungrammatical. However, in the nominative the article preceding the adjective has the same form irrespective of whether the noun is definite or not, i.e. *gur-i i bardhë* is 'the white stone' and *gur i bardhë* is 'a white stone', so there is no agreement in definiteness. In Albanian, then, agreement in definiteness crucially depends on case: It exists in the accusative, but not in the nominative.

A typologically unusual agreement in transitivity is found in some Panoan languages of the Western Amazon (called "transitivity concord" by Loos 1999: 235–40). This agreement pattern is shown in different ways elements of the clause are modified depending on whether the main verb of the clause is transitive or intransitive. For example, in Capanawa the adverbial suffixes meaning 'abruptly, rapidly, completely' have the form *-kaʔin-* for intransitive verbs and *-baʔin-* for transitives (Loos 1999: 239):

(36a)   *mapí-kaʔin-i*
        go.up-rapidly(INTR)-conjunction
        'He goes up rapidly'

(36b)   *biʔ-baʔin-kin*
        grab-rapidly(TRANS)-conjunction
        'He grabs it rapidly'

Similar transitivity agreement markers occur on locative phrases, which are independent of the verb. To the best of our knowledge, this agreement pattern does not occur except in Panoan.

In Korean, and possibly in other languages with extensive honorific systems, there is a phenomenon that has been labeled "honorific agreement" (Sohn 1999: 416). Korean has honorific suffixes added to verb stems that index the addressee and the subject. If the addressee and the subject are identical, the subject agreement ranges over the whole sentence, as in (37):

(37)   *Kim sensayng-nim   kkeyse o-sy-ess-e.yo*
        Kim professor-HON NOM   come-HON-PST-PTC
        'Professor Kim came'

The verb in (37) effectively agrees in the use of the appropriate honorific suffix with the subject (*Kim sensayng*). However, the honorific suffix on the verb can also agree with a nominal which is not the subject of the sentence, as in (38), where the subject of the sentence is *somay* 'clothes', but the honorific *-usey-* "agrees" with *apeci* 'father' (Sohn 1999: 416–17):

(38)   *Apeci uy   somay ka ccal-usey-yo*
        Father GEN clothes NOM short-HON-PTC
        'The sleeves of your clothes are short, Dad'

A particular problem is posed by sequence of tenses (*consecutio temporum* of classical grammar), which exists in Latin, Romance languages, Old Irish and several other Indo-European languages (and probably in other language families). It is essentially a rule stating that the choice of the tenses of verbs in dependent clauses is determined by the tense of the main verb, and it can also be formulated in terms of agreement between the tenses of the main and the subordinated verb. In Latin, for example, the present tense of the verb in the main clause requires that the verb in certain subordinate clauses be in the present subjunctive, while the use of the perfect or imperfect in the main clause requires the use of the imperfect subjunctive, hence the contrast between (39a) and (39b):

(39a) *Cognosc-o*   *quid*   *faci-as*
       find.out-1SG.PRES what   do-2SG.PRES.SUBJUNCTIVE
       'I am finding out what you are doing'

(39b) *Cognosc-ebam quid fac-eres*
       find.out-1SG.IPF what do-2SG.IPF.SUBJUNCTIVE
       'I was finding out what you were doing'

In (39a), the present indicative of *cognosco* 'I know' is matched by the present subjunctive of *facias* 'you are doing', while in (39b) the imperfect *cognoscebam* requires the use of imperfect subjunctive of the subordinated verb (*faceres*, cf. Gildersleeve and Lodge 1895: 315). One possible analysis of this rule would be to say that the main verb is the controller and the subordinated verb the target, and that the target agrees with the controller in the category of tense. However, it is also possible to claim that the main verb governs the subordinated verb and assigns to it the subjunctive mood, and that the choice of the subcategory (present or imperfect subjunctive) depends on the tense of the main verb, whereby the use of the same tenses is the consequence of the temporal logic of the situation rather than grammar: If both the main and the subordinated verb refer to situations in the past, it is appropriate that both are in the past tense. The most intuitive approach in our opinion is to combine the two analyses and say that the Latin construction involves government in terms of mood and agreement in terms of tense. In any case, even if sequence of tenses is considered to represent agreement in the same sense as, say, agreement in number and person, it appears to be a rather rare phenomenon, best described in the syntax of European languages. It is, however, attested elsewhere (e.g. in Malagasy), but of particular typological interest is Kayardild (Tangkic), in which not just verbs but some nominal arguments as well agree with their verbs in tense, mood, aspect and even polarity[17] (Evans 2003b: 215):

(40a) *ngada*   *waa-jarra wengarr-ina ngijin-maru-tharra thabuju-maru-tharra*
       1sg.NOM sing-PST   song-M.ABL   my-V.DAT-PST   brother-V.DAT-PST
       'I sang a song for my brother'

(40b) *ngada waa-n-da*   *wangarr-inja*   *ngijin-maru-n-da thabuju-maru-n-d*
       1SG.NOM sing-NMSR-NOM song-A.OBL   my-V.DAT-NMSR-NOM brother-V.DAT-NMSR-NOM
       'I am singing a song for my brother'

---

[17] That is, if the verb is negated, the verb's argument must also be marked with a negative affix.

Table 2 *Categories and domains of agreement*

	NP	Clause	Controller	Target
Number	+	+	N/Pro	V, Modifiers
Gender	+	+	N/Pro	V, Modifiers
Person	(+)[a]	+	N/Pro	V, (Modifiers)
Case	+	−	N/Pro	(N), Modifiers

[a] Only in languages with possessive agreement in the NP, on which see Section 4.6.

Both elements of the NP 'my brother' in (40a–b) agree in tense (past tense in (40a) and the unmarked present in (40b)) with the verb *waa-* 'to sing'. This pattern of agreement of nominals in verbal categories *par excellence* appears to be found only in Kayardild,[18] a language noted for its many typologically unusual features (see also Evans 1995).

It is quite possible (even probable) that other typologically unusual agreement patterns exist, but they are not found in our sample and will not be treated in the present investigation. From the areal–typological point of view, we can only record the existence of such patterns and admit that they are rare and do not show – as far as we can tell at present – any genetic or areal pattern in their distribution.

3.3   Summary

We can now summarize, in Table 2, how various categories combine with various domains of agreement, as well as with different types of controllers and targets.

We see from the table that case is indeed a divergent category when compared with the Phi-features (person, number and gender). The NP is the sole domain of case agreement and, moreover, its target is never the verb, whereas all of the Phi-features may be (but need not be) expressed on the verb. This anomaly of case agreement, as well as the problem whether it should be treated as agreement at all, will be discussed further in Section 4.5.

---

[18] The Kayardild data appear to refute Lehmann and Moravcsik's universal claim (2000: 742) that nouns cannot agree with verbs in tense.

4   Problems with Agreement

We have mentioned in Chapter 2 that our definition of agreement includes constructions with omissible controllers and those with referential targets, as well as some phenomena that are sometimes not considered to instantiate agreement (case agreement and person agreement in possessive constructions). Moreover, there are some other challenges to typological research of agreement systems: Agreement may be optional in some languages, in the sense that the occurrence of agreement markers on targets is not obligatory, and the nature of those markers varies considerably in different languages, since they can belong to different kinds of bound morphemes and clitics. We shall now examine how such problems affect our research and, in particular, our sampling of languages used in this study.

4.1   Optionality of Agreement

In some languages agreement is optional. That means that agreement markers assigned by controllers may, but need not, appear on targets. For example, in Mian (Ok branch of the Trans-New Guinea family), adjectives agree in gender with the head noun optionally, so that the agreement marker can, but need not, be attached to the adjective stem. It must, however, be added to the final element of the NP (Foley 1986: 82):

(41)   *til-(e) nama-(e) sum-e*
        dog-M white-M big-M
        'big white dog'

This type of system should be analyzed as gender agreement, as long as the agreement marker has to be present at least on one word (target) different from the head noun itself (the controller). On the other hand, Yoruba (Niger-Kordofanian, Nigeria) has optional number agreement in the NP. The plural word *àwọn* can co-occur with the plural marker on the demonstrative (Aboh 2010: 19):

(42a)   *àwọn iṣu wọn-yẹn*
         PL   yam PL-DEM
         'those yams'

However, constructions without agreement are also grammatical (42b):

(42b)   *àwǫ̀n iṣu yẹn*
        PL   yam DEM
        'those yams'

This syntactic pattern does not satisfy our definition of agreement, because the target *does not have to* be morphologically modified when it is part of the same constituent (here the NP) as the controller. Similarly, in Awtuw (a language of the Upper Sepik family spoken in Papua New Guinea), demonstrative pronouns cannot have number marking if the referent of the head noun in the NP is singular or dual, but if it is plural, the demonstrative pronouns may bear plural marking (Feldman 1986: 123):

(43)   *tader/tadum tale-m liwke*
       this/these   woman-PL many
       'these many women'

On the other hand, a determiner (or article) must agree with the head noun in number, and it has to be in the non-female form if the referent of the noun is either animate or male; but if it is female, then both the female and the non-female form of the determiner can be used:

(44)   *rey/tey*   *tale*
       3M.SG/3FEM.SG   woman
       'the woman'

(45)   *rey*   *yaen*   *naydowo*
       3M.SG   child   one
       'the one child'

The female form of the article *tey* would be ungrammatical in (45), but if the referent is female, the choice between *rey* and *tey* is optional (44). Although the rules of agreement are underdetermined in Awtuw, we would still acknowledge that this language has gender agreement in the NP, because the choice of the head noun necessarily affects the choice of the form of at least some of its modifiers.

In Tarascan, an isolate spoken in Mexico, the plural suffix in an NP consisting of a noun and an adjective is regularly on the adjective, but since the noun is uninflected, there is no agreement: 'fat women' is *wáṛi tepáṛatii-ča* (woman fat-PL); however, the plural suffix *-ča* can optionally occur on the head noun, so *wáṛi-ča tepáṛatii-ča* is also grammatical (LeCron Foster 1969: 70). One might object that our analysis is inconsistent, since we claimed above that Mian has gender agreement as long as the gender marker has to appear on at least one modifier in the NP. But gender, unlike number, is an inherent category of nouns, which means that the gender feature is copied from the head noun to one of its modifiers, which constitutes agreement. Number, on the other hand, is not inherent to nouns in the sense that gender is,[1] so we can say that number is marked on the noun modifier rather than that it agrees with the noun, provided that the noun itself is unmarked for number.

Finally, optionality of agreement can be a matter of degree. In Turkish, verbs normally agree with their subjects in number and person (46a–b). However, when the subject is inanimate, the verb tends to agree in person, but not in number (47a), and when the subject is higher animate, but non-human, as in (47b), both the construction with agreement and without it are common.

(46a)   *Ben koş-tu-m*
        I   run-PRET-1SG
        'I ran'

(46b)   *Adam-lar   koş-tu-lar*
        man-PL   run-PRET-3PL
        'The men ran'

(47a)   *Gün-ler   geç-ti-0*
        day-PL   pass-PRET-3SG
        'The days passed'

(47b)   *At-lar   koş-tu-0   / At-lar   koş-tu-lar*
        horse-PL run-PRET-3SG   horse-PL   run-PRET-3PL
        'The horses ran'

This pattern of agreement in Turkish is similar to the so-called *tà zõ̃ia trékhei* rule in Ancient Greek: Neuter nouns (which almost always denote inanimate referents) usually occurred with verb person markers in the singular (i.e. the agreement in number was cancelled), but in Homer, as well as in many writers from the fourth century BC and later, there are many exceptions to this rule. Ultimately, in many languages the presence or absence of agreement in a construction can depend on the sociolect,[2] or even the idiolect of the speaker.

These examples show how deciding whether a language has agreement or not is often far from trivial, and many grammars do not even bother to state whether a particular agreement pattern is obligatory or optional, and under

---

[1] An exception might be *pluralia tantum*, nouns that are inherently plural, which exist in many languages.

[2] Upadhyay (2009) argues that sociolinguistic factors, especially the perception of women and their social standing in society, govern the use of gender/person agreement in non-standard Nepali.

which circumstances. From our survey of the literature it appears, though, that optional agreement is rather rare cross-linguistically. It is undoubtedly found (i.e. it is explicitly stated in grammars that such agreement exists) in less than 3 percent of the languages in our sample.

4.2 Omission of Controllers

In many languages, irrespective of whether their verbs are marked for person/ number/gender, arguments of verbs can be omitted. This applies to both actor and undergoer arguments[3] and to languages that mark only subjects on verbs (e.g. Italian), as well as those that mark both subjects and objects, sometimes also indirect objects (e.g. Kabardian, a NW Caucasian language). For example, in Japanese the verb is unmarked for arguments, but they can nevertheless be omitted from the sentence:

(48) *Boku-wa eigo-o   wakar-imasu*
     1SG-TOP English-ACC understand-PRES
     'I understand English'

(49) *Eigo-o   wakar-imasu*
     English-ACC understand-PRES
     '(I) understand English'

(50) Wakar-imasu
     understand-PRES
     '(I) understand (it)'

Similarly, in Kabardian (Northwest Caucasian, Matasović 2010), which is a polysynthetic language, both the subject and the object argument can be omitted from the sentence:

(51) *sa wa   wə-s-łaġʷ-ā-ś*
     1SG 2SG   2SG-1SG-PRET-AFF
     'I saw you'

(52) *wə-s-łaġʷ-ā-ś*
     'I saw you'

And in Italian, which marks only the subject argument on the verb, the independent subject NP can be omitted:

---

[3] The terms "actor" and "undergoer" refer to semantic macro-roles, generalizations over individual semantic roles in the sense of Van Valin (2005).

(53)   *(Io) veng-o*
        I   come-1SG.PRES
        'I am coming'

As Camacho (2013: 34) notes, there are transitional types, in which the omissibility of an argument depends on which discourse participant (i.e. which person) is involved: In Finnish it is only possible to omit the subject (the controller of person/number agreement on the verb) in the 1st and 2nd person:

(54a)   *Nousi-n   junaan*
         stop-1SG.PST   train.into
         'I boarded the train'

(54b)   **Nousi-0   junaan*
         stop-3SG.PST   train.into
         'He/she boarded the train'

(54c)   *Hän   nousi   junaan*
         he/she stop-3SG.PST   train.into
         'He/she boarded the train'

The same condition on person agreement applies in Hebrew, but in Shipibo-Konibo (a Panoan language spoken in Peru and Brazil) the reverse is true: The 1st and 2nd persons are obligatorily overt, and the 3rd person is optionally zero. Shipibo-Konibo verbs are not inflected for person (as in Japanese), cf. Camacho (2013: 35):

(55a)   *E-ra   Lima-n   noko-ke*
         1SG-EVID Lima-DIR arrive-PERF
         'I arrived in Lima'

(55b)   *Lima-n-ra   (ja)   noko-ke*
         Lima-DIR-EVID (he)   arrive-PERF
         'He arrived in Lima'

In Marathi (an Indo-Aryan language spoken in Western India) only the 2nd person allows the omission of subjects, and in Brazilian Portuguese, Finnish and Marathi indefinite subjects can be null, but definite subjects generally cannot. There may be other such conditions on the obligatory presence of controller, but as long as the presence of the (subject or object) controller necessarily triggers the presence of the person/number(/gender) argument indices, we are dealing with agreement. Needless to say, in languages such as Japanese all subjects are omissible, but there is no person/number/gender agreement on the verb, since verbs are uninflected for these categories.

Languages in which independent arguments (including both nouns and pronouns) may be omitted are usually called *Pro-drop languages*. We have seen that, in one type of such languages, verbs are obligatorily marked for person (e.g. in Italian), while in the other type this is not the case (e.g. in Japanese).[4]

Non-Pro-drop languages can also belong to two types, distinguished with respect to the syntactic behavior of verbs with zero-valence (i.e. verbs without a semantic argument). In languages such as English, such verbs receive a "dummy subject," i.e. a syntactic argument that does not have a semantic interpretation. In (56), the verb *to thunder* does not have an agent ("thunderer") in its semantic representation, but it has to receive a pronoun *it* as its syntactic argument.

(56)   *It thunders*

In the other type of non-Pro-drop languages, such as Russian, verbs without a semantic argument do not get a "dummy subject":

(57)   *Grem-it*
       thunder-3SG.PRES
       'It thunders'

In English, we would say that the verb agrees with the dummy subject in person and number, but in Russian, where overt arguments are impossible in such constructions, we would probably have to say that verbs with zero-valence do not show agreement; rather, their person/number marking verbal affixes are purely morphological and play no part in the syntax of the language.

It should be mentioned, finally, that argument omissibility is a scalar, not an absolute category: Although Russian verbs require an overt subject, as a rule, in discourse one finds many subjectless sentences, but less than, e.g., in other Slavic languages such as Croatian or Czech. A sentence such as the following is perfectly grammatical in Russian:

(58)   *Esli xoč-eš,   poid-ëm   vmeste*
       if   want-2SG.PRES   go-1PL.FUT together
       'If you want, we'll go together'

---

[4] It has been claimed (Huang 1984) that Pro-drop languages either have no argument-indexing verbal morphology (like Japanese), or have full-fledged morphological paradigms that index verbal arguments (like Italian and Kabardian), but that the type is essentially incompatible with languages having impoverished verbal morphology (or marginal verbal agreement, as we would call it), such as English and French. Although this observation might be correct as a statistical universal, it is in dire need of large-scale empirical confirmation. Moreover, defining "impoverished" verbal morphology is a tricky business: French certainly has more of it than English.

Moreover, while English is more rigorously a non-Pro-drop language than Russian, even in English colloquial speech subjects are omissible in some contexts:

(59)   *Been there, done that*
       'I've been there and (I've) done that'

In typological investigations, where many languages are analyzed simultaneously, it is important to apply the same standards for all of the sampled languages. In practice, some subjectivity cannot be avoided, but it is fortunate that for the large majority of languages it is quite clear whether they are more like English or like Italian, i.e. whether they are Pro-drop or not. However, it is still necessary to note if a language is not as clear-cut a case as the more prototypical ones, and in any statistical analysis such transitional types must be counted separately.

4.3   Referentiality of Targets: Pronominal Argument Hypothesis

We have seen that our definition of agreement implies that controllers can be freely omitted, provided that, when they are present, targets are marked with a morpheme expressing the agreeing category. It is often assumed that controllers are referential elements, while targets are not. In an NP such as *those big men* it is the noun that refers to a group of entities (certain big men), while the agreeing demonstrative *those* only contributes deixis and/or definiteness to the NP, but it is semantically empty and non-referential. Likewise, in the clause *The man walk-s* it is the controller *man* that refers to the entity that performs the action of walking, while the 3rd sg. present ending *-s* merely agrees with the controller, but does not refer to anything. Hence, apparently, it may be taken for granted that controllers are referential, while targets are not.

   However, our definition of agreement does not make such a statement. Indeed, targets can also have referential status and/or meaning. It can be argued that number agreement morphemes, unlike pure agreement markers, have a semantic component. Namely, their function is not purely syntactic but also to express quantity. Likewise, it can be asserted that person/number markers in polysynthetic languages are not pure agreement markers, but that they behave like incorporated pronouns, in that they also refer to speech-act participants (Baker 1996). The full NPs are always optional in such languages, and can be freely omitted, as in Kabardian examples (51) and (52) above, repeated here as (60) and (61):

(60)   *Sa wa   wə-s-łaǵʷ-ā-ś*
       I you   2SG-1SG-see-PRET-AFF
       'I saw you'

(61)   *wə-s-łaġʷ-ā-ś*
         2SG-1SG-see-PRET-AFF
         'I saw you'

In languages like Kabardian, it appears that the person/number markers *refer* to speech-act participants, rather than agreeing with the omissible full NPs. However, this last claim, known also as the *Pronominal Argument Hypothesis*, is highly controversial. Bresnan and Mchombo (1987) have shown that in some languages bound person/number markers can be both referential (i.e. incorporated pronouns) and non-referential agreement markers. This is the case in Chichewa, a Bantu language, where object markers are incorporated pronouns but subject markers are just agreement markers without referential properties (Bresnan 2001: 151f.):

(62a)   *Njûchi   zi-ná-lúma   a-lenje*
         CL.10.bee CL.10.SUBJ-PST-bite CL.2-hunter
         'The bees bit the hunters'

(62b)   *Zi-ná-lúma   a-lenje*
         CL.10.SUBJ-PST-bite CL.2-hunter
         'They bit the hunters'

(62c)   *Njûchi   zi-ná-wá-lúma   a-lenje*
         CL.10.bee CL.10.SUBJ-PST-CL.2.OBJ.-bite CL.2-hunter
         'The bees bit them, the hunters'

(62d)   *Njûchi   zi-ná-wá-lúma*
         CL.10.bee CL.10.SUBJ-PST-CL.2.OBJ.-bite
         'The bees bit them'

(62e)   **Njûchi   zi-ná-lúma*
         'The bees bit'

As we see from the examples (62a–e), the object prefix is optional when the object is expressed with the full NP (as in 62b), but the subject prefix is obligatory, irrespective of whether the subject is expressed by a full NP (as in 62a) or not (as in 62b). However, when the object of a transitive verb is not expressed by a full NP, then the use of the object prefix becomes obligatory (as illustrated by the contrast between (62d) and (62e)). The argument that object markers, in contrast to subject markers, are true incorporated pronouns with referential properties relies on the fact that objects are obligatorily post-verbal in Chichewa (62a), so the subject normally cannot follow the verb (63a). But when the object is expressed by a prefix in the verbal complex, the subject NP can be directly post-verbal (63b):

(63a) *Zi-ná-lúma   njûchi   a-lenje
       CL.10.SUBJ-PST-bite   CL.10.bee   CL.2-hunter

(63b) Zi-ná-wá-lúma   njûchi   a-lenje
       CL.10.SUBJ-PST-CL.2.OBJ.-bite   CL.10.bee   CL.2-hunter
       'The bees bit them, the hunters'

Note also that free-standing object pronouns in Chichewa cannot be used except to introduce a new topic, or for contrast (as in *I saw* him, *not her!*), which is consistent with the fact that referential object pronouns are incorporated in the verb. Thus, it follows that object prefixes in Chichewa can truly replace free-standing object NPs and have referential properties (for other arguments in favor of this thesis see Bresnan 2001: 152–6). But would we have to say that the verb *agrees* with its object in Chichewa? From our definition of agreement, it follows that we would say that object agreement is optional, because the presence of the controller (the full object NP) may, but need not, trigger the presence of the target (the object prefix), as can be seen in the contrast between (62b) and (62c).

In contrast to Chichewa, Evans (1999) has argued that bound person markers in Bininj Gun-wok, a Gunwinyguan language of Australia, are *not* incorporated referential pronouns, since the incorporated adverbs such as "again" do not have scope over them:

(64)   wanjh bi-yawoyh-yam-i   na-buyika
       then 3>3.PST-again-spear-PST.IPF   M-other
       'And then he speared another (man) again'

This example (Evans 1999: 271) is from a tale in which it is told that a cannibal would spear a man, and then spear another, different man, not the same man again, as we would expect if the 'portmanteau' morpheme *bi-*, expressing that the 3rd person actor is acting on a 3rd person undergoer, were referential. In English, where free personal pronouns are referential, this is the natural interpretation of the sentence *He speared him, and then speared him again* (the pronoun *him* must refer to the same man in both of its occurrences). One should not conclude from this that bound person markers are necessarily not referential in head-marking, polysynthetic languages such as Bininj Gun-wok. Mithun (2003: 262ff.) shows that in Navajo (Eyak-Athabaskan), which is strongly polysynthetic, bound person markers are just as referential as free pronouns in English; Navajo verb *tá-náá-0-ní-gis* (involving.water-REPETITIVE-3.OBJ-2.SG.SUBJ-rub.IPF) "Wash it again" must be a request to wash the same object again, which shows that the 3.sg object marker (-0-) is referential, just like the English free pronoun *him* and unlike the Bininj Gun-wok portmanteau 3rd person subject and object marker *bi-* in (64). Moreover, there is another important difference between Bininj Gun-wok and Navajo. In Bininj Gun-wok, the sentence *al-ege daluk gaban-du-ng bedda* (FEM-DEM woman 3.SG/3.PL-scold-NON.PAST) is ambiguous, as it can be interpreted both as "That woman scolds people" and "That woman scolds them," showing that the portmanteau person/number prefix *gaban-* is not necessarily referential (Evans 1999: 266). In Navajo, the equivalent of such a sentence would not have a generic reading ("That woman scolds people"). It would necessarily mean "That woman scolds them," which shows that person/number prefixes in Navajo are referential.

Thus, there may well be languages in which person/number (and sometimes gender) marking morphemes are referential, but there are others in which they certainly are not, and there is nothing wrong with the hypothesis that in some languages there are both kinds of person/number marking morphemes. Apparently, this is the case in Hungarian, where, according to Wechsler (2015), person markers in the definite conjugation are referential, while those in the indefinite conjugation are not (for a similar argument about person markers in Ngalakgan, an Australian language, see Baker 2002). What is relevant in our investigation is that the *rule of obligatory agreement* can apply to both types of person/number(/gender) markers. In Bininj Gun-wok as well as in Navajo, in Kabardian as well as in Chichewa, speakers of those languages have to learn the rule according to which, if the clause contains the free argument NP, that argument must be expressed on the verb as well.

To this one could object that, if person/number (/gender) markers on the verb are referential in some languages, then the independent NPs in such languages are not in the clause but rather outside of it, provided only one occurrence of referential elements per clause is assumed. This would mean that there is agreement in such languages, and that it does not obtain within the domain of the clause but rather within the sentence. If this is the case, then we run the risk of comparing two different things across different languages, since the domain of verbal agreement is the clause in languages where agreement targets are not referential, and it is the sentence in languages where they are. We might attempt to distinguish the two cases in our sample, by including the information about the referential status of person/number markers for all the sampled languages, but the practical difficulties of this approach would be overwhelming. In many languages – and in many grammars describing them – the referential status of person/number markers is unclear. For example, it is certain that in Colloquial French the clitic pronouns (*je*, *tu*, *il*, etc.) are developing toward the status of agreement markers.

(65)   *Moi, je   parle   français*
        I   1SG speak.1.SG.PRES French
        'I speak French'

In Literary French, the pronoun *moi* in (65) would be represented in the sentence, but outside of the clause, and it would be used only when it was topical. The clitic pronoun *je* would be represented within the clause as the referential argument. In Colloquial French, on the other hand, it could be argued that the use of the pre-verbal pronoun *moi* has become obligatory, and that it has become referential, while the clitic pronoun *je* is a pure marker of agreement and that it does not have referential status. It is, however, quite unclear at exactly which point the re-analysis of such pronouns occurred and, needless to say, there are many intermediate varieties between Literary and the Colloquial French in which the status of pre-verbal pronouns is likewise blurred. This shows that the question of which element has referential status is quite complex even in familiar languages such as (Colloquial) French, and it can be far more difficult to answer in languages for which we have much less reliable information.

Therefore, it is probably best to treat languages with referential person/number markers together with those in which those markers are not referential, and not just for practical reasons: The very proposal that there can only be one occurrence of referential elements per clause might be plainly wrong. Some syntactic theories, e.g. Role and Reference Grammar (see, e.g., Van Valin 2005 and above, Section 3.1), systematically distinguish the core, as a syntactic domain consisting only of the predicate (or "nucleus") and its arguments, from the clause, which is a broader domain consisting of the core together with adjuncts and elements in the "precore slot" (or "postcore slot" in some languages). These are usually fronted question words (as in *What did John say?*) and NPs fronted for topicalization (as in *Bean soup I can't stand*). This leaves open the possibility that both independent NPs and (referential) agreement markers are elements of the same clause, although agreement markers are elements of the core, while independent NPs are not. Van Valin convincingly shows (Van Valin 2005: 16–17) that independent NPs in Tzotzil (a head-marking Mayan language) are part of the clause, rather than extra-clausal elements such as preposed nominals in English constructions of the type *John, I saw him yesterday.* In fact, they are comparable to elements in the English precore slot, e.g. the stressed NP *bean soup* in the sentence *Bean soup I can't stand.* If this is accepted as a general principle for the status of independent, referential arguments in languages which also have referential verbal agreement markers – and we think that this is a reasonable hypothesis – then we are justified in considering the clause as the universal domain of verbal agreement.

The discussion of verbal agreement so far leads us to the following conclusions:

1. In languages with person/number(/gender) marking on verbs (by affixes or clitics, as will be explained below), it is possible to have both the clause and the sentence as domains of agreement (see Section 3.1).
2. Since many grammatical descriptions do not explicitly state whether free pronouns and NPs expressing verbal arguments are omissible or not (and under which conditions), it is plausible to make separate statistics for languages in which targets of verbal agreement are certainly omissible and for those in which they may not be (or certainly are not) omissible (see Section 4.2).
3. Although it should be possible, in principle, to distinguish between referential and non-referential verbal agreement markers, in practice it is too difficult to obtain reliable information about the referential status of agreement markers in the sampled languages. Hence, no attempt to do so will be made in this book, and both types will be subsumed under a general notion of "verbal agreement markers." It is assumed that both types of verbal agreement markers have the clause as their proper domain of agreement (see Section 4.3).

4.4   Markedness of Targets

Our definition of agreement stated that the agreeing feature has to be "present" on the target, but we did not say what exactly that was supposed to mean. We did not specify by which means this "presence" can be signaled on the target. It is generally assumed that agreement, as a type of morphosyntactic rule, involves a morphological alteration of targets, i.e. that agreement markers are morphological elements. By this one usually has affixation in mind, but Ablaut, tone change, and other forms of non-linear morphology, are quite commonly involved in agreement as well. For example, in Mbembe (a Cross River language of the Niger-Kordofanian family, spoken in Nigeria), there is number agreement in the NP, and plural forms of nouns and determiners are mostly formed by Ablaut and tonal changes (Kemmermann 2015: 68ff.). Likewise, in many Afro-Asiatic languages, gender and number are differentiated by Ablaut on both controllers and targets, and a similar pattern is found in Marind, a Papuan language spoken in southern Irian Jaya (Foley 1986: 83). Case is marked by Ablaut alone in a few languages, mostly in Australia (e.g. in Baardi, a Nyulnyulan language, cf. Bowern 2012: 169ff.) and Africa (e.g. in Nuer, a Nilo-Saharan language, Frank 1999), and at least one of those (Baardi) has case agreement. Hence non-linear morphological marking should obviously count as indicating the "presence" of the agreeing feature on the targets of agreement.

A more difficult problem in determining what should be counted as "the presence of agreeing feature" on the target involves the distinction between affixes and clitics. This is particularly problematic in the case of verbal agreement markers. In the grammars of some languages, the same elements that could be called verbal person markers are treated as independent pronouns, because they are not, strictly speaking, affixes on verbs. To avoid confusion, we have chosen to adopt the terminology of Haspelmath (2013a) and speak about argument indices rather than person/number/gender markers.

Argument indices can be recognized by applying the following criteria (Dixon 2002: 381; Haspelmath 2013a):

1. They are not part (or all) of an NP.
2. They cannot take modifiers.
3. They have a fixed position (or a number of possible positions) in the clause.
4. They are not complete words (they cannot stand alone in the utterance, but must co-occur with a morphological "host").

Being able to determine whether a language has pronominal clitic agreement, or no verbal agreement at all, is particularly difficult in many African languages (Creissels 2006). In the Africanist tradition it is usual to treat clitic person/number(/gender) markers as independent pronouns, and therefore to claim that languages with such clitics do not have verbal agreement. However, on closer inspection, these languages often have two "sets of pronouns," and their use differs depending on pragmatic factors. One set is regularly used when the speech-act participant is focused or otherwise emphasized, and the other set is used in pragmatically unmarked constructions. Moreover, the pragmatically marked pronouns usually do not have a fixed position in the clause, while the other pronouns do. Finally, while the pragmatically marked pronouns can freely be omitted, the use of the other pronouns is obligatory (except in some particular cases, as omission under co-reference in coordinated constructions). This is the situation we find in Babungo (Schaub 1985: 195), a Bantu language that distinguishes "subject pronouns" and "emphatic pronouns":

(66)   à   sang   ngwə́ mū?
       you   beat.PERF him   INTERR
       'Did you beat him?'

(67)   sàng   ghɔ́ sang   ngwə́ mū?
       beat.PERF you beat.PERF him   INTERR
       'Did *you* beat him?'

It is important to note that the subject forms of pronouns (such as à 'you') cannot be used in emphatic contexts. If the subject is in focus, the emphatic forms (such as *ghɔ̃*) have to be used, and their structural position in the sentence is different (and less fixed). Thus, subject forms are indeed clitic argument indices, i.e. we can treat them as person agreement markers.

Of course, the criteria for identifying argument indices mentioned above can be partially conflicting. It is possible to have bound pronouns that cannot take modifiers but that are, indeed, complete words. For example, this is the case with the English personal pronouns *I, you, he, she, it,* etc., which cannot take modifiers (hence the ungrammaticality of *this I or *big it), but they are complete words in that they do not take affixes and do not need to be attached to any verbal or nominal stem. Indeed, their position is not completely fixed in the clause (they may take a number of fixed positions according to criterion (3)). Moreover, in some languages we find pronominal elements that have a fixed position (thus satisfying criterion (3)), but they must be part of an NP (thus violating criterion (1)). This is the case with personal pronouns in some Khoisan languages. Here are some illustrative examples from Nama (Hagman 1977: 43):

(68a)   *tií kxòe-ta*
        I person-1SG
        'I the person'

(68b)   *saá kxòe-ts*
        you person-2SG.M
        'you person (m.)'

(68c)   *saá kxòe-s*
        you person-2SG.FEM
        'you person (fem.)'

(69a)   *sií !noná kàó'aok-e*
        we   three king-2PL.EXCL.M
        'we three kings (exclusive)'

(69b)   *saá á   !noná   kàó'aok-o*
        you PL   three   king-3PL.M
        'you three kings'

The head noun is inflected for person/gender/number, and it agrees with the pronoun in those features. Forms such as *tií* 'I' cannot be used independently, i.e. unless they are a part of an NP in which the noun (often a "generic noun" such as *khòe-* 'person') agrees with it.[5] This strange system of adnominal

---

[5] This applies only to the 1st and 2nd person pronouns. The 3rd person pronouns are never part of an NP.

gender agreement is found, as far as we know, only in Khoisan languages and in some Papuan languages such as Alamblak, an East Sepik language of Papua New Guinea (Bruce 1984: 96). In Alamblak, the system seems rather similar to Nama, with clitic person/gender/number markers following the last element of the NP (Bruce 1984: 90).[6]

(70a)   ïnd bro fëh-r
       DEM big pig-3SG.M
       'the big pig'

(70b)   ïnd fëh   bro-r
       DEM pig   big-3SG.M
       'the *big* pig'

Unlike in Nama, in Alamblak the person/gender/number marker need not be attached directly to the noun, but may rather be added after the adjective. However, their position is fixed and the agreement pattern is the same, with person being one of the agreeing categories (besides gender and number); moreover, the person/gender/number markers cannot be used independently, as heads of NPs. A similar system may also have existed in the extinct and unclassified Elamite language spoken in ancient Iran in the third and second millennium BC (Stolper 2008).

In Norwegian (Bokmål, Marm and Sommerfelt 1967), verbs are uninflected for person, but personal pronouns cannot take modifiers (criterion (2)) and they have a very limited number of possible positions in the clause, which is reminiscent of argument indices according to criterion (3). However, they are arguably complete words (thus violating criterion (4)), and there does not exist a separate set of personal pronouns with a "freer" position in the clause, as there is in Babungo. Moreover, although personal pronouns generally occur immediately preceding the verb (e.g. *Jeg kom* 'I come (am coming)'), they may follow it in interrogative clauses (*Kom jeg?* 'Am I coming?') and in other constructions (*For en uke siden kom han* 'A week ago he arrived'), as well as in subordinate clauses (*Hvis jeg får tid, skal jeg komme* 'If I get time, I shall come'); in subordinate clauses the verb can even be separated from the pronoun by the negation *ikke*, e.g. *Jeg visste at han ikke ville komme* (1SG knew that he NEG will come) 'I knew that he would not come'. Thus, it is probably best to treat Norwegian as a language without verbal agreement, although it might be reasonably argued that it is in the process of acquiring a new agreement pattern as its personal pronouns are being reduced to argument indices.

---

[6] Manambu (Ndu, cf. Aikhenvald 2008) also has person/gender/number-marked non-possessive NPs, but apparently only in some constructions, i.e. the system seems to be more limited than in Alamblak or Nama.

Again, it must be stressed that in coding the information about agreement patterns in individual languages some subjectivity cannot be avoided. In most languages it is clear whether they have argument indices or not, and for the purpose of this book these will be counted as verbal agreement markers, be they affixes or clitics. Doubtful cases will be recorded and discussed separately, and they will be excluded from statistical analyses where their inclusion would crucially affect the validity of hypotheses we are trying to test.

We have seen that, in verbal agreement, it is often difficult to show whether targets (verbs) contain bound morphemes (affixes or clitics) expressing agreement. In cases where no bound morphemes used as argument indices can be discovered, we do not have agreement in the sense in which we are using the term. In such languages, arguments are coded only once per clause, on independent pronouns or nouns, and the distinction between controllers and targets of person(/number) agreement cannot be maintained. In adnominal agreement, a similar problem occurs. It is sometimes the case that targets (noun modifiers) are not independent words but rather clitics modifying the controllers (i.e. the nouns themselves). We find this, for example, in Somali (Saeed 1999: 174):

(71a)   *gèed-kán*
        tree-this.M
        'this tree'

(71b)   *mindi-dán*
        knife-this.FEM
        'this knife'

In examples (71a–b), the demonstrative has a different shape depending on the gender of the noun, but it is cliticized on the noun rather than being a separate word. Possessive pronouns and interrogative pronouns behave in a similar manner in Somali. Should this count as gender agreement in the NP? Well, if we decide *not* to treat this as gender agreement, then we would clearly have to say that this is a thoroughly different syntactic process from adnominal gender agreement in, say, Italian, *just because* demonstratives happen to be clitics in Somali, rather than free words. As this is counter-intuitive, we have decided to treat such rare patterns[7] as instantiating adnominal agreement. This decision also has the merit of being consistent with our treatment of argument clitics expressing person/number(/gender) as agreement markers on verbs.

---

[7] A similar type of adnominal agreement exists in Bella Coola, a Salishan language (Davis and Saunders 1997). In Kuliná (Arawan, Dienst 2014: 73), the adnominal clitic topic marker agrees in gender with the noun it is attached to. However, in that language, other adnominal modifiers agree with the head noun, not just clitics.

4.5   Case Agreement

Although "case agreement" is a term common in traditional grammars, case is a feature that is often excluded from typological accounts of agreement. Thus neither Corbett (2006) nor Wechsler (2015) include case as one of the features that play a role in agreement systems, on the grounds that in languages where nominal modifiers agree in case, their case is not assigned by the head noun, but independently by the element that assigns case to the head noun itself – usually by a verb or an adposition. According to this view, case is a feature that falls in the domain of government rather than agreement, both with respect to nouns and noun modifiers. In Section 3.3 we have already stated that case is unlike Phi-features (person, number and gender) in a number of respects.

However, the fact remains that there is a typological contrast between languages in which case agreement exists and those where it does not, and case agreement is usually found in precisely those languages that have other forms of adnominal agreement, while it is usually absent in languages that otherwise do not have adnominal agreement.[8] Moreover, the rules for case agreement can be formulated in exactly the same manner as the rules for agreement in other features, such as number or gender. It is not a priori clear how these rules are implemented in the minds of the speakers of languages with agreement, but in the absence of strong psycholinguistic or neurolinguistic evidence to the contrary, it is quite possible that case agreement rules in the NP work identically to the gender and number (adnominal) agreement rules. We could say that case is assigned by government rules to nouns, and then indirectly by agreement rules to noun modifiers. If this is indeed so, then case should be included in a comprehensive typological study of agreement systems, and we would be wrong to omit data on case agreement in our typological database.

Optionality of case agreement appears to be more common, cross-linguistically, than the optionality of agreement of other categories. In Australian languages, case agreement is often lacking in NPs in which all the elements are adjacent to each other. In split NPs,[9] case agreement is more common. Moreover, case affixes can be added to different elements of the clause (not necessarily those belonging to the same NP) for semantic reasons. For example, in Muruwari, a Pama-Nyungan language of Australia, the genitive suffix *-ka* can be added to the possessed noun "to emphasize possession" (Oates

---

[8] There are exceptions to this claim, such as the Uralic languages spoken in Europe, like Finnish, or the Pama-Nyungan languages in Australia. Those will be treated in Chapter 8.

[9] That is, in NPs whose elements are separated from each other by other words or clitics. A split NP is found in the first verse of Virgil's *Aeneid*: …*Troiae qui primus ab oris* 'who first from the shores of Troy', where *Troiae* 'of Troy' is separated from *ab oris* 'from the shores'.

1988: 117), and the possessed noun then effectively shows case agreement with the possessor, which is also marked with the genitive suffix:

(72)   *kuntarl-ka thi-ka*
        dog-GEN 1SG-GEN
        'my dog'

A similar agreement pattern is found with the allative case marker (*-ku*), which may be added to the subject of the clause to agree with the case marking of the adjunct referring to the goal of movement (Oates 1988: 118):

(73)   *ngathu-ku   ya-n-ta-yu   Brewarrina-ku   Lightning Ridge-ngu*
        1SG.NOM-ALL go-REAL-PST-1SG Brewarrina-ALL   Lightning Ridge-ABL
        'I went to Brewarrina from Lightning Ridge'

Since such agreement patterns seem always to be optional, it is probably best to disregard them in statistical analyses of different types of agreement. However, they should be mentioned when they cluster in a number of languages and show an areally significant distribution.

There are also languages in which modifiers of the head noun must be case marked but do not appear with the same case marking as the head itself. We have this in Maiduan languages, formerly spoken in California, e.g. in Nisenan (Mithun 1999: 456f.). In that language, all modifying nouns in the NP must appear in the nominative case, regardless of the case of the head, even when the head is a numeral, as in (74):

(74)   *hyyny-im   laj-im   peen-i*
        small-NOM child-NOM two-ACC
        '[She left her] two small boys'.

Here we would not say that the adjective *hynny-* agrees with the noun *laj-* in case, since the head of the NP, the numeral *peen-* is in the accusative case. It appears more intuitive to say that the default case marker of the modifiers is the nominative *-im*.

Another challenge is presented by languages with split-ergative case marking. In such languages, demonstratives and articles sometimes have accusative case marking, while full nouns have ergative case marking. Thus, in complex NPs with demonstratives modifying nouns, the demonstratives may be in the nominative, while the nouns are in the ergative case. Should we say that in such languages the noun in the ergative agrees with the demonstrative in the nominative case? This kind of system is found, e.g., in Uradhi (Paman branch of Pama-Nyungan), where articles have nominative, and nouns ergative alignment (Crowley 1983: 364, 371, cf. also Legate 2014):

(75) *uluβa   ama:lu aniβa   aru-nyangka*
     ART.SG.NOM man.ERG 1SG.ACC hit-FUT
     'The man will hit me'

(76) *ulaβa   mupa   unyaβa:ni-n*
     ART.3.NON.SG.NOM child.ABS hide-REFL.PST
     'The children were hiding'

Claiming that elements of the NP agree in case, although they are in *different* cases is clearly counter-intuitive. However, there is an alternative analysis of such case systems. Goddard (1982) and others have argued that in such languages, the case system is basically tripartite, with an accusative, a nominative, and an ergative case. The accusative is the case of the undergoer in transitive clauses, the nominative expresses the single argument of intransitives, and the ergative is the case of the actor of transitive verbs. For pronouns (and articles), there is syncretism of the nominative and the ergative, while the nouns attest to syncretism of the nominative and the accusative. If this is accepted, we can change the gloss of nominative to ergative in example (75) and Uradhi will exhibit a very commonplace pattern of case agreement, with *uluβa ama:lu* 'the man' agreeing in the ergative case (which, for *uluβa*, happens to be syncretic with the nominative). Likewise, if we change the label absolutive to nominative in (76), *mupa* will agree in the nominative with its modifier *ulaβa*.

Therefore, for reasons stated above, information about case agreement should be included in our comprehensive typological study of agreement systems. However, for purposes of specific analyses, we can and will choose to exclude case agreement, given its theoretical status is contested.

4.6   Person/Number Agreement in the NP

In some languages, the possessed noun agrees in person (usually also in number) with the possessor. This is often the case with inalienably possessed nouns, e.g. in Amele (a Papuan language of the Trans-New Guinea stock, Roberts 1987: 86):

(77) *Naus uqa mela-h-ul   ho-gi-na*
     N.   3SG son-3SG-POSS come-3PL-PRES
     'Naus' sons are coming'

In (77), the name *Naus*, modified by the 3sg pronoun *uqa*, is the controller, the possessed noun *mela* is the target, and the suffix *-h-* is the agreement marker. The expression of number in the subject NP is not obligatory, but it is marked on the verb by the 3pl suffix *-gi-*. On the other hand, the person/number agreement in the NP is obligatory, so the presence of the possessor *Naus uqa* automatically triggers the presence of the 3sg possessive *-h-ul-* on the possessum.

In most languages with possessive person/number agreement in the NP, the presence of the overt possessor is not obligatory. For example, in Hungarian, 'the man's house' is *az ember ház-a* (the man house-3SG.POSS), 'my house' is *az én ház-om* (ART I house-1SG.POSS), but *a ház-om* (ART house-1SG.POSS) 'my house' is also perfectly grammatical. This is, in itself, not a problem, since we have already decided to treat verbal argument indices in languages with Pro-drop as agreement markers (see Section 4.2). We can say that forms like Hungarian *a házom* show agreement with omitted controllers, just as the Italian clause *Vogli-amo cant-are* 'We want to sing' (want-PRES.1PL sing-INF) shows agreement with the omitted first person plural pronoun (*noi*).

However, this pattern is unlike the other kinds of agreement discussed so far, in that we only find it in one particular type of construction (the possessive construction, often only in case of inalienable possession), and not in all types of NPs. Treating this as the same type of phenomenon as adnominal gender agreement, which does not depend on the semantics of the NP, would clearly be counter-intuitive. With gender, number and case agreement, the default situation is that all NPs in a language show agreement in those categories, not just a subset of them. We do find languages in which certain types of agreement are restricted to NPs headed by nouns denoting humans, or where gender agreement obtains only with singular, but not with plural, nouns, but restrictions on agreement to certain types of NPs do not tend to occur, e.g. we do not expect languages in which gender agreement is found only in NPs containing quantifiers or numerals. Actually, saying that person agreement in possessive NPs is just like any other type of adnominal agreement would be like saying that numeral nominal classifiers should be treated like genders, although they are tied to one particular type of NP, namely to NPs containing numerals (Allen 1977). Indeed, non-restrictedness to one type of NP is one of the criteria for distinguishing gender agreement from constructions with numeral classifiers.

However, there is one particular type of possessive person agreement that deserves special attention and that is very like other uncontroversial agreement systems; in languages such as Navajo, some nouns cannot be used alone, they are "bound" to possessive affixes, i.e. they are obligatorily possessed (see the map WALS 58A, Bickel and Nichols 2013). For example, in Navajo, the noun *-be'* 'milk' must be possessed. One cannot say just 'milk', but one must rather specify whose milk it is, e.g. *bi-be'* 'her milk' or (with an 'indefinite possessor') *'a-be'* 'someone's milk'. Here one must note that *any* NP with a particular noun (an "obligatorily possessed noun") must show a possessive affix, which can be said to agree in person with the possessor. The possessor, in turn, may, but generally need not, be expressed. Such languages with obligatorily possessed nouns are rare in Eurasia and Africa, but they seem to be rather common in the Americas. Their areal distribution will be further discussed in Chapter 8.

Another kind of adnominal agreement that involves the category of person is the unusual system found in Khoisan languages (discussed in Sections 3.2.2 and 4.4), where each NP contains a person/number/gender clitic, which agrees with the head noun in these categories (or rather marks the whole NP for them). We have argued earlier (see Section 3.2.4) that the "obviation agreement" in Algonquian languages, where adnominal modifiers share the obviation marking of the head noun, is a similar phenomenon. In any case, our overview of the languages in our sample and the relevant typological literature assures us that person agreement in the NP is not a very common phenomenon in the languages of the world, but it must be included in a large-scale investigation of areal distribution of agreement patterns. Consequently, we have decided to examine the languages in our database for the presence vs. absence of the Navajo-type possessive agreement in the NP, in which certain nouns are obligatorily possessed and must have a possessive affix to show agreement with the possessor.

5   Grammatical, Ambiguous and Anaphoric Agreement

We have seen in the preceding chapters that the NP and the clause are the two main domains of agreement, and that, consequently, adnominal and verbal agreement are the two principal types of agreement. But how comparable are they? This chapter argues that, although there are differences between the two types, there is also a parallelism in the way they are realized, showing that we are dealing with a well-defined grammatical rule applicable in a variety of languages.

Our definition of agreement, presented in Chapter 2, was deliberately formulated in rather broad terms, in order to be applicable to a wide range of related phenomena in different languages. It required that there is a systematic covariance between some (semantic or formal) property of controllers and a morphological marking on targets. However, our definition did not exclude instances where the controller of agreement was omitted, as is the case with person agreement on the verb in Pro-drop languages and with person agreement in possessive NPs. It required only that the agreeing feature be present on the target, not that the controller be present in the actual utterance. It can be omitted, if it can be unambiguously retrieved from the context. Thus, we can say that in the Latin sentence *Venit* 'he/she/it is coming' the verb agrees with the 3rd person singular subject, which is unexpressed. Likewise, if we imagine a discourse in which someone is talking about a certain man (Lat. *homo*) and then the question is asked about his height, the answer *Altus est* '(He) is tall' may be appropriate. In this case we would say that the adjective *altus* agrees in masculine gender with the subject *homo*, which is retrievable from the context, but unexpressed. Let us now discuss the types of agreement constructions that can be deduced from the presence vs. absence of controllers.

Siewierska (1999) distinguished three types of person agreement, depending on whether the controller of agreement is obligatorily present or not. Since person/number agreement is the most common kind of verbal agreement,[1] it

---

[1] Although Siewierska developed her typology with just person(/number) agreement in mind, it can easily be extended to gender verbal agreement as well, and the analogous definitions of the three types would apply.

is tempting to look at all three types and determine in advance whether to count them all as parallel to adnominal agreement in gender, number, case and person.

1. Grammatical agreement: The controller has to be present and the agreement marker is likewise obligatory. Grammatical agreement on verbs is found in languages that do not allow Pro-drop, such as English:[2]

(78)   *Jack sings / *Sings*

2. Ambiguous agreement: The controller may or may not be present, but the agreement marker is still obligatory.[3] Ambiguous verbal agreement in person is found in languages that allow Pro-drop, such as Croatian (Slavic):

(79)   *Ivan   ide / Ide*
        Ivan   goes / goes
        'Ivan goes / (He) goes'

3. Anaphoric agreement: The controller and the agreement marker are in complementary distribution, i.e. the latter occurs on the target only if the former is not present. Macushi (Cariban) is a language with verbal agreement of this type (Abbott 1991: 24):

(80)   *t-ekînera'   ma-'pî   paaka   esa'ya*
        REFL-pet.ABS   see-PRET   cow   owner
        'The owner of the cow saw his own pet'

(81)   *i-koneka-'pî-ya*
        3SG-make-PRET-3SG.ERG
        'He made it'

It is clear that anaphoric agreement is different from the other two types in one crucial respect: The "agreement markers" occur on the verb only when there is no NP in the clause for the verb to *agree* with (as in (81)). Rather, the agreement is with some NP elsewhere in the discourse, which is the proper

---

[2] It has been argued that in some Australian languages (Austin and Bresnan 1996) the obligatory presence of true (i.e. non-referring) agreement markers does not imply that the controller is obligatory, as it can be omitted in contexts of zero-anaphora. Such languages can be said to combine grammatical agreement with Pro-drop. In essence, this means that if a language does not allow Pro-drop, this implies it has grammatical agreement, but the converse probably does not hold: Languages with Pro-drop can also have grammatical agreement.

[3] This type has three sub-types, distinguished with respect to the status of the affix(es) expressing agreement. This affix can always be an incorporated pronoun (e.g. in Kabardian, a NW Caucasian language), it can never be an incorporated pronoun (e.g. in Croatian, under most analyses), or it can be an incorporated pronoun only when there is no phrasal argument (e.g. in Welsh).

domain of this type of agreement. Moreover, as we will claim below, this type of verbal agreement probably does not have any analog in the domain of adnominal agreement. Since the domain of agreement in anaphoric agreement is the discourse, rather than the clause or sentence, this type of agreement is similar to "anaphoric" gender/number agreement, in which pronouns agree in these categories not with their head noun in the NP, but rather with some nominal antecedent previously mentioned in the discourse (cf. the English gendered pronouns *he, she, it*). This type, which we may call *pronominal gender agreement*, is not considered as instantiating adnominal agreement in this book, and for this reason, in order to preserve the consistency of our treatment of agreement systems, we have decided to disregard Siewierska's anaphoric agreement in our discussion of verbal agreement. However, grammars do not always allow us to decide with certainty which type a language belongs to, so there are cases where it is difficult to decide whether it has an anaphoric or ambiguous verbal agreement system.[4] Still, such languages were identified in the sample, and their special status was taken into account in the statistical analyses discussed below.

Siewierska's typology was based on the intuition that there is a diachronic progression from anaphoric to ambiguous agreement, and hence to grammatical agreement, as person pronouns become agreement morphemes, thereby losing their referential properties and becoming purely grammatical markers of agreement. As we will argue in Chapter 10, no such diachronic progression is probable for adnominal agreement markers, which is why it is difficult to establish types of adnominal agreement analogous to Siewierska's types of verbal (person) agreement. However, some parallelism can still be said to exist.

In order to see how adnominal agreement constructions are comparable to verbal agreement constructions, we obviously need some more fine-grained distinctions. We believe that three grammatical parameters have to be distinguished:

1. whether the grammatical category (number, person, gender, case) can be "displaced," expressed on some other element of the syntactic unit than the controller (i.e. the element that is usually the controller of agreement for that category)
2. whether the presence of the controller is obligatory or not
3. whether it is possible to express the grammatical category twice in a syntactic unit.

---

[4] It would be difficult to distinguish between anaphoric and other kinds of verbal agreement in a principled way because, as Siewierska says (2004: 126), "the distinction between pronominal and ambiguous agreement markers and thus between anaphoric and grammatical agreement is a scalar one," and the sources of our data seldom note that distinction explicitly. In any case, the inclusion of languages with anaphoric agreement does not affect our general conclusions, since clear instances of this type are very rare.

Table 3 *A typology of verbal agreement systems (for number)*

Agreement in the V (number)	Displaceable Phi-features	Controller obligatory	Categories doubly expressible
Kabardian	+	−	+
Italian	+	−	+
Kayardild	+	−	+
Turkish	+	−	+
English	+	+	+
Japanese	−	−	−
Macushi	+	−	−
Welsh	+/−	−	+/−

These parameters are partly independent of each other, and their values can be combined in different manners in different languages. With respect to number agreement on verbs (the commonest kind of verbal agreement, along-side person agreement), we can distinguish the types of languages shown in Table 3.

All languages in Table 3 are Pro-drop, except for English. English is the only one that has grammatical verbal agreement (in Siewierska's terms), while Macushi is the only one that has anaphoric agreement (the agreement marker is on the verb only if there is no overt controller). Japanese has no verbal agreement at all, and Italian, Kayardild and Turkish, although very different languages in almost every respect, all have ambiguous agreement: The agreement marker must be on the verb, irrespective of whether the controller is present or not. This is cross-linguistically the most common type of verbal agreement.

We have deliberately formulated the third parameter in terms of double *expressibility* of categories, because there are languages in which they *can*, but need not, be expressed twice in the clause. There is usually a grammatical condition stating when certain grammatical categories are expressed twice. One such language is Welsh, where number agreement occurs only with pronouns, but not with nouns:

(82) *Daeth*   *y dynion*
      come.3   ART man.PL
      'The men come'

(83) *Daethan (nhw)*
      come.3PL they
      'They come'

A similar restriction on person agreement exists in Maxakalí, a Macro-Jê language spoken in Brazil, where verbs get a person marking prefix only if the subject is not immediately before an intransitive verb (Rodrigues 1999: 186):

(84a) *pɨtšap tšipep*
       duck arrive
       'The duck arrives'

vs.

(84b) *ʔɨ-tšipep pɨtšap*
       3-arrive duck
       'The duck arrives'

In Breton, too, the verb may be inflected or uninflected for person depending on its position with respect to the other elements of the clause:

(85)   *Me   a skriv*
       1SG PTC write
       'I am writing'

(86)   *Ul lizher a skrivañ*
       ART letter PTC write.1SG
       'I am writing a letter'

Note that both *Ul lizher a skriv* and *Me a skrivañ* would be ungrammatical.

In Arabic, the verb normally agrees in person, gender and number with its subject, but if the subject is human, there is number agreement only if the subject precedes the verb, not if it follows it (Ryding 2014: 130):

(87a) *al-banaatu   daras-na   fii   l-maktabat-i*
       ART-girls.NOM   studied-3.PL.F   in   ART-library-GEN
       'The girls studied in the library'

(87b) *daras-at   al-banaatu   fii   l-maktabat-i*
       studied-3.SG.F ART-girls.NOM   in   ART-library-GEN
       'The girls studied in the library'

In Arabic, the verb still agrees in gender and person with its subject, irrespective of its position in the clause, but the number agreement is dependent on the position of the verb. Conditions may vary across languages, but in all such languages the category of number is expressible twice in a clause.

Let us review the possible combination of parameters in Table 3: The specification of parameters for grammatical agreement is [+displaceability of features +obligatoriness of controllers +double expressibility of categories], for anaphoric agreement the specification is [+--], for ambiguous agreement [+-+] and, of course, for no agreement it is [---]. The combination [+/-- +/-], which is found in Welsh, defines a language type similar to the one with anaphoric agreement, but in which a Phi-feature (number) is displaceable and doubly expressible only for some subjects (the pronominal subjects), but not for others (the nouns). It could, in principle, be considered as a sub-type of ambiguous agreement. Some combinations of features do not seem to occur: [--+] and [-++] are logically impossible, since a feature cannot be doubly expressible if it is not displaceable, i.e. if it is not expressible on an element other than the referring NP. The combination [++-] is likewise impossible since, if the "controller" is obligatorily present, it has to be specified for Phi-features (person, number, and in some languages also gender) and, if some or all of these Phi-features are doubly expressible, they have to be expressed on some element other than the controller, i.e. they have to be displaceable. Finally, the type [-+-] is logically possible, but somewhat incongruent, since it would be odd to call "controller" the element which does not control anything (for the features it "controls" are neither displaceable nor doubly expressible). Notionally, it would be a language with verbs that are not inflected for gender/person/ number (and without clitics expressing those categories), in which every sentence must have an overt subject. There do not appear to be any such languages in our sample: Prototypical isolating languages without verbal agreement, such as Thai, freely omit their subjects, as well as other arguments, if the referents are retrievable from context. Thus, example (88) is completely grammatical in Thai, although neither subject, direct object nor indirect object are stated (Smyth 2002: 117):

(88)   tôŋ   rîip   pay   súuu   hây
       must hurry go   buy   give
       'I must rush off and buy some for her'

Let us compare this typology of verbal agreement systems with agreement patterns in the domain of the NP. The category of number was chosen again, as the most common adnominal agreement category (see Table 4).

Apparently, there are no languages in which all elements of the NP must contain the controller, i.e. the noun. Kayardild (Tangkic) is close to this potential type: In this language adjectives agree in case and number, but cannot occur without nouns in an NP (Gil 2013), but even in Kayardild, demonstratives bearing case and number markers can appear as heads of NPs (Evans 1995: 205). A language with grammatical adnominal agreement would be

Table 4 *A typology of adnominal agreement systems (for number)*

Agreement in the NP (number)	Displaceable number marking	Controller obligatory	Doubly expressible number marking
Kabardian	+	−	−
Italian	+	−	+
Kayardild	+	(+)	+
Turkish	−	−	−
English	+ (marginal)	−	+ (marginal)
Japanese	−	−	−
Macushi	−	−	−

just like Kayardild, except that it would not allow case and number marked demonstratives (or any other modifiers of nouns) as heads of NPs. Hence, there appears to be no equivalent to Pro-drop languages in the NP domain.

There are, again, languages with no agreement in the NP, such as Turkish and Japanese. In Turkish, for example, there is no gender, and the number marker (*-lar/-ler*) marks only the head noun in the NP, not the modifiers, as shown in (89a–b) (see also the discussion in Chapter 2):

(89a)   *ev   bu ev   bu büyük ev*
        'house' 'this house' 'this big house'

(89b)   *ev-ler   bu ev-ler   bu büyük ev-ler*
        'houses' 'these houses' 'these big houses'

The Turkish examples (89a–b) show that the plural morpheme in that language is not displaceable, i.e. it has to mark the head noun in the NP. A language like Turkish, but with a displaceable plural morpheme, might appear to be the equivalent of anaphoric agreement on the NP level, but it is difficult to apply Siewierska's terminology in this case, and this will become apparent if we contrast Turkish with Kabardian. In Kabardian (90a–b), the number morphemes are displaceable, in that they can mark the adjective rather than the noun in the NP:

(90a)   *pśāśa-r pśāśa dāxa-r*
        girl-ABS girl beautiful-ABS
        'girl'   'beautiful girl'

(90b)   *pśāśa-xa-r pśāśa dāxa-xa-r*
        girl-PL-ABS girl beautiful-PL-ABS
        'girls'   'beautiful girls'

Although the plural morpheme -*xa*- is on the adjective, if it is not on the noun (i.e. it can be displaced), we would not say that a language such as Kabardian has number agreement – rather, we say that the number morpheme in that language is attached to the last lexeme in the NP. That lexeme is not the target of agreement, since the number morpheme (-*xa*-) is not controlled by the head noun, inherently marked for number: Nouns are not inherently marked for number in the sense that they are assigned to a particular gender in languages with gender. This is why it is implausible to analyze the Kabardian data as displaying anaphoric adnominal agreement. Kabardian is, indeed, just like Turkish, but in Turkish the last element of an NP is, by default, the noun, and so it bears the number marker. Saying that Kabardian has anaphoric adnominal agreement, while Turkish lacks any adnominal agreement, would hide this structural similarity between these two languages. We could also imagine a language with adnominal agreement in which the agreement marker is present on a modifier of the noun (say adjective and/or demonstrative) only when there is no controller. This would be the proper equivalent of the anaphoric type of verbal agreement, but there appear to be no such languages (at least in our sample).

Finally, since grammatical verbal agreement is possible only in languages that have obligatory controllers in every clause (i.e. in languages without Pro-drop), it would appear that languages cannot have grammatical adnominal agreement, since we saw that there seem to be no languages in which all NPs have obligatory nominal heads. Hence, we can conclude that adnominal agreement, unlike verbal agreement, cannot be grammatical. It follows, then, that adnominal agreement is always ambiguous, i.e. languages with adnominal agreement always have the specification of parameters [+displaceability of features –obligatoriness of controllers +double expressibility of categories] as in languages with ambiguous verbal agreement.

Therefore, it is clear that comparing types of agreement patterns in both domains (the clause for verbal, the NP for adnominal agreement) makes sense only if we limit our investigation to ambiguous agreement. In our database, we have collected data for languages that have grammatical verbal agreement, and also for those very rare languages with anaphoric agreement. We have compared the areal patterning of those languages with the areal patterns found for languages with other types of agreement (adnominal and verbal) and some interesting results concerning grammatical verbal agreement will be discussed in Chapter 9. However, unless it is specifically claimed otherwise, in what follows "language with agreement" will mean language with ambiguous agreement, as defined by Siewierska (and above).

6   Marginal Agreement

It is clear that agreement plays a major role in grammars of some languages, whereas it affects the grammar of others only marginally. In a language such as Swahili, agreement is a pervasive phenomenon: All modifiers of the head noun must agree with it in gender/number, and verbs also agree in gender/number with their subjects. Moreover, the nouns are also marked for gender/number (i.e. there is overt agreement):

(91) *ki-kapu*   *ki-kubwa*   *ki-moja*   *ki-lianguka*
      CL.7-basket CL.7-large   CL.7-one   CL.7-fall(PRET)
      'One large basket fell'

On the other hand, in English, adnominal agreement in number exists, but it is limited to just a few lexical items: The demonstratives *this* and *that* have to agree in number with the noun they modify (*this man* but *these men*, *that horse* vs. *those horses*). Besides that, English has traces of gender agreement, as relative pronouns have to agree in animacy, but this "agreement" is by suppletion, since different stems are used: cf. *the man who came*, but *the stone which lies on the ground* (**the stone who lies on the ground*). Thus, when compared with Swahili, English clearly has marginal number agreement.

In Hungarian, the marginality of adnominal agreement is particularly radical, as there are only two words, the demonstratives *ez* 'this' and *az* 'that', that agree in case and number (Rounds 2001: 132–3):

(92) *az-t*   *a*   *film-et*   *akar-om*   *meg-néz-ni*
      this-ACC ART   film-ACC   want-1SG.PRES   PERF-seen-INF
      'I want to watch that movie'

(93) *E*   *ház-ban*   *lak-ott*   *az*   *egész család*
      this   house-INESS live-PRET.3SG   ART   whole family
      'The whole family lived in this house'

In (92), the demonstrative *azt* has the accusative marker *-t* and agrees with the head noun (*film-et* 'film'), but a different demonstrative *e* in (93) carries no case marking and does not agree with the head noun *ház-ban* 'in house', which is in the inessive case. Similarly, the definite article and adjectives do not agree with the head noun, so 'in the big house' would be *a nagy ház-ban*, with the adjective *nagy* and the definite article *a* both uninflected.

In Ngiti (a Nilo-Saharan language spoken in the Democratic Republic of the Congo), only some modifiers have plurals, and these are formed by reduplication or suppletion. Adjectives meaning 'big', 'small' and 'other' form their plurals by suppletion, and, with human nouns (which have special plural forms), there is agreement in number (Kutsch Lojenga 1993: 345):

(94a)   *ngátsi ngbángba*
         other   child
         'another child'

(94b)   *ngɯkpà nzónzo*
         'other children' (both the adjective and the noun have suppletive plurals)

Again, this kind of number agreement is confined to a small set of lexical items, so it is clearly marginal.

In Sarcee (Athabaskan-Eyak), only human nouns and the nouns *tłí(tc'á)* 'dog' and *ìstłí* 'horse' occur with numerals which may carry a plural marker, thus agreeing with the head noun in number (Rijkhoff 2002: 37):

(95)   *gūnìsnóní-ká   tłí-ká*
         nine-PL   dog-PL
         'nine dogs'

This pattern of number agreement is marginal not just because it is limited to humans and two higher animates, but also because it shows only on numerals, which behave as a kind of appositional noun. That is, not only is the number of controllers of agreement lexically limited, the number of targets is limited too, which justifies the decision to treat this pattern as marginal.

However, it is impossible to say precisely how limited a lexical class showing agreement should be to call it marginal. Any decision is arbitrary. For example, Makalero (Trans-New Guinea) has a limited number of verbs that show subject number agreement; they do not appear to be a semantically coherent class, except that they are all monovalent (they include verbs for running, sleeping, standing and being big). In her grammar of Makalero, Huber (2011: 130) cites five verbs that exhibit number agreement, but implies that there are more such verbs; in the absence of an exhaustive list, it is probably better to conclude that the pattern is not truly marginal.

There surely are dubious, borderline cases. In Georgian (Kartvelian), adjectives agree with the nouns they modify in case and number only if they are postposed (96a), but not if they are preposed (96b) (Testelec 1998: 652):

(96a) *kal-eb-s*   *lamaz-eb-s*
woman-PL-DAT   nice-PL-DAT
'to the nice women'

(96b) *am*   *or lamaz*   *kal-s*
that.OBL two nice   woman-DAT
'to those two nice women'

Testelec (1998: 249) claims that the postposition of adjectives is now found only in "archaizing" style and, moreover, he argues that constructions with postposed adjectives show some characteristics of appositions (1998: 652, 677), so that (96a) might also be translatable as 'to women, to the nice ones'. Note, however, that the demonstrative pronoun (*am*) has a special oblique form even when it is preposed, distinguishing it from the nominative/absolutive form, which would have been used before a nominative/absolutive noun. It is for this reason that it is probably better not to treat Georgian case agreement as a marginal phenomenon.

An agreement pattern should not be called "marginal" just because its morphological expression is minimal and restricted to just one form (or a handful of forms) within a paradigm. The fact that in the English present tense of regular verbs only the 3rd person singular is morphologically marked (*goes, sings* as opposed to the *go, sing* in the other persons) makes person/number agreement less conspicuous in the English verbal system. However, the syntactic rule of agreement is strong, obligatory and exceptionless, and in the irregular verb *to be* different endings are found in all persons of the singular. Hence, we would not call this agreement pattern marginal, because, as a syntactic rule, it plays a major role in the structure of English.

Agreement can be both optional *and* marginal. In Chukchi (Chukchi-Kamchatkan), case/number agreement is common (but optional) only when both the noun and its attribute are in the nominative case, e.g. *načgen-(at) k'or-at* (old.man's-NOM.PL elk-NOM.PL) 'elks of the old man'; in the oblique cases, case agreement is exceptional (marginal), since Chukchi usually incorporates modifiers, cf. *n'evysket-in evirr-yn* (woman-GEN clothes-GEN) 'of the clothes of a woman' vs. *n'evysk'et-evirr-yn* 'of the woman's clothes', where the possessor *n'evysk'et* 'woman' is incorporated (Skorik 1968: 268).

Finally, we must note that there are languages in which only borrowed lexical items are subject to agreement. In Bengali (Indo-Aryan), only adjectives borrowed from Sanskrit show gender agreement (Bykova 1981), and in Tagalog (Austronesian), this holds only for adjectives borrowed from Spanish (Schachter and Otanes 1972: 166 ff.). To say that these languages have gender agreement just like Russian (where all adjectives, irrespective of their origin, agree) may be correct in principle, but it tends to miss an important difference in the status of agreement in those languages. Hence, it seems appropriate to say that gender agreement in languages like Bengali and Tagalog is marginal.

In any empirical work the question always arises how to treat such "marginal" phenomena. To dismiss them as irrelevant can be interpreted as cheating or putting inconvenient data under the carpet. Certainly, dismissing marginal agreement patterns would not be as empirically adequate as including them in an investigation of the areal typology of agreement systems. Moreover, dismissing "marginal" agreement is bound to be somewhat subjective, because it is difficult to give an exact definition of what should be counted as a marginal agreement pattern. On the other hand, to say that English and Hungarian are languages with adnominal agreement just like Italian or Swahili disguises important differences between these two groups of languages. Therefore, we think that the best approach is to note, for each language studied, whether the agreement patterns it has are marginal and in exactly what sense. The distribution of agreement patterns can then be studied separately for all languages with agreement and only for those in which agreement is not marginal, and then it can be tested if the two approaches result in any empirical or statistical differences. This is, indeed, how we have approached "marginal" agreement patterns in this book.

Part II

Empirical Results

7   The Sample of Languages

7.1   The Construction of the Sample

This study aims to discover patterns in the areal distribution of particular types of agreement. Establishing that certain linguistic types are especially rare, or unexpectedly common, in a particular area, requires two things: First, that areas be defined independently, before the sample of languages is determined, and second that the language sample be representative, in the sense that every area should contain a number of languages proportional to its overall linguistic diversity.

In this study we chose to divide the world into five macro-areas that make sense from the geographic point of view: 1. Eurasia, 2. Africa and the Middle East, 3. North America, 4. South America and 5. Australia and Oceania. Our list of areas thus corresponds to a large extent to the list of continents, with four exceptions: First, Middle East was included in a single area with Africa because it did not make sense to separate the Semitic languages of the Middle East (Hebrew and Arabic) from the Semitic and other Afro-Asiatic languages in Africa. Second, Eurasia was treated as a single unit, since it is very difficult to separate Europe from Asia when it comes to the spread of particular languages. For example, do the languages of the Caucasus belong to Europe or to Asia? Any decision would seem to be arbitrary, and the same applies to many Uralic, Turkic and Iranian languages. Third, languages of Oceania, New Zealand and New Guinea were treated together with the languages of Australia within a single macro-area (Australia and Oceania), and, finally, Antarctica was not surveyed for obvious reasons. We did not want to include in our list of macro-areas those regions for which there is already ample evidence that they behave as zones of linguistic diffusion, e.g. the Indian Subcontinent (Masica 1976), the Caucasus (Klimov 1986), Central America (Campbell, Kaufman and Smith-Stark 1986), etc. Defining the exact borders of such areas is somewhat arbitrary, and there is always danger that the areas will be defined in such a manner as to confirm the initial hypothesis that the researcher has about the areal distribution of the features under investigation. To avoid begging the question in this way, it was decided that the areas would be defined geographically, rather than (geo-)linguistically. Therefore, the Indian Subcontinent, Mainland Southeast Asia and the Caucasus are all treated as parts of Eurasia. However, each of the five major areas contains independently established micro-areas, so our data allow us to examine linguistic micro-areas such as Mainland Southeast Asia in order to determine if languages spoken there also share some common properties when it comes to agreement systems. In what follows, we shall have a number of occasions to do so (see especially Chapter 8).

The question of how to collect a representative sample of languages, both globally and with respect to particular areas, is not an easy one. First, there is the question of the number of languages to include. The whole project on language universals started with just 30 carefully selected languages (Greenberg 1963), but now the consensus seems to be that at least one hundred languages is the desirable number (cf. the 100-language core sample in WALS). Most WALS chapters are based on at least 200 languages, and there are some for which more than 1000 were collected.[1] Of course, the more complex the research topic, the more difficult it is to obtain the relevant data, and therefore larger samples become less practicable. Also, if one needs to make a thorough examination of certain aspects of grammar (e.g. determine exactly which nominal modifiers agree with the head noun in the NP), then large samples are difficult to collect, as thorough descriptive works containing the relevant information are scarce. In spite of their authors' best efforts, grammars of languages often reflect what their authors were interested in, rather than what the readers may want to find out about the language in question. In doing research for the present work we have read several grammars counting more than 400 pages that do not give information on whether demonstratives agree in number with their head nouns, even if it is clear that both the noun and the demonstratives can be inflected for number. The more languages one collects, the greater the chance that non-reliable and non-comprehensive sources will have to be used. It is for this reason that we have limited the number of languages in our sample to 300. If it is accepted that around 6000 languages are spoken in the world today,[2] these languages represent around 5 percent of the world's linguistic diversity, and the examination of relevant descriptions brought us to the conclusion that reliable information can be found about approximately this number of languages. Of course, there are reliable descriptions of many more than 300 languages, but these tend to be well-studied languages of Europe and Asia, and to include them would bias the sample toward the Old World. Which brings us

---

[1] Bakker (2011) calculated that the average sample of WALS samples (in the 2005 version of the site) was 417, while 39 samples consisted of over 500 languages.

[2] Ethnologue gives the number of 7102 languages, but this source is on the splitting side of the continuum between the lumpers and the splitters in counting languages of the world. Other sources give lower figures, e.g. Ruhlen (1991: 1) and Hagège (2000: 1) estimate that there are 5000 languages in the world.

to the question of collecting the representative sample for our study from the areal point of view.

The basic idea was that the number of languages in the sample from any area should be proportional to the overall linguistic diversity of that area.[3] In terms of numbers of languages, here is how the languages of the world are distributed in our chosen areas. First we give the numbers of (living) languages spoken in different continents according to Ethnologue:

> Africa: 2138 (30%)
> The Americas: 1064 (15%)
> Eurasia (separated into Europe and Asia in Ethnologue): 2587 (36%)
> Pacific (with Australia): 1313 (19%)

Of course, these numbers do not give us the whole picture of the relative linguistic diversity of individual areas. Firstly, the number of languages spoken in an area does not have to correspond with that area's genetic diversity, if most (or exceedingly many) languages in that area belong to a single family (or to a small number of families). Thus, for example, although Africa appears to be the most diverse continent in terms of the number of languages spoken there (and also in terms of the number of languages divided by square kilometers), its genetic diversity is actually lower than that of most other continents. According to Greenberg's classification (still found in some relevant sources, e.g. Ruhlen 1991 and Heine and Nurse 2000), the languages of Africa can be attributed to only four indigenous families: Niger-Kordofanian, Nilo-Saharan, Afro-Asiatic and Khoisan, plus a few isolates (e.g. Laal in Chad). There are also a few recent intruders, such as Austronesian Malagasy on Madagascar and Indo-European English and Afrikaans in South Africa, plus some other Indo-European languages, remaining as a part of Europe's colonial heritage in Africa. Even if most Africanists today would agree that Khoisan should be rather seen as a number of different families, and many doubt whether Nilo-Saharan is a valid genetic grouping, it is nevertheless true that the number of language families in Africa is much smaller than in other inhabited continents. Here it must be mentioned that Glottolog, which is otherwise an up-to-date resource for genetic classification, is extremely conservative with respect to African language classification. Although it is difficult to assume only four native language families in Africa, as in Greenberg's original classification noted above, 59 (as proposed by Glottolog) is almost certainly an overblown number.

Likewise, the number of language families in South and North America appears to be higher than the average, even if not all genetic groupings have been discovered already. This also holds for New Guinea and Australia, where

---

[3] On the use of macro-areas in linguistic sampling see Hammarström and Donohue (2014).

the genetic classification of languages is notoriously controversial. As many as 50 language families, comprising around 830 languages, are estimated to be present in New Guinea alone. To offset for the factor of genetic diversity, we have decided to also take into account the number of language families in individual areas. Here are the numbers from Glottolog:

> Africa: 59
> Australia and "Papunesia" (roughly corresponding to our Australia and Oceania): 178
> Eurasia: 46
> North America: 82
> South America: 117

Obviously, these data mean that the Americas, where more than a third of the world's genetic diversity of languages is found (as compared to only 15 percent of the world's languages),[4] need to be represented by more languages than would be the case if we looked only at the number of languages spoken in particular areas.[5]

Moreover, not all families were created equal. Some language families comprise several hundreds of languages (e.g. Sino-Tibetan, Indo-European and Austronesian), while others, such as Kartvelian, have only a few members. And then there are the isolates, such as Basque and Ainu, which also have to be well represented in a properly assembled database.[6] Large linguistic families such as Indo-European usually tend to have more time-depth than small ones (although this is not an absolute rule), so languages from different primary branches of large families may be structurally as different as languages belonging to different language families. This fact should also be captured in our sample, and one possibility would be to use the sampling method advocated by Matthew Dryer (1989, 1992), in which *genera* rather than individual languages are elements of the sample. Genera are units of genetic classification of approximately the same time-depth, corresponding, roughly, to Romance or Slavic languages in the Indo-European family. In this method of sampling, when languages belonging to a genus agree with respect to some feature (say, the order of O and V) the genus is characterized as having the feature in question. When the genus is internally inconsistent, the genus is counted as two

---

[4] Östen Dahl (2009: 216) reaches a similar conclusion: "My claim, then, is that any method that gives the Americas less than 35 percent of the languages in a sample underrepresents them."

[5] The exact number of families in both Americas is disputed, but it is in the order of magnitude of the number suggested by Glottolog. Campbell and Grondona (2012) list 108 language families and isolates for South America, and Marianne Mithun (1999) lists only 55 families and isolates for North America, but excludes the families of Central America.

[6] Our sample contains thirteen isolates.

units in the sample, one having and the other lacking the feature. The idea is that by using genera rather than languages, the linguistic diversity of the world will be divided into comparable linguistic units, which will give us an objective basis for sampling. However, Dryer's method is more appropriate for typological investigations with rather simple objectives where genera are likely to agree with respect to the presence or absence of a feature, such as the order of syntactic units. In examining more fine-grained linguistic features, where internal inconsistency of genera is more common, it is much more difficult to use this method of sampling. Besides, deciding which units of genetic classification have approximately the same time-depth is difficult and time-consuming for many language families, so the costs of using Dryer's sampling method appear to exceed its benefits in terms of having a genetically unbiased sample.

But still, the fact that some families are disproportionately large, and should not be treated in the same manner as smaller families, has to be addressed in some way. Therefore, as a matter of principle, we have decided to take at least three languages from those families that have more than a hundred languages. Here is a list of those language families from Ethnologue: Afro-Asiatic (374), Austronesian (1257), Austro-Asiatic (169), Australian (269), Indo-European (439), Nilo-Saharan (205), Niger-Congo (1532), Oto-Manguean (177), Sino-Tibetan (449), and Trans-New Guinea (477).[7] Note that Nilo-Saharan, Trans-New Guinea and Australian families are not generally accepted in the literature, but we have nevertheless included more than three languages from these families in our sample. On the other hand, increasing the number of languages from areas with high genetic diversity would not make sense if languages from only one or two families were included, so care was taken to maximize the number of language families in the sample in those areas where genetic diversity was highest, especially in the Americas and in Australia and Oceania.

Then there is the question of extinct languages. It is a general principle in contemporary linguistics that languages spoken today are in all respects comparable to languages spoken many millennia ago, i.e. we do not expect extinct languages to be in any way structurally more different from living languages than living languages are different among themselves. Indeed, this principle is almost certainly correct, but it does not imply that only living languages should be used in typological studies, while extinct languages

---

[7] The list of these families from Glottolog.org is similar, although this source avoids controversial higher-order groupings such as Australian or Niger-Kordofanian: Atlantic-Congo (1432), Austronesian (1275), Indo-European (584), Sino-Tibetan (472), Afro-Asiatic (372), Nuclear Trans New Guinea (315), Pama-Nyungan (240), Oto-Manguean (178), Austro-Asiatic (164). Again, all of the families from this list are represented with at least three languages in our sample.

should be excluded. Actually, including extinct languages, provided they are extensively described, contributes to the diversification of languages in the sample, so in our previous work (Matasović 2014a) we decided to include a number of well-studied extinct languages such as Ancient Greek, Ancient Egyptian and Classical Armenian. However, including extinct languages in a sample designed to show areal patterns is objectionable because the maps will not show the areal distribution of linguistic features at the same time level. Therefore, in our present sample, ancient extinct languages have been generally excluded. We have included a few recently extinct languages, e.g. Biloxi (Siouan), Yintyingka (Pama-Nyungan), Timucua (isolate) and a few languages for which it is uncertain whether they still have any speakers, e.g. Manchu (Tungusic branch of Altaic). We believe that their inclusion does not significantly affect the consistency and comparability of the areal distribution of features we were looking at.

Finally, in collecting any sample of languages it is difficult to avoid unconscious personal biases. Having studied agreement systems in different languages and in different parts of the world for more than a decade, I subconsciously know where particular types are likely to be found, so I must be careful to avoid taking more languages from those areas where one can expect to find types that would confirm my preconceived hypotheses. Some subconscious bias can probably never be completely excluded, but it is, in practice, offset by the random availability of good linguistic descriptions. Some languages, rather than others, are always included in our samples simply because some linguists, sitting in a tropical jungle with the native speakers, did a good job writing the grammars that we can use, while other languages were less "lucky" in that respect.

To conclude this chapter, we present a table in which our sample is divided into the five macro-areas mentioned earlier. The table also contains the number of language families in each macro-area,[8] and the data in our sample are compared with the data about linguistic (and genetic) diversity from Ethnologue and Glottolog.

We see from Table 5 that the percentage of languages from particular macro-areas in the sample roughly corresponds to the percentage of languages in those macro-areas according to Ethnologue, except that the number of languages in Eurasia and in Africa and Middle East was reduced, while the number of languages from the Americas was increased, because of the relative difference in genetic diversity in those continents. On the other hand, the percentage of language families in different areas roughly corresponds to the percentages found in Glottolog, except for Africa and Australia/Oceania. This is because,

---

[8] Isolates were counted as families with a single member.

Table 5 *The proportions of languages in the sample by macro-areas*

Area	No. of languages in the sample	% of languages in Ethnologue	No. of language families in the area (Ethnologue)	No. of language families (Glottolog)
Eurasia	85 (28%)	36%	17 (16%)	46 (10%)
Africa and Middle East	67 (22%)	30%	7 (6%)	59 (12%)
Australia and Oceania	51 (17%)	19%	21 (20%)	178 (37%)
North America	52 (17%)	15% (both N and S America)	30 (29%)	82 (17%)
South America	45 (15%)	15% (both N and S America)	30 (29%)	117 (24%)

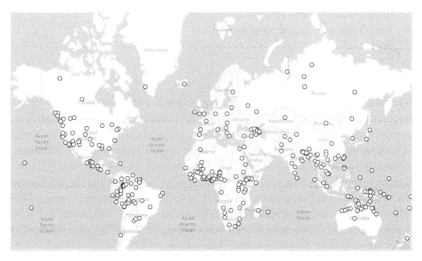

Map 1 Languages in the sample
Initial versions of Maps 1–13 were made with the help of ZeeMap, an online cartographic tool.

in our opinion, Glottolog greatly overestimates the number of families in the former, and underestimates it in the latter.

7.2   The Design of the Database

The preceding discussion of the phenomena relevant to agreement largely determined the selection of information to be included into our typological database and the very design of the database. Our database is divided into the following fields:

1. Language[9]
2. Genus
3. Family
4. WALS/ISO code[10]
5. Macro-area[11]
6. Micro-area[12]
7. Number agreement in the NP
8. Gender agreement in the NP
9. Case agreement in the NP
10. Verbal number agreement
11. Verbal gender agreement
12. Verbal person agreement
13. Grammatical verbal agreement
14. Adnominal possessive agreement
15. Notes
16. References
17. Reliability

In Field no. 3, we also noted if the language was selected for the smaller database in which we checked the areal and genetic stability of agreement patterns (see Section 8.7). For fields 8–13 the principal values are binary, i.e. YES and NO, showing whether a language has the specified feature or not. However, because the grammatical descriptions used were not always completely unambiguous, some fields also contain a question mark, showing that the attribution of a feature to a language was not altogether certain. If a feature is present, but only marginally, this was also noted (and indexed as M), and in the fields on "verbal agreement" it was noted (and indexed as C) if the language expressed any of those feature by clitics rather than affixes.

Field 15 contains notes explaining why a particular analysis was adopted and why a particular language was classified one way or another, when alternative analyses seemed possible. Field 16 shows the references from which data for a particular language were taken, and Field 17 shows how reliable

---

[9] The name quoted in WALS was used by default; if the language is not in the WALS database, the Ethnologue name was used.

[10] For languages not in WALS, the ISO code was used. For one language (Yintyingka), for which no code exists, a new code was invented (yin1).

[11] See Section 7.1 for the list of the macro-areas and how they were selected.

[12] Languages belonging to ten well-documented micro-areas were marked in this field. See the next chapter for the list of micro-areas and how they were used to check the areal and genetic stability of agreement patterns.

the data for a particular language appear to be (i.e. whether the grammatical description used was exhaustive, whether two or more independent sources were consulted, etc.). The fields of the database most relevant for the statistical analyses in the following chapters are included in the Appendix (for reasons of space, some fields, such as Field 15, could not be included).

There are some languages for which we were unable to find all the information needed to include it in the database. In the database the relevant fields were simply left blank in this case, and in the Appendix to this book they are marked with a question mark. It should also be mentioned that we have collected data for many more languages than the 300 included in the database, but most of those languages are from Eurasia and they belong to some of the best-studied language families in the world (especially Indo-European, Afro-Asiatic, Uralic and Altaic). Although data from such languages are mentioned where relevant, enlarging the database to include them would bias it from the areal and genetic point of view and render it unusable for objective statistical analyses.

8   Areal and Genetic Patterns in Agreement Systems

Our investigation of the languages in our sample revealed that some categories involved in agreement have a very unexpected areal distribution. For example, gender is much more widespread in Africa and the Middle East than we would expect a priori. It is attested in 38 of the 67 languages in that macro-area, which is statistically significant (p = 0.0472).[1] However, it is not always the case that whole areas (as defined in our database) are characterizable in terms of the presence (or absence) of a particular pattern of agreement. For example, gender is common in Northern Australia, but virtually absent in Oceania; it is common only in parts of Amazon, rather than in South America as a whole, and – as argued already in Matasović (2004) – gender characterizes only the southwestern half of Eurasia, while it is rather rare in its northeastern half.

In what follows we will look at the areal and genetic distribution of different agreement patterns. Each section deals with one of our macro-areas, as defined above, and it is recapitulated by a table showing which language families can be characterized as either having or lacking a particular feature. Some of the families selected (e.g. Sahaptian) are not represented in our 300-language sample, but they were nevertheless included if data were available about their agreement systems. Availability of reliable data also determined the choice of features represented in the tables (gender agreement,[2] number agreement in the NP, case agreement, person agreement on verbs and possessive agreement in the NP). If a family is marked with [+], this means that the overwhelming majority of its members have the feature in question, and that it can be reasonably supposed that the proto-language also had it. This is the case, e.g., with gender agreement in Indo-European languages, which mostly inherited

---

[1] The calculation was done by applying the chi-square test and using a table with the expected number of languages from Africa with gender (28) and the attested number (38). For these values, $X^2 = 3.939$ with 1 degrees of freedom. On the chi-square test see further Chapter 9.

[2] The tables refer to the presence or absence of gender agreement in general, not specifically adnominal or verbal gender agreement. This is because few families can be characterized as having exclusively adnominal or verbal gender agreement.

their gender systems from Proto-Indo-European (although some languages, such as Armenian and a number of Iranian languages, lost it). Likewise, if a family is marked with [−], this means that the feature is either entirely lacking in the respective family, or that it is exceptional, and that the proto-language can safely be reconstructed without it. For example, case agreement is attested in a number of Finnic languages of the Uralic family, but the overwhelming majority of languages in that family lack it, and it is very probable that this type of agreement did not exist in Proto-Uralic. Finally, when a feature is present in a non-negligible number of languages of a family, and it cannot be established whether it was present in the proto-language, the family was marked with [+/−] for that feature. For example, of the five languages belonging to the NW Caucasian family, gender agreement exists in two (Abkhaz and Abaza) and is lacking in the other three (Adyghe, Kabardian and the recently extinct Ubykh). Although it is often assumed that the Abkhaz/Abaza gender system is inherited, and ultimately related to the gender systems found in NE Caucasian languages (Matasović 2017), this is a very speculative hypothesis, so NW Caucasian was marked with [+/−] for gender agreement.

Our lists of language families are not meant to be exhaustive, and we are well aware of the problem that not all language families have the same time-depth. In Africa, where many fewer language families are found than in other macro-areas, we have decided to include also the sub-families of the two major genetic groupings (Niger-Kordofanian and Nilo-Saharan, both of which have been doubted). In Australia, where all languages may belong to a single ("Australian") language family, we have decided to take the conservative view and retain the old division into Pama-Nyungan and non-Pama-Nyungan languages, whereby the latter are not a genetic, but an areal grouping containing several language families. For New Guinea, where genetic relationships of languages are still poorly understood (for a recent attempt at classification, see Wichmann 2013), no attempt was made to provide a comprehensive overview of the families and the agreement patterns they have.

In many cases the available information was insufficient to reliably classify a family or an isolate with respect to the presence vs. absence of particular features. Therefore, some families/isolates were not included in our overview (e.g. the isolates Kusunda and Nahali in Eurasia, or some small language families of Northern Australia), and in some cases our tables contain question marks. This is an unfortunate consequence of the present state and extent of our knowledge of agreement systems found in the world's languages.

Every section also contains maps in which features with the most biased distribution (from the areal point of view) are represented. Representing the areal distribution of all the features surveyed in the tables would not have made sense for reasons of space.

8.1   Eurasia

In Eurasia, gender agreement is found, roughly, in the southwestern half of that huge land mass (Matasović 2004, cf. also Janhunen 2000). Exceptions in the northeastern part of Eurasia are rare: Ket, the only surviving language of the Yeniseian family, has extensive gender agreement (Krejnovič 1961). Uralic, Altaic, Chukchi-Kamchatkan and Tai-Kadai families are generally genderless,[3] as well as the isolates Ainu, Japanese (with Ryukyuan), Korean, Yukaghir (Maslova 2003) and Nivkh. Languages of the large Sino-Tibetan family also generally lack gender, but a rather marginal gender system distinguishing mas-culines and feminines is reported for Limbu, a Mahakiranti language, and sim-ilar systems probably exist in some other languages of that group. In Limbu, some adjectives take either a masculine suffix (*-pa/-ba*), or a feminine suffix (*-ma*), and agree with the head noun in gender (Van Driem 1987: 20f.):

(97a) *yəm-ba   yɛmbitcha*
        big-M   man
        'big man'

(97b) *yəm-ma   mɛnchuma*
        big-FEM   lady
        'big lady'

Since gender distinctions affect only animate nouns (adjectives modifying inan-imate nouns receive the masculine suffix *-pa/-ba* by default), and agreement does not occur in pronouns and verbs, this system can indeed be characterized as marginal. It may have developed rather recently in contact with the speakers of Nepali and possibly other Indo-Aryan languages, but, at present, this cannot be proved.

In southwest Eurasia, gender agreement is found in Dravidian (except in Toda, Kurruba and Brahui), two of five NW Caucasian languages (Abkhaz and Abaza), and in most NE Caucasian languages (except in Udi, Lezgian, Agul, and some dialects of Tabasaran). A two-gender system, probably with the opposition of male humans vs. neuters (including female referents) is generally reconstructed for Proto-Dravidian (Krishnamurti 2003); in some languages this system developed into a three-gender system, with masculines, feminines and neuters. Proto-Northeast Caucasian also had a gender system probably with four genders (for male humans, female humans, higher animates and

---

[3] Traces of grammatical gender were suggested for Mongolian (Sanžeev 1956), but it is much more likely that these represent remnants of an honorific system in which females and males had different honorific markers. In any case, there is no proof that there was ever a gender agreement system in Mongolian.

inanimates, cf. Alekseev 2003). In NW Caucasian the comparative recon-struction is very difficult, but there are indications that a three-gender system existed in the proto-language (Matasović 2017).

In the Austro-Asiatic family, Munda languages, as well as some other languages spoken in India and Bangladesh (e.g. Khasi) have gender agreement, while those languages that are spoken in Mainland SE Asia (e.g. Khmer and Vietnamese) lack it. In Munda, gender agreement opposing animate and inanimate genders is mostly limited to verbs and (some) demonstratives (Bhattacharya 1976). It is at present impossible to tell whether gender can be posited for Proto-Austro-Asiatic. A curious gender system, with verb agreement and body-part terms as the basis of gender assignment, has been reported for Great Andamanese (isolate, see Abbi 2013: 68), but this claim needs further clarification and definite proof. Gender agreement is also found in the isolate Burushaski, and it was attested in some extinct languages of ancient Anatolia and Mesopotamia, such as the isolates Hattic, Sumerian and Elamite. Gender is lacking in the isolate Basque, as well as in the small Kartvelian family (Georgian and its relatives). The extinct language Hurrian (spoken in northern Mesopotamia in the second millennium BC), and its only known relative, Urartean (spoken in and around Armenia in the early first millennium BC), were genderless.

Indo-European languages, which are spread over most parts of western and central Eurasia, are generally gendered, but some languages (e.g. Armenian, as well as some Indo-Iranian languages) lost gender. Of 144 members of the Indo-European family listed by Ruhlen (1991), gender is preserved in at least 109 (Matasović 2014b: 235), but it was lost in more than 30 languages, and the large majority of them are Indo-Iranian. Gender loss affected a rather compact group of Iranian languages stretching from eastern Turkey, where some Kurdish dialects are genderless (Thackston 2006), across much of Iran and the Caucasus (gender was lost in Persian and its close relatives Dari and Tajiki, as well as in Ossetic) to central Pakistan, but it was preserved in a number of languages on the fringes of the Iranian area, e.g. in Pashto (see Efimov 1975, Abaev 1981 and Èdel'man 1990, 1999). Gender agreement can certainly be reconstructed for Proto-Indo-European (Matasović 2004), and there are indications that the two-way opposition between the animate and inanimate genders preceded the development of the three-gender system (with masculine, feminine and neuter genders) familiar from languages such as Greek and Latin.

Most gender agreement systems in Eurasia show up on verbs (e.g. in Dravidian and Burushaski), or on both verbs and some modifiers in the NP (e.g. in NE Caucasian). Languages (and families) in which gender agreement is mostly limited to the NP are a distinct minority (this is typical of Indo-European and Yeniseian families). In Abkhaz and Abaza, the gendered members of the NW Caucasian family, gender is expressed only on verbs, on some numerals and in the possessive NPs, where the possessum agrees with the possessed in gender (Aristava 1968: 70):

(98a)   *sara sə-gʷə*
         I   1.SG.POSS-heart
         'my heart'

(98b)   *yara yə-gʷə*
         he   3SG.M-heart
         'his heart'

(98c)   *lara lə-gʷə*
         she   3SG.F-heart'
         'her heart'

We know that case systems are very widespread in Eurasia, and we also know that adnominal agreement is quite common in that macro-area. And languages with case agreement in Eurasia are quite a lot more common than statistically expected: 20 are attested and 13 would be expected a priori, which is statistically significant (p = 0.047, with X^2 = 3.94).[4] It is highly significant that, in our sample, most of the languages with case agreement in Eurasia belong to the Indo-European family. In Uralic, case agreement is found in Finnish, which has probably acquired it as the result of intensive contact with the neighboring Indo-European languages that have it (Schlachter 1958); it is found in other Baltic Finnic languages such as Estonian, but not in the other branches of Uralic. Likewise, case agreement (for a class of adjectives) is attested in Brahui, the northernmost Dravidian language spoken in Pakistan, but not in its relatives in the south of India. Brahui case agreement may have been the result of the influence of Indo-Iranian languages with which it has been in contact for several millennia. Elsewhere in Eurasia, we find case agreement in the Nakh branch of NE Caucasian and in Kartvelian languages. Although case agreement is somewhat marginal in contemporary Georgian (see Chapter 6), Old Georgian had a full-fledged system of case (and number) agreement with adjectives and demonstratives, and in Zan adjectives show full agreement with the head noun if they are postposed (as in Modern Georgian); in Svan, on the other hand, case agreement appears to be optional (Tuite 1997; Hewitt 2004: 146–7). Quite marginally, case agreement also exists in Chukchi, spoken in the far northeast of Siberia.

---

[4] Three languages (Brahui, Chukchi and Hungarian) are classified as having marginal case agreement. If they were included in the calculation, the statistical significance of the frequency of case agreement in Eurasia would be even greater. For the procedure for calculating probabilities of random distributions see Chapter 9.

In Eurasia, possessive person agreement is very rare. It is found in some Sino-Tibetan languages spoken in the Himalayas (e.g. Belhare and Limbu, cf. Van Driem 1987: 22), in the isolate Burushaski and in Evenki, a Tungusic language spoken in Siberia. WALS (Map 58A, Bickel and Nichols 2013) also reports it for Ossetic (an Iranian language spoken in the Caucasus), but we have not been able to confirm this in the sources available to us. Since proper person agreement in the NP, as defined in this book (see Section 4.6), is difficult to detect, it may be that it exists in other Eurasian languages as well, perhaps even in some languages included in our sample. Yet it seems safe to conclude that it is indeed a rare phenomenon in Eurasia.

Among the 85 languages spoken in Eurasia that were included in our database, gender agreement (in general, not just in the NP) exists in 32 (38%), number agreement in the NP exists in 33 (39%),[5] case agreement in 20 (24%), and verbal agreement in person/number/gender agreement exists in 60 languages (71%).[6] Grammatical verbal agreement (i.e. verbal agreement with obligatory controllers, see Chapter 5) is attested in 11 languages (13%), most of them Indo-European languages spoken in Western Europe (e.g. English, German, French), and a handful of NE Caucasian languages (Ingush, Chechen and Khwarshi).[7]

Table 6 tentatively represents the distribution of agreement patterns among the language families of Eurasia. It can be observed that person agreement characterizes the largest number of families, while possessive agreement is the rarest pattern, followed by case agreement.

8.2 Africa and the Middle East

In Africa and the Middle East, languages with gender agreement are very common.[8] In the large Afro-Asiatic family, the opposition between masculine and feminine gender is very old and can be posited for the proto language. It was preserved in most branches, including Ancient Egyptian (Menu 2002), Semitic, Berber and Cushitic (Diakonov 1988); in those branches the presence of gender would seem to be universal. In Chadic, gender was lost in a number of languages (e.g. Goemai, Wandala and Hdi), but it was preserved in others (e.g. Hausa). Omotic languages are not well studied, and there are doubts whether they represent a single branch or rather a number of independent branches of Afro-Asiatic. Gender has been preserved in at least some Omotic languages (e.g. Dime).

---

[5] In one language of those 33 (Hungarian), number agreement in the NP is marginal.

[6] In five of these languages, verbal agreement is expressed by clitics, and in one language (Sinhala) it is marginal.

[7] In two languages, Semelai and Batsbi, the existence of this feature is probable, but uncertain.

[8] For a survey, see, e.g., Hurskainen (2000).

Table 6 *Agreement in the languages of Eurasia*

Family	Gender (in any domain)	Number (NP)	Case	Person (V)	Poss. agreement
Indo-European	+	+	+	+	–
Basque	–	–	–	+	–
Uralic	–	–	–	+	–
Altaic	–	–	–	+/–	–
Yukaghir	–	–	–	+	–
Yeniseian	+	+	–	+	–
Chukchi-Kamchatkan	–	+	–(?)	+	–
Nivkh	–	–	–	+	–
Ainu	–	–	–	+	–
Japanese	–	–	–	–	–
Korean	–	–	–	–	–
NW Caucasian	+/–	–	–	+	–
NE Caucasian	+	+	+/–	–	–
Kartvelian	–	–	–	–	–
Dravidian	+	–	–	+	–
Burushaski	+	+	+	+	+ (?)
Sino-Tibetan	–	–	–	+/–	–
Hmong-Mien	–	–	–	–	–
Tai-Kadai	–	–	–	–	–
Austro-Asiatic	–	+/–	–	+/–	–

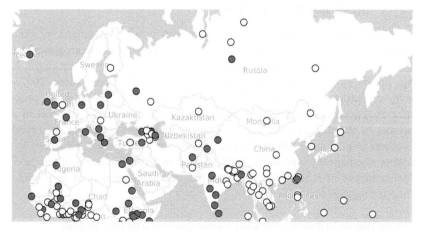

Map 2 Languages with gender (in any domain) in Eurasia (black)

Map 3 Languages with case agreement in Eurasia (black)

In Niger-Kordofanian, gender agreement is pervasive, and gender markers are one of the defining features of that family. However, gender has been lost in a number of branches, including Mande[9] (e.g. Bambara, Bobo, Vai), in many Kwa languages (e.g. Ewe, Fon, Akan), in Igboid languages (e.g. Igbo), in some Adamawa-Ubangian languages (e.g. Mambay), some Kru languages (e.g. Grebo),[10] in some Defoid languages (e.g. Yoruba), in several Kordofanian languages (e.g. Katla, cf. Tucker and Bryan 1966),[11] and it is residual in Dogon (some Dogon languages have agreement in animacy on adjectives and demonstratives in the NP). In many Cross River languages gender agreement is reduced to the point of being rather marginal, e.g. in Efik and Ogoi (Demuth, Faraclas and Marchese 1986), and it is completely lost in others (e.g. Gokana). However, in some languages of that branch gender is well preserved (e.g. the Bendi group of languages). Some Bantoid languages (e.g. Mfumte, spoken in Cameroon, or in Mambila) also lost gender agreement (McLean 2014), but others preserved it, especially in the southern group (e.g. Tiv). Bantu languages, which represent a low-level grouping within Bantoid and Niger-Kordofanian,

[9] Some linguists doubt whether Mande languages are really a branch of the Niger-Kordofanian family, but we accept the traditional classification found, e.g., in Ruhlen (1991).
[10] Loss of gender in Kru may have been triggered by contacts with South Mande languages (on areal features shared by Kru and South Mande languages see Vydrine 2009).
[11] However, many Kordofanian languages have gender, e.g. the Heiban group and Utoro.

generally have extensive gender agreement. As they are spread over much of central and southern Africa, they significantly contribute to the overall impression that the continent is covered by gendered languages.

Likewise, gender agreement is generally present in Atlantic languages (e.g. Fula, Wolof, Serer; some of those languages have as many as 25 genders, or even more) as well as in Gur languages (e.g. Supyire, Koromfe). In many parts of Western Africa languages with and without gender are found side by side, but it appears that languages without gender are more common in the coastal areas near the Gulf of Guinea, especially in Ghana, Côte d'Ivoire and Liberia (see Map 4).

In many Niger-Kordofanian languages gender is marked on verbs by means of prefixes, but in some languages verbs have gender-marking suffixes (e.g. in many Gur languages), or both prefixes and suffixes (in some Gur languages); most languages with gender also mark it on modifiers in the NP, and some of the most extensive gender agreement systems are found in Bantu languages such as Swahili, Chichewa and Xhosa.

In Nilo-Saharan, some languages have gender (e.g. the Nilotic languages Luo and Maasai),[12] but some do not, e.g. Berta, Songhay languages and Sudanic languages such as Ma'di and Kunuz Nubian. Laal, an isolate spoken in Chad, distinguishes masculine, feminine and neuter (inanimate) genders, expressed primarily in pronouns (including relative pronouns which agree with the head noun, Boyeldieu 1982). Bangime, an isolated language spoken by a small group of ethnic Dogon in Eastern Mali, is a thoroughly isolating language with very little morphology and, consequently, no gender (Hantgan 2013).

Khoisan languages are mostly gendered (Vossen 2012). Gender is attested in Hadza, Sandawe (which may not be a member of the Khoisan family), in the Khoekhoe languages and in Central Khoisan (or Ju), as well as in !Ui-Taa (or Southern Khoisan). The only Khoisan language that certainly lacks gender is ≠Hoan, which may be related to Central Khoisan, but the relationship is not obvious. Although it does not have gender, ≠Hoan seems to have number agreement in the NP (Vossen 2012),[13] so it does not entirely lack adnominal agreement.

African languages with gender agreement in the NP usually also have gender agreement on verbs, but there are exceptions, e.g. Wolof (Niger-Kordofanian, Atlantic), which has the former, but lacks the latter: It has person/number agreement on verbs, but no gender. Conversely, there are languages in which

---

[12] Generally, gender is more common in Eastern Nilotic than in Western and Southern Nilotic languages.

[13] However, I was unable to confirm this in the grammar of ≠Hoan by Collins and Gruber (2014). From the examples they give (2014: 118–20) it seems that the language has only number agreement with adjectives in the predicative position.

gender agreement is found only on verbs, e.g. Zande (Niger-Kordofanian, Adamawa-Oubangui, cf. Claudi 1985).

Nearly all languages with adnominal gender agreement also have number agreement in the NP, and almost all languages with person agreement on verbs also have number agreement on verbs, as argument indices show fusion of the categories person and number (often also gender). However, in a few languages we find number agreement in the NP without gender agreement, e.g. in Bobo (Mande). Fur, a Nilo-Saharan language spoken in Darfur (Sudan), appears to have optional number agreement of adjectives with head nouns, while it lacks gender (Jakobi 1989). Laal, an isolate spoken in Chad, has object clitics attached to verbs (though the verb is uninflected for subject). It has number agreement on verbs that is expressed by suffixes different from its argument indices.

In Africa and the Middle East, case is a rather rare category. Most Niger-Kordofanian languages lack it, and it is not very common in Nilo-Saharan and Khoisan languages either. However, it does occur in Fur, as well as in several Saharan languages and in many Nilotic languages such as Maasai, Dinka and Teso. When it comes to case agreement, it is virtually limited to the Cushitic branch of Afro-Asiatic: It is found in languages such as Beja, Sidamo and Alaaba. Example (99) illustrates case agreement for Sidamo (Kawachi 2007: 487). Both the demonstratives *hakku* 'that' and *konní* 'this', as well as the adjectives *seedu* 'tall' and *dančǔ* 'good' agree in case with the nouns they modify (*hanaat'ičči* 'carpenter' and *hakkimiččira* 'doctor', respectively).

(99) *hakku*   *seed-u*   *hanaat'ičč-i*   *šiimá*
      that.NOM.M   tall-NOM.M   carpenter-NOM.M   little.ACC

      wot'é   *konní*   *danč-u*   *hakkimičči-ra u-0-i*
      money.ACC this.GEN.M good.GEN.M doctor.GEN.M give-3SG.M-PERF.3SG.M
      'That tall carpenter gave a small amount of money to this good doctor'

Person marking on verbs is very common in Africa, although many grammars of individual languages may give a different impression. This is because of the long-standing tradition of treating clitic subject and object markers, which are clearly different from independent pronouns, as free rather than bound morphemes (either clitics or affixes, see Creissels 2000, 2006, and see Section 4.4). However, there are some languages that have absolutely no verbal agreement in person, e.g. Mande languages in Western Africa (e.g. Bambara, Vai)[14] and Zarma (or Djerma, a Songhay language in Niger). In many cases it is difficult to decide whether a language has clitic verbal agreement or no verbal agreement at all; in our database, it is assumed that Yoruba (Defoid,

---

[14] See, however, Idiatov 2010 for discussion.

Niger-Kordofanian), Sango (Adamawa-Ubangi, Niger-Kordofanian), Fon (Kwa, Niger-Kordofanian), Goemai (Chadic, Afro-Asiatic) and Nama (Khoisan) have no verbal agreement whatsoever (i.e. not in person, gender or number), although for some of these languages a different analysis may have been possible.[15]

Among the 67 languages from Africa and the Middle East in our sample, gender agreement (in any domain) is attested in 39 (58%), number agreement in the NP in 45 (67%),[16] case agreement in only 4 languages (6%), and verbal agreement (in any category) is attested in 57 languages (85%), of which 19 languages (28%) use clitics rather than affixes to express verbal agreement. Grammatical verbal agreement appears to exist in 10 languages (15%), but for as many as 6 this cannot be shown conclusively. In any case, we must conclude that it is a rare phenomenon, as elsewhere in the world. Possessive agreement is generally absent in Africa.

Table 7 shows the distribution of agreement patterns in language families in Africa and the Middle East; for the three large families (Afro-Asiatic, Nilo-Saharan and Niger-Kordofanian) their branches were included as well (in italic).

8.3   North America

In North America, gender is found in some large language families, such as Iroquoian and Algic (in the eastern part of the USA and Canada), as well as in some small ones, especially in the northwestern USA and in Canada. This applies above all to Salishan languages (except Interior Salishan) and some Chinookan and Chemakuan languages, as well as to some Athabaskan-Eyak languages (e.g. Sarcee, Slave and Koyukon), where gender systems interact with a typologically unusual system of classificatory verbs (see Section 3.2.3). Gender is also found in the isolates Tunica (last spoken in Louisiana, see Haas 1941) and Yuchi (in Oklahoma), and a marginal gender system exists in the small Chumash family (last spoken in California). In Central America, gender agreement is widespread in the Oto-Manguean family (e.g. in Chalcatongo Mixtec). In languages that have gender agreement in the NP, it is also found on verbs, e.g. in Blackfoot (Algonquian, Frantz 1991: 38–9):

(100a)   *amo-yi   náápioyis-i*
         this-INAN house-INAN
         'this house'

---

[15] Malagasy (spoken on Madagascar) also lacks verbal agreement, but Austronesian languages are generally counted as languages of Australia and Oceania in our database.

[16] In two languages, Beja and Gaahmg, alternative analyses are possible, but they have been counted as having number agreement in the NP.

Table 7 *Agreement in the languages of Africa and the Middle East*

Family	Gender	Number (NP)	Case	Person (V)	Poss. agreement
Central Khoisan	+	?	−	+	−
Northern Khoisan	+	+		+	−
Southern Khoisan	+	+	−	+	−
Sandawe	+	?	−	+	−
Niger-Kordofanian	+/−	+/−	−	+	−
Kordofanian	+/−	+/−	−	+	−
Mande	−	+/−	−	−	−
Atlantic	+	+	−	+	−
Adamawa-Ubangi	+/−	+/−	−	+	
Cross River	+/−	+/−	−	+	−
Dogon	−	−	−	+	−
Igboid	−	−	−	+	−
Kru	+/−	+/−	−	+	−
Gur	+	+/−	−	+	−
Kwa	−	−	−	+	−
Bantoid	+	+	−	+	−
Laal	+	+	−	+	−
Nilo-Saharan	+/−	+/−	−	+	−
Berta	−	−	−	+	−
Fur	−	+/−	−	+	−
Gumuz			−	+	
Nilotic	+	+	+/−	+	−
Saharan	+/−	+/−	−	+	−
Songhay	−	−	−	−	−
Afro-Asiatic	+	+	+/−	+	−
Semitic	+	+	+	+	−
Egyptian	+	+	+	+	−
Berber	+	+	+	+	−
Chadic	+	+	−	+	−
Cushitic	+	+	+	+	−
Omotic	+/−	+/−	?	+	−

(100b) *amo-istsi   náápioyi-istsi*
this-INAN.PL house-INAN.PL
'these houses'

(101a) *soká'p-ss-iwa*
3SG-ANIM-good
'He/she/it (animate) is good'

(101b) *soká'p-i-iwa*
3SG-INAN-good
'It (inanimate) is good'

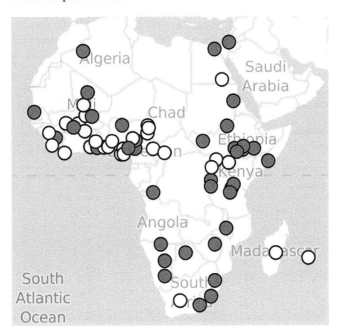

Map 4 Languages with gender in Africa (black)

Languages that have gender agreement in the NP also have number agreement in the NP; there are some languages having number agreement in the NP, but no gender. This pattern is found in some Hokan languages (mostly in the Yuman branch, e.g. Diegueño, Maricopa), as well as in some Uto-Aztecan languages (Chemehuevi, Luiseño), and in Coast Tsimshian.

Thus, in North America, just like in Africa and Eurasia, the distribution of languages with gender agreement shows a clear genetic and areal pattern (see Map 5). As elsewhere, gender agreement in the NP is usually accompanied by number agreement.

In North America, case systems are not very common (they exist in 15 out of 52 languages in our sample, which is 28.8%), and case agreement is very rare. It exists in the Takic branch of the Uto-Aztecan family (e.g. in Cupeño and Luiseño),[17] in Sahaptian, as well as in the isolates Tarascan and Tunica. It is also attested in West Greenlandic and in other Eskimo-Aleut languages. There does not seem to be an areal pattern in the distribution of languages with case agreement in North America: Tunica was spoken in the Gulf of Mexico, Eskimo-Aleut languages are located in the far north, Tarascan is spoken in Mexico, and the Uto-Aztecan languages with case agreement are spoken in

---

[17] Marginally also in Chemehuevi, which is in the Numic branch of Uto-Aztecan.

California. Moreover, case agreement seems to be rather limited in some languages. We have not been able to find instances of extensive case agreement of the Indo-European type. For example, in Tarascan, only the article agrees in the objective case with the noun it modifies (LeCron Foster 1969: 183):

(102)   imá-ni   k'wínčekwa-ni
        the-OBJECTIVE   fiesta-OBJECTIVE
        'the fiesta'

Somewhat more extensive is case agreement in Nez Perce (Sahaptian). In that language, case suffixes appear on every modifier in the NP, as well as on the head noun (Mithun 1999: 480):

(103)   kon-nyá yaʔwic-pa kús-pe
        that-LOC cold-LOC water-LOC
        'in that cold water'

Person agreement (usually fused with number agreement) is almost universal in North America; languages without this agreement pattern on verbs are very rare; some are creoles (e.g. Haitian French and Negerhollands, which may have some residual person agreement, see Muysken 2003), and in some the presence of verbal agreement depends on the analytic approach taken, e.g. in the isolate Kutenai and in Wappo, of the small Wappo-Yukian family. We classified both these languages as having no verbal person agreement. In some Uto-Aztecan languages argument indices are best treated as clitics, so in that sense they have person agreement of the clitic type (e.g. Chemehuevi and Cupeño); finally, Eastern Pomo seems to lack person agreement on verbs altogether.

Possessive person agreement is widespread in North America; it is found in isolates such as Haida, Kutenai, Chitimacha and Tunica, in Caddoan languages (e.g. Pawnee), in Sahaptian languages (e.g. Nez Perce), in Chimakuan (Quileute), in some Muskogeean languages (e.g. Koasati), in some Algonquian languages (e.g. Plains Cree, Dahlstrom 1991), in some Athabaskan-Eyak languages (e.g. Navajo), in the isolate Salinan (California, cf. Mason 1918) and in some languages of Mesoamerica (e.g. in Totonacan and in some Mayan languages such as Tzutujil), etc. On the whole, the impression is that this type of agreement is more common on the western coast and in the southeast of the USA than in the interior of the continent.

Among the 52 North American languages in our sample, gender exists in 16 (31%),[18] number agreement in the NP is attested in 10 languages (19%),[19]

---

[18] In two of these languages, Ineseño Chumash and Wichita, gender agreement can be considered as a marginal phenomenon.

[19] In one language, Wappo, number agreement in the NP is marginal.

case agreement is attested in 7 languages (13%),[20] and verbal agreement is attested in 48 languages (92%). In 4 of those 48 languages (8% of all languages with verbal agreement) verbal agreement is of the clitic type. Grammatical verbal agreement seems to be very rare: It can tentatively be posited for only three languages in our sample (Cupeño, Ojibwa and Haitian Creole French), but even that is not beyond all doubt. Possessive agreement in North America appears to be more common than on average, but it is difficult to give the exact figures because for too many languages data are insufficient or unclear.

Table 8 shows the distribution of agreement patterns in a selection of language families from North America. It can be observed that person agreement on verbs is by far more common than any other type of agreement.

8.4   South America

In South America, different types of nominal classification systems are found, and in a number of languages it is difficult to distinguish between gender and classifier systems (see Fedden and Corbett 2017). One such language is Kwaza, an isolate spoken in Rondônia (Brazil). The standard reference grammar of that language (Van der Voort 2004) analyzes it as having classifiers, rather than gender, but the use of classifiers in all NPs is obligatory (Van der Voort 2004: 128–9), and they are also marked on verbs. For non-classified nouns there is the "neutral class marker -$h\tilde{y}$," so that, in essence, all NPs contain a morphological marking that agrees with the head noun. Hence, Kwaza can be regarded as a language with gender, albeit with a very large number of genders which is highly reminiscent of languages with numeral classifiers. Similarly, in Káro, a Tupian language, there are ten nominal classifiers, and the basis of nominal classification is the shape of referents. However, classifiers must be used following both a noun and its modifier in the NP, and this shows that we are dealing with an agreement system (Rodrigues 1999: 117):

(104)   *wayo   nāk   pap tʃú   pap*
         alligator mouth CL   big   CL
         'alligator's big mouth'

Paumarí, an Arauan language spoken in Brazil, is unusual in having two different gender systems superimposed on each other (Aikhenvald 2012: 285–6). It has masculine and feminine genders, but it also classifies referents according to shape. Masculine and feminine agreement markers are found on articles, demonstratives, some modifiers and some verbal forms. In addition, some

---

[20] In one language, Chemehuevi, case agreement is marginal.

Table 8 *Agreement in the languages of North America*

Family	Gender	Number (NP)	Case	Person (V)	Poss. agreement
Eskimo-Aleut	−	+	+	+	−
Athabaskan-Eyak	+/−	−	−	+	+/−
Algic	+	−	−	+	+/−
Iroquoian	+	−	−	+	−
Yuchi	+	+ (?)	−	+	−
Muskogean	−	−		+	?
Tunica	+	−	+	+	+
Chitimacha	−	−	−	+	+
Coahuilteco	+/−	?	−	+	−
Caddoan	+	−	−	+	−
Siouan	−	−	−	+	−
Kiowa-Tanoan	−	−?	−	+	−
Keresan	−	−	−	+	−
Zuni	−	−	−	+	−
Uto-Aztecan	−	+/−	+/−	+/−	−
Wakashan	+	−	−	+	−
Salishan	+/−	+/−?	−	+	−
Chemakuan	+/−	−	+/−?	+	+
Coosan	−	−	−	+	?−
Sahaptian	−	−	+	+	+
Kutenai	−	−	−	+/−	−
Hokan	−	+/−	−	+	−
Wappo-Yukian	−	+/−?	−	+/−?	−
Salinan	−	−	−	+	?+
Chumash	+ (marginal)	−?	?−	+	−
Oto-Manguean	+/−	+/−	−	+	−
Tarascan	−	− (optional)	+	+	−
Totonacan	−	−	−	+	?
Mixe-Zoque	+/−	+/−	−	+	?
Mayan	−	−	−	+	+
Misumalpan	−	−	−	+	?
Huave	−	−	−	+	?
Pomoan	−?	−	−	−	?

nouns trigger the so-called "ka-agreement" on some modifiers, and on some verbs. Those referents which trigger ka-agreement are flat in shape, they may consist of many parts, or contain seeds, or be extended. The ka-gender interferes with the masculine/feminine system. A turtle is flat, so it belongs to the ka-class, but it can be male or female:

(105a) *ada*   *ojoro*   *ka-hoara-na*
        that.M.SG turtle(male) KA.CLASS-one-M
        'that one male (flat) turtle'

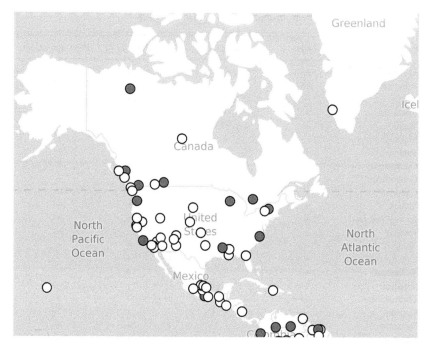

Map 5 Languages with gender in North America (black)

(105b)   *ida*   *ojoro*   *ka-hoara-ni*
         DEM.FEM   turtle(FEM)   KA.CLASS-one-FEM
         'that one female turtle'

However, if a noun does not belong to the ka-class, its agreement is in gender only:

(106)   *ada*   *kawina hoara-na*
         DEM.M monkey(M) one-M
         'that one monkey'

As far as we are aware, this type of system, with two independent genders, is attested only in South America.[21]

In the Amazon, many (if not most) language families are gendered, including Arauan (Kulina, Jarawara), Wari-Chapacuran (Wari'), Witotoan (Bora) and

---

[21] Michif, a Pidgin language spoken in Canada and northern USA also has two independent gender systems as the result of language mixing: In the NP, the gender system is basically French (with masculine and feminine genders), while the verbal morphology displays the Algonquian animate/inanimate gender opposition (Bakker 1997). This is different from Paumarí where, as we see, the two genders both show up in the NP.

most Tucanoan languages (Desano, Kotiria, Cubeo). Gender is also found in the small Makú family (e.g. Hup), as well as in the equally small Guahiban, Guaicuruan, Mosetenan and Moviman families. Likewise, gender systems are widespread in the large Arawakan family (e.g. Arawak, Tariana),[22] the members of which are scattered mostly in the northern part of South America, and in the eastern Amazon. In the Guaicuruan language Mocovi, we find gender agreement in the NP reminiscent of the Indo-European languages (Grondona 1998: 48):

(107)   *e-na   ?tagaki lawerag-ayk*
        M-DEICTIC   mug   black-ADJ.M
        'that black mug'

(108)   *a-na   ?we:na lawerag-ay*
        FEM-DEICTIC   pot   black-ADJ.FEM
        'that black pot'

Note, however, that (unlike in Indo-European languages) number agreement is optional, and not all adjectives agree in gender (one exception is *tog-* 'red', Grondona 1998: 87–8):

(109a) *qo?ole tog*
        bird   red
        'red bird'

(109b) *qo?ol-qa   tog-er*
        bird-PAUC   red-PAUC
        'red birds'

(109c) *qo?ole tog-er*
        bird   red-PAUC
        'red birds'

Peba-Yaguan languages (e.g. Yagua) have nominal classifiers that function as suffixes (and infixes) on dependent elements in the NP, effectively agreeing with the head noun in what should be considered gender. Most classifiers classify their referents on the basis of shape, but there are also classifiers for male and female persons, which function as gender markers. The closely related Yanomami languages on the border of Venezuela and Brazil also have classifiers, but they are expressed by bound morphemes chiefly on verbs. Their use

---

[22] Some Arawakan languages spoken in the Upper Xingu region in Brazil (e.g. Waurá-Mehinaku) have lost gender, presumably under the influence of the neighboring Tupí and Carib languages (Seki 1999).

is obligatory, so the verbs effectively agree with the subject of the intransitive clause, or the object of the transitive clause by the use of the appropriate classifier (see Dixon and Aikhenvald 1999: 347–8). In such languages some terminological clarification would be in order, since their classifier systems apparently have several features of gender systems, and the only surprising feature is that the number of genders is rather large. Both a gender system and a classifier system are reported for Ayoreo, a language belonging to the understudied Zamucoan family, spoken in Paraguay and Bolivia (Bertinetto 2009).

Tupian languages (e.g. Tupí and Guarani), which used to be spoken in large territories of Brazil (especially the state of Rondônia, which may have been their homeland) and in Paraguay, generally lack gender.[23] Likewise, gender is absent in the languages of the small Nambiquaran family (e.g. Sabanes), on the border of Brazil and Bolivia; however, these languages have classifiers – usually expressing the shape of the referent, but also animacy and sex. These occur in the form of suffixes attached to adjectives in adnominal position, and can also be used for de-verbal nominalizations, i.e. to form participial forms which, when adnominal, agree with the head noun (Lowe 1999: 280–1). Cayuvava, an isolate spoken in the Bolivian part of the Amazon, has neither gender nor classifiers (Dixon and Aikhenvald 1999: 369), and the same holds for Warao, an isolate spoken in Venezuela. At least some Matacoan languages, spoken in northern Argentina, western Paraguay and southeastern Bolivia, have gender (e.g. Nivaclé, cf. Campbell and Grondona 2012: 281).

Languages of the Andes mostly lack gender, which is unattested in the two large families of the area (Quechuan and Aymaran). Uru-Chipayan languages, a small family of languages spoken around Lake Titicaca, are an exception to the generalization that gender is not found in the Andes: In Chipaya, there is a distinction of masculine and feminine gender, which is shown overtly on nouns, but also in possessive constructions, where the possessor must agree in gender with the possessed noun (Adelaar 2004: 362). There is also verbal agreement in gender, but gender markers are clitics that do not attach directly to verbs; rather, they follow adverbs preceding the verbs (Adelaar 2004: 369):

(110)   *ni:-nak-ki*   *maxn^ya=š*   *t^hax-a-ki-ča*
         that-M.PL-TOP   early=M   sleep-FUT.NON.SPEAKER-DECL
         'They (those men) will sleep early'

---

[23] However, nominal classifiers (with extensive agreement) are reported for Káro and Mundurukú (Rodrigues 1999: 116), and, although the number of classifiers is large (over 120 in Mundurukú), it is probable that these systems would qualify as gender under our definition of the term. In Tupí-Guarani, the largest branch of the Tupian languages, such systems are apparently not found.

Mapudungun (also known as Mapuche, an Araucanian language spoken in southern and central Chile and western Argentina) has a marginal gender system which distinguishes animate and inanimate nouns. However, this opposition shows up only in the use of different plural markers and a special form of animate definite article, which can be said to agree in gender with the head noun in the NP. It is possible that gender agreement disappeared in Jivaroan, a small language family on the border of Peru and Ecuador, under the influence of its Quechuan and Aymaran neighbors (Aikhenvald 2012: 280, see also Adelaar 2004: 432–40), and gender is also generally lacking in Panoan languages and in some isolates such as Tacana (in Bolivia). Yate (Fulniô), a Macro-Jê language, is unusual in having two genders, but the large majority of the languages of that family, spoken mostly in eastern Brazil, do not have gender. Finally, languages of Patagonia, although most of them are inadequately documented, seem to be mostly genderless (this is certainly so in Yahgan).[24]

In the north of South America gender also appears to be lacking in most families. Barbacoan languages (in Ecuador and Colombia) lack it, and Chibchan languages spoken from Colombia to Costa Rica are also genderless. Cariban languages (e.g. Hixkaryana, Carib, Tiriyo), spoken in Venezuela, Guyana, Surinam and parts of northern Brazil, mostly lack gender, but in Panare (Payne and Payne 2013), demonstratives agree in animacy with the head noun in the NP. Could this be due to the influence of the Arawakan languages, such as Maipure, which are spoken nearby? In the absence of more detailed research, we can only speculate that this is indeed the case.

Therefore, gender agreement seems to be both genetically and areally restricted in South America (see Map 6). As a rule, languages with gender agreement have number agreement, and this applies to both the NP and the clause (i.e. to both adnominal and verbal agreement).

In South America, case systems are found in Quechuan and Aymaran families in the Andes, in Tucanoan and in some Panoan languages, as well as in isolates such as Warao, Mochica and Kwaza (with a very marginal case system), scattered here and there on the continent. In our sample at least, case agreement is found only in the Mosetén language, of the small Mosetenan family spoken in Bolivia.

Person agreement is nearly ubiquitous in South America; however, it is lacking in Pirahã (Pirahã), Shipibo-Konibo (Panoan) and in the isolate Trumai, all of which are spoken in different parts of the Amazon. Chocoan languages (e.g. Waunana), spoken on the border of Panama and Colombia, also lack person marking on verbs. Nambiquaran languages (e.g. Sabanes) have only

---

[24] Campbell and Grondona (2012: 282) report that Chonan languages, except Puelche (Gününa Küne) distinguished masculine, feminine and neuter genders, but it is unclear whether they had a pronominal gender system (as in English) or a full system of gender agreement.

bound object person markers on verbs, while subjects are expressed by free NPs. Some languages in the western Amazon, such as Bora (Witotoan) and Cavineña (Tacanan) have clitic verbal agreement, and this is also the case in Uru-Chipayan languages. In some Tucanoan languages (e.g. Orejón), it is possible to account for all of verbal argument indices just in terms of gender/number, without invoking the category of person (Baerman and Corbett 2013: 6), but this is not the only possible analysis. Their agreement system can also be represented as having person agreement, but apparently this would be a less economical approach.

Some languages do not have person agreement, but still have number agreement on the verb. This is the case in Cuna, an isolate spoken in Colombia (Adelaar 2004: 65):

(111)   *akkʷa-kine make-sa-mala*
         stone-INST hit-PST-PL
         'They hit them with a stone'

In South America, most languages have some sort of possessive affixes (or clitics attached to the possessum) which could qualify for person agreement markers. However, it is often difficult to establish whether there are obligatorily possessed nouns and constructions in which possessive person agreement is obligatory. A full system of possessive suffixes exists in Cariban languages, where inalienably possessed nouns obligatorily carry them. Similar systems of possessive prefixes exist in Tupian languages. On the other hand, there are exceptions, e.g. Nambiquaran languages usually express possession by simple juxtaposition (Lowe 1999; de Araujo 2004). Thus, it cannot be said that this pattern is universal in South America. For example, Barbacoan languages (spoken in Ecuador and Colombia) do not have anything resembling possessive agreement. But it is fair to say that many languages have possessive person agreement, including Arawakan (e.g. Campa, Resígaro, Arawak), Macro-Jê (e.g. Caneba-Krahó), Tucanoan (e.g. Barasano), Chocoan (Epena Pedee), Cariban (e.g. Hixkaryana), etc.

Among the 45 languages from South America in our sample, gender agreement (in any domain) is found in 22 (49%), number agreement in the NP in 14 (31%),[25] case agreement in 1 (2%), and verbal agreement is attested in 42 languages (93%), of which 3 (7%) have verbal agreement of the clitic type. Grammatical verbal agreement exists in at least two languages (Warao and, probably, Berbice Dutch Creole), but reliable data are lacking for so many languages that no exact statistics can be given.

---

[25] For one language, Tucano (Tucanoan), the analysis is somewhat doubtful.

Table 9 *Agreement in the languages of South America*

Family	Gender	Number (NP)	Case	Person (V)	Poss. agreement
Chibchan	−	−	−	+	−
Chocoan	+	−	−	+	+?
Barbacoan	−	−	−	+	?
Wari-Chapacuran	+	+	−	+	?
Guahiban	+	−	−	+	?
Tucanoan	+	+	−	+	+
Witotoan	+	−	−	+ (clitic)	+/−
Warao	−	+	−	+	?
Yanomam	−	−	−	+	+
Mura-Pirahã	−	−	−	−	?
Peba-Yaguan	−?	?	−	+	?
Jivaroan	−	−	−	+	−
Panoan	−	−	−	+/−	?
Quechuan	−	−	−	+	−
Aymaran	−	−	−	+	−
Makú	+	−	−	+	+ (?)
Arawakan	+	+?	−	+	+
Cariban	−	−?	−	+	?
Tupian	−	−	−	+	?
Macro-Jê	+	−	−	+ (?)	+
Trumai	−	−	−	−	−
Nambiquaran	−?	−	−	+	−
Kwaza	+?	−	−	+	?
Arauan	+	−	−	+	?
Tacanan	−	−	−	+ (clitic)	?
Movima	+	+	−	+	?
Mosetenan	+	+	+	+	?
Uru-Chipayan	+	+	−	+ (clitic)	−
Matacoan	+	−	−	+	+/−
Guaicuruan	+	+	−	+	?
Araucanian	−	−	−	+	−

Table 9 shows the distribution of agreement patterns in a selection of families of South America. It can be seen that person agreement on verbs is nearly omnipresent, and that gender agreement is fairly common. For number and case agreement no reliable conclusions can be drawn at present, and further research is needed.

8.5   Australia and Oceania

In Australia and Oceania, gender agreement (mostly on verbs, less commonly on adnominal modifiers) is consistently found only in the non-Pama-Nyungan

Map 6 Languages with gender in South America (black)

languages of Northern Australia.[26] It is attested in West Barkly languages (e.g. Wambaya), Mangarayi, Wororan, Gaagudju, and others, but there are also some language families spoken in the area without gender agreement (e.g. Garrwan and Tangkic languages, such as Kayardild).[27] Non-Pama-Nyungan languages are probably not related to Pama-Nyungan, and it is also unclear which of them are mutually related. Only low-level language families are universally recognized, and, at present, it is best to use this low-level genetic classification.

Among the Pama-Nyungan languages, gender is attested only in a minority of them, mostly in those languages that are spoken in the northern part of Australia. In Dyirbal, spoken in Queensland, the gender system seems to be

[26] Non-Pama-Nyungan is, of course, an areal rather than a genetic grouping. On the other hand, Pama-Nyungan languages do represent a genetic unit (i.e. a family) *pace* Dixon (2002). For a criticism of Dixon's skeptical position on Pama-Nyungan, see Evans (2005).

[27] On nominal classification in Australian languages in general see Harvey and Reid (1997); for Non-Pama-Nyungan see Evans (2003a), who posits a shared system of four or five genders for most languages of this group. Heath (1978: 87ff.) argues that gender markers in at least some languages of the Arnhem Land (Nungubuyu, Warndarang, Ngandi) were borrowed from other Australian languages.

a recent development (Plaster and Polinsky 2007). It is expressed only on (some) nominal modifiers in the NP, and the gender markers follow the case suffixes. Dyirbal's closest relative, Warrgamay, lacks gender markers, and it should be noted that at least some of Dyirbal's gender markers seem to go back to "generic nouns." For instance, the generic noun *mayi* 'vegetable food', is probably the source of the class suffix *-m* in Dyirbal, denoting precisely edible plants. Besides Dyirbal, gender is also attested in a few other Pama-Nyungan languages such as Wangkumara and Bandjalang chiefly in the north and northeast of the continent. Thus, in Australia, gender agreement seems to be an areal phenomenon.

In New Guinea and the surrounding islands, gender agreement is found in some languages of Bougainville (e.g. Motuna, Nasioi), on the Solomons (Lavukaleve, Savosavo), in some languages of the Sepik river area (e.g. Ambulas, Yimas)[28] and elsewhere, e.g. in Mian (Ok branch of the Trans-New Guinea family), Maybrat (Bird's Head family), in Alamblak, Arapesh, etc. On the whole, it appears that gendered languages are very widespread on New Guinea, but there are also several languages lacking gender agreement, e.g. Makalero, Dani and Amele, all belonging to the putative Trans-New Guinea family. Alor-Pantar languages, spoken in eastern Indonesia, also lack gender (Klamer 2014). Some languages, e.g. Tobelo (North Halmaheran, Fedden and Corbett 2017: 47), have both a gender system and a system of numeral classifiers. In any case, the genetic relationships among the languages of New Guinea are still too poorly understood for any general conclusions to be drawn about the presence or absence of gender in that island's language families.

Languages of Oceania that belong to the Austronesian family generally lack gender. However, Schapper (2010) shows how gender arose in some Austronesian languages spoken in East Indonesian islands (e.g. Suvai, Roon) under the influence of Papuan languages[29] spoken in that area. The opposition is between neuter and non-neuter, and it is usually shown on demonstratives and verbs. Moreover, a number of Austronesian languages in eastern Oceania and western Melanesia, but also some languages spoken on New Guinea (Holzknecht 1989: 115, with references), show a pattern that might be analyzed as gender agreement in possessive constructions. Such languages have two sets of possessive markers for edible (or "consumable") and non-edible (or "non-consumable") possessed nouns. It may be argued that these represent two genders (consumable and non-consumable) and that the possessive marker agrees in gender with the possessed noun. This pattern is found in Sinaugoro, an Austronesian language spoken in

---

[28] According to Foley (1986: 77), gender is particularly common in the Sepik basin and the adjoining lowland areas of Irian Jaya.

[29] Under "Papuan languages" we subsume all non-Austronesian languages spoken in New Guinea and the surrounding parts of Oceania. This is a purely areal, not a genetic, grouping.

Papua New Guinea (Tauberschmidt 1999: 61). In that language, the possessive marker *g'a-* is used for edible possessed nouns, and *g'e-* is used for all other (alienably) possessed nouns:

(112)   *(au) g'e-gu vanug'a*
        1SG POSS-1SG village
        'my village'

(113)   *(au) g'a-gu   bai*
        1SG POSS(EDIBLE)-1SG pig
        'my pig (to eat)'

(114)   *(g'ia) g'e-na bai*
        3SG   POSS-3SG pig
        'his pig'

Australian languages usually have rich case systems. Case affixes can often be attached only to one word in the NP, usually the last one.[30] Case agreement is widespread in several families, including the largest one, Pama-Nyungan (e.g. in Dyirbal, Yidiny, Bilinarra, Western Desert, Jiwarli), but it is also attested in several families of Arnhem Land and the neighboring areas, e.g. in Tangkic (Kayardild) and in Mangarayi. In some languages, especially in Pama-Nyungan languages which lack gender, case agreement is obligatory only in split NPs, but optional (or impossible) otherwise. The data provided by Dixon (2002: 144) do not reveal an areal pattern in the distribution of languages with case agreement in Australia; the phenomenon is found in the extreme west of the continent (Kanjara, Ngarla), in the center (e.g. in Kalkatungu and Wangkumara) and in the northeast (Yidiny, Dyirbal). In many languages case agreement seems to be optional (e.g. in Ngalakgan, a non-Pama-Nyungan language, see Merlan 1983: 38).

On the other hand, case systems are much rarer in Oceania, and none of the Oceanian languages in our sample have case agreement. In New Guinea, languages with case exist (although they are not as common as in Australia), and case agreement is attested only in one language from our sample. This is Motuna, spoken on Bougainville (Onishi 2012: 221–2):

(115)   *ti-ki*   *sikuulu-kori-ki*
        ART.LOCAL.GENDER-ERG school-LOCAL.GENDER-ERG
        'in the school'

---

[30] However, the case-marked word can also be the nominal head, as in Anguthimri, the first word of the NP, as in Bunuba, or just any word of the NP, as in Gooniyandi (Dixon 2002: 144).

(116) *hoo-nno   onu-nno   kaakoto*
       ART.M-COMIT DEM.M-COMIT   white.man
       'with this white man'

In (115), the article *ti-* agrees in the ergative case with the noun *sikuulu-* (there is also agreement in the so-called "local gender"); in (116), both the article *hoo-* and the demonstrative pronoun *onu-* appear to agree in the comitative case (as well as in the masculine gender) with the head noun *kaakoto* 'man', which is itself unmarked for case. This type of case agreement is unusual, since noun modifiers have to share a case marker (*-nno*) that the head noun itself lacks.

Possessive person agreement is attested in some languages of New Guinea, e.g. in Dani, Asmat, Salt-Yui (only for body-part terms, see Irwin 1974: 29) and in many Finisterre-Huon languages, cf. McElhanon (1973: 12), in some peripheral Malayo-Polynesian languages (Paamese), and in Tiwi, an Australian isolate. In Australia, this pattern of agreement seems to be rare, as most languages express possession by special case forms (usually the genitive), or by juxtaposition of possessor and possessum (especially for inalienable possession). However, many languages have possessive affixes (or clitics), which are sometimes used only on body parts and kinship terms. Dixon (2002: 395) estimates that slightly more than 70 Australian languages have possessive affixes (or clitics), but in only some of these languages is there possessive agreement. In Wemba-Wemba (Pama-Nyungan), body-part terms and kinship terms must obligatorily take possessive suffixes, and the possessum may be further specified by the possessor NP taking genitive case (Dixon 2002: 394):

(117) *wilenngidj-gad ginja barinng-ug*
       possum-GEN   this track-3SG.POSS
       'This is a possum's track'

Possessive affixes/clitics exist both in Pama-Nyungan and in non-Pama-Nyungan languages, but languages that have them almost always also have person marking on verbs, i.e. they have verbal agreement in person (usually also in number, and sometimes in gender as well). In a few languages this is not the case, e.g. in Wemba-Wemba and in the Gurnu dialect of Baagandji (both spoken in southeastern Australia). Other languages of this type, spoken in central Australia (e.g. Arrernte and Kaititj) use possessive affixes only marginally and exclusively with kinship terms.

Among the 51 languages from Australia and Oceania in our sample, gender is attested in 17 (33%), number agreement in the NP is found in 16 (31%),[31]

---

[31] Among these languages, the existence of number agreement in one (Ambulas) is uncertain.

Table 10 *Agreement in the languages of Australia*

Family	Gender	Number (NP)	Case	Person (V)
Anson Bay	+	+	+/−	+
Bunuban	−	?	?	+
Eastern Daly	+	+	+/−	+
Gaagudju	+	−	−	+
Garrwan	−	−	−	−
Gunwinyguan	+	+	+	+
Iwaidjan	+	+	+/−	+
Mangarayi-Maran	+	+	+	+
Mirndi	+	+	+	+
Northern Daly	+	+	+/−	+
Nyulnyulan	−	?	+/−	+
Pama-Nyungan	−	+/−	+/−	−
Southern Daly	+	+	+/−	+
Tangkic	−	−	+	−
Wagiman	+	+	+/−	+
Western Daly	+	+	?	+
Wororan	+	+?	+	+

case agreement is found in 12 languages (24%),[32] and verbal agreement is attested in 38 languages (75%). This figure includes languages with clitic verbal agreement (7 languages, 18%). Grammatical verbal agreement is found in at least three languages (Ambulas, Samoan and, probably, Wambaya), but the actual number may be higher because reliable data about this feature are lacking for several languages.

Table 10 shows the distribution of agreement patterns in selected language families of Australia.[33] The typological contrast between Pama-Nyungan and non-Pama-Nyungan languages, spoken in the north of the continent, is clearly visible.

8.6   Differences among the Macro-Areas

To conclude, we can compare the frequencies of different patterns of agreement in different macro-areas. Table 11 shows the frequencies of the agreement patterns for languages in our 300-language sample.

These data show, for all their limitations, that different agreement patterns do have areal biases. Gender is considerably more common in two areas (Africa/

---

[32] In one, Worora, the analysis is inconclusive.

[33] For some language families the available data are too scant, so they were not included in the table. Likewise, data on possessive agreement in the NP were often too unreliable to be included in the table.

Table 11 *Frequency of agreement patterns in different macro-areas*

	Eurasia	Africa and the Middle East	North America	South America	Australia and Oceania
Gender	38%	58%	31%	49%	33%
Number (NP)	39%	67%	19%	31%	31%
Case	24%	6%	13%	2%	24%
Verbal agreement	71%	85%	92%	93%	75%
Grammatical verbal agreement	13% (?)	15% (?)	>= 6%	>= 4%	>= 6%

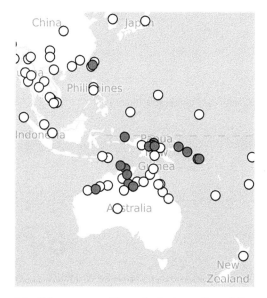

Map 7 Languages with gender in Australia and Oceania (black)

Middle East and South America) than elsewhere. Number agreement in the NP shows a similar pattern, although it is slightly less common in Eurasia and more common in Africa and the Middle East. Case agreement is not particularly common anywhere, but two areas (Eurasia and Australia/Oceania) stand out when compared to the others (see Map 8). It appears that the distribution of languages with case agreement is the same as the distribution of languages with other kinds of adnominal agreement (gender and number), except in areas where case as a category is rare to begin with (chiefly in Africa). Finally, verbal person agreement is much more common than all other agreement patterns in all areas, although in Eurasia and Australia/Oceania the percentages

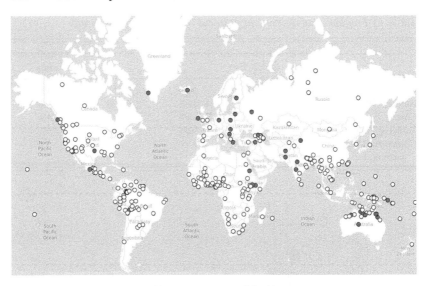

Map 8 Languages with case agreement (black)

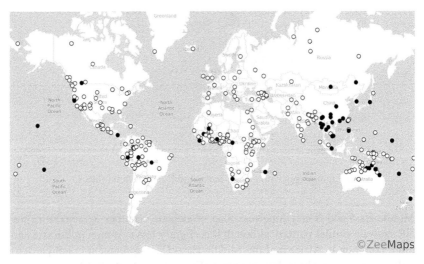

Map 9 Languages without verbal agreement (black)

of languages with this feature are slightly lower than elsewhere (see Map 9). It is difficult to speculate about the relative frequency of grammatical verbal agreement, because our data for several languages are incomplete and often not reliable enough, but it appears that this is indeed a rare phenomenon in all areas

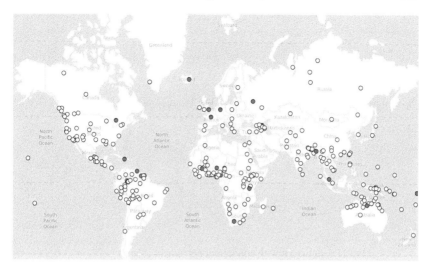

Map 10 Languages with grammatical verbal agreement (black)

(Map 10). The number of languages with this pattern does not exceed 15 percent in any area, and it is lower than 4 percent in one area (South America). Although grammatical agreement is rare, it is somewhat more common than reported by Siewierska (1999: 238) for her sample. She found as little as 1 percent of languages with grammatical verbal agreement.

In contrast to verbal agreement, adnominal agreement (whether in gender, number, or case) is clearly an areal phenomenon: It is common in western Eurasia and in the whole of Africa, Northern Australia, northwestern America and parts of the Amazon, but rather rare elsewhere (Map 11).

8.7   Areal and Genetic Stability of Agreement Patterns

When we say that a linguistic feature is diachronically stable, this can actually mean several different things, but two senses of diachronic stability are particularly important (Nichols 1995, 2003). Firstly, a feature can be diachronically stable if in normal situations of language transmission (i.e. without language shift) languages are unlikely to lose it or acquire it. Or, since likelihood is a relative concept, it is more precise to say that such diachronically stable features are less likely to be lost or acquired than other, diachronically unstable, features. Diachronically stable features in this sense will be homogeneous across language families with respect to their presence or absence, since, if such a feature was present in the proto-language of a family, its descendants will usually preserve it; if the proto-language did not have it, its descendants will be

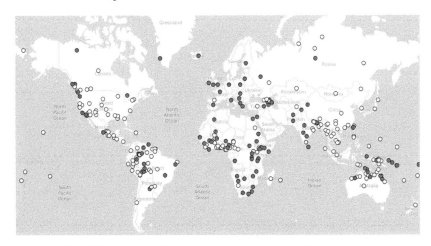

Map 11 Languages with adnominal agreement (black)

unlikely to acquire it. Secondly, a feature can be diachronically stable if it is easily acquired or lost in situations of intensive language contact. Since most languages are spoken in a single area over a long period of time, languages will tend to preserve the same value of such features for longer periods of time than the values of features that are not diachronically stable in this sense. Diachronically stable features in this sense will be homogeneous across language micro-areas (we use the term "micro-areas" to distinguish them from the five continent-sized areas in our 300-language sample).

In order to examine the diachronic stability of individual agreement patterns in language areas and in language families, we decided to select ten language families and ten language areas and see how homogeneous they are with respect to agreement patterns. We selected the largest families with five or more languages in our 300-language sample, and from each family we randomly chose five languages. If at all possible, languages were selected from different branches of each family. We also selected ten language (micro-)areas which have been well documented in previous research, areas in which intensive language contact is either attested or deduced with a high degree of probability (see Chapter 7). From each area we selected five languages, if at all possible from different families (or from distant branches of the same family). The ten families we selected are: Indo-European, Altaic, NE Caucasian, Sino-Tibetan, Afro-Asiatic, Niger-Kordofanian, Austronesian, Austro-Asiatic, Pama-Nyungan and Uto-Aztecan. The ten micro-areas are: Caucasus, SE Asia, South Asia, the Himalayas, East Africa, Northern Australia, Northwestern America, Mesoamerica, Amazonia, and the Andes.

Table 12 *Selection of languages from ten large families*

Family					
Indo-European	Italian	Icelandic	Greek	Oriya	Russian
Altaic	Khalkha	Japanese	Korean	Enets	Turkish
Sino-Tibetan	A'tong	Belhare	Burmese	Dhimal	Karen (Sgaw)
Afro-Asiatic	Arabic	Hausa	Tamashek	Iraqw	Dime
Niger-Kordofanian	Degema	Ewe	Grebo	Mambay	Supyire
NE Caucasian	Batsbi	Chechen	Ingush	Khwarshi	Kryz
Austronesian	Hawaiian	Ilocano	Malagasy	Tsou	Cham
Austro-Asiatic	Khmer	Semelai	Kharia	Chrau	Vietnamese
Pama-Nyungan	Biri	Duungidjawu	Jiwarli	Warlpiri	Bilinarra
Uto-Aztecan	Chemehuevi	Cupeño	Nahuatl	Shoshone	Pipil

Table 13 *Selection of languages from ten micro-areas*

Micro-area					
Caucasus	Armenian	Georgian	Abkhaz	Khwarshi	Chechen
SE Asia	Chrau	Vietnamese	Khmer	Lao	Nung
South Asia	Tamil	Telugu	Kharia	Hindi	Oriya
Himalayas	Khasi	Newari	Nepali	Kulung	Lepcha
E Africa	Alaaba	So	Dime	Iraqw	Gaahmg
N Australia	Gooniyandi	Gaagudju	Mangarayi	Bilinarra	Tiwi
Mesoamerica	Rama	Tarascan	Tzeltal	Zapotec	Pipil
Amazonia	Hixkaryana	Wari'	Kwaza	Pirahã	Jarawara
Andes	Mapuche	Aymara	Quechua (Cuzco)	Mochica	Uru
NW America	Quileute	Tsimshian	Kwak'wala	Halkomelem	Chinook

Tables 12 and 13 show which languages were selected in the genetic and areal groupings.

Tables 14 and 15 show how individual agreement patterns are distributed in the samples taken from the selected families and micro-areas. In both tables, means and modes were calculated: The "mean" refers to the number obtained by dividing the sum of the numbers of languages in each grouping having a particular agreement pattern by ten (the number of families and micro-areas). For example, the mean for case agreement in families is 1.4 = (3×4 +2)/10, as there are three families with four (out of five selected) members with case agreement, one family with two members (Uto-Aztecan) and six families with zero members having case agreement. The mode is the most frequent number of languages having a particular agreement pattern within a grouping (for families as well as for micro-areas). For example, the mode for case agreement in

Table 14 *Means and modes for selected agreement patterns in families*

	Verbal agreement (in any category)	Adnominal agreement (in any category)	Case agreement	Gender agreement (NP or V)	Number agreement (NP)
Indo-European	5	5	4	5	5
Altaic	2	0	0	0	0
Sino-Tibetan	3	0	0	0	0
Afro-Asiatic	5	5	0	5	5
Niger-Kordofanian	5	3	0	2	3
NE Caucasian	5	5	4	5	5
Austronesian	1	0	0	0	0
Austro-Asiatic	2	0	0	0	0
Pama-Nyungan	4	4	4	0	0
Uto-Aztecan	5	2	2	0	1
Mean	**3.7**	**2.4**	**1.4**	**1.7**	**1.9**
Mode	**5**	**0**	**0**	**0**	**0**

Table 15 *Means and modes for selected agreement patterns in micro-areas*

	Verbal agreement (in any category)	Adnominal agreement (in any category)	Case agreement	Gender agreement (NP or V)	Number agreement (NP)
Caucasus	5	3	3	3	3
SE Asia	0	0	0	0	0
South Asia	5	2	2	4	2
Himalayas	4	2	0	2	1
E Africa	5	4	1	4	4
N Australia	5	4	2	3	3
Mesoamerica	4	1	1	0	0
Amazonia	4	3	0	3	2
Andes	5	0	0	0	0
NW America	5	1	0	3	2
Mean	**4.2**	**2.0**	**0.9**	**2.2**	**1.7**
Mode	**5**	**–**	**0**	**3**	**2**

families is zero, as six out of ten families do not have any members (out of five selected languages) with case agreement.

If we compare the modes across the two groupings, it emerges that 0 is the most common mode for families, but not for micro-areas, except in the case of verbal agreement. For verbal agreement, 5 is the most common mode for both areas and families, since verbal agreement is so common cross-linguistically: A randomly selected language is much more likely to have it than not to have it. If we look at the mean values, it transpires that they are consistently higher for areas than for families, but this does not show us whether the examined patterns are more areally or genetically stable. A mean value of a feature can be high in a grouping (say, in micro-areas) not because the presence of that feature is particularly stable in that grouping, but because the selected groupings are just as likely to have it as not to have it, in which case the mode for such a feature will be 2 or 3 (as it is, e.g., for number and gender agreement in micro-areas). What we need to do is compare the homogeneity of the units comprising the two populations, where the populations are areas and families. In homogeneous units, we expect their values (the number of languages having an agreement pattern) to be closer to the extremes (0 or 5), while in non-homogeneous units, the values will be closer to 2 or 3 (the median). What is also relevant is how common a pattern is cross-linguistically, as both families and areas will be more homogeneous with respect to the presence of more common patterns, such as verbal agreement. To deal with this problem, we first calculated the mean values for the number of languages having individual agreement patterns in ten randomly selected groups of five languages (the first fifty languages in our sample, in alphabetical order). Then we calculated the deviations of areas and families from those means, and finally we compared the obtained deviations between areas and families. For example, the mean for case agreement in ten randomly selected groups of five languages is 0.9, and Indo-European deviates from this mean by 3.1 (since there are four Indo-European languages with case agreement in our selection, see Table 14). Such deviations were calculated for the other selected features and for the other language families, and the results are represented in Table 16. Then these calculations were repeated for language micro-areas, and the results can be seen in Table 17.

If we compare Tables 16 and 17, it is immediately visible that, for most patterns, micro-areas tend to diverge from the means found in random groupings less than families, i.e. they are less homogeneous by this metric. However, we cannot be sure if this difference is the result of random distribution: Maybe the micro-areas are indeed less homogeneous than language families, but not enough for us to conclude that chance cannot be responsible for this. In order to test the statistical significance of our observation, we have applied the standard t-test for two independent variables. This test is normally used in statistics to compare the means or averages of two separate groups or populations. Table 18 shows the result.

Table 18 shows that, for all of the surveyed features except for verbal agreement (which is the most common agreement pattern), the difference in the behavior of areal and genetic groupings is statistically significant. We interpret

Table 16 *Deviations from the means obtained for randomly selected languages (for families)*

	Verbal agreement	Adnominal agreement	Case agreement	Gender agreement (NP or V)	Number agreement (NP)
Indo-European	0.5	3.1	3.1	3.0	2.9
Altaic	2.5	1.9	0.9	2.0	2.1
Sino-Tibetan	1.5	1.9	0.9	2.0	2.1
Afro-Asiatic	0.5	3.1	0.9	3.0	2.9
Niger-Kordofanian	0.5	1.1	0.9	0	0.1
NE Caucasian	0.5	3.1	3.1	3.0	2.9
Austronesian	3.5	1.9	0.9	2.0	2.1
Austro-Asiatic	2.5	1.9	0.9	2.0	2.1
Pama-Nyungan	0.5	2.1	3.1	2.0	2.1
Uto-Aztecan	0.5	0.1	0.9	2.0	2.1
Mean[a]	**4.5**	**1.9**	**0.9**	**2.0**	**2.1**

[a] For ten groups of randomly selected languages (with five languages in each group).

Table 17 *Deviations from the means obtained for randomly selected languages (for micro-areas)*

	Verbal agreement	Adnominal agreement	Case agreement	Gender agreement (NP or V)	Number agreement (NP)
Caucasus	0.5	1.1	1.1	1.0	0.9
SE Asia	4.5	1.9	0.9	2.0	2.1
South Asia	4.5	0.1	1.1	2.0	0.1
Himalayas	0.5	0.1	0.9	0	1.1
E Africa	0.5	2.1	0.1	2.0	1.9
N Australia	0.5	2.1	1.1	1.0	0.9
Mesoamerica	0.5	0.9	0.9	2.0	2.1
Amazonia	0.5	1.1	0.9	1.0	0.1
Andes	0.5	1.9	0.9	2.0	2.1
NW America	0.5	0.9	0.9	1.0	0.1
Mean[a]	**4.5**	**1.9**	**0.9**	**2.0**	**2.1**

[a] For ten groups of randomly selected languages (with five languages in each group). The mean values are, naturally, the same as in Table 16.

these findings to mean that families, more than areas, tend to be homogeneous with respect to the presence or absence of the selected agreement patterns (except for verbal agreement). This is in accordance with the findings of Nichols (1992), who showed that gender is a diachronically stable feature and that language families tend to be homogeneous with respect to the presence

Table 18 *Statistical significance of divergences between areas and families with respect to patterns of agreement*

Patterns	t value	p value	Statistical significance
Verbal agreement	0	0.5	not significant
Adnominal agreement	−2.08013	0.026038	significant
Case agreement	−2.04735	0.02753	significant
Gender agreement (NP or V)	−1.97557	0.031873	significant
Number agreement (NP)	−2.67176	0.007778	very significant

or absence of that category. We now see that two other categories involved in adnominal agreement (number and case) pattern the same way.

Our conclusion does not mean that the selected features are not *both* areally *and* genetically stable. Indeed, they are, as we have argued in the preceding chapter. The presence of agreement features can be said to characterize linguistic areas as well as language families, but we believe that our analysis shows that the nature of their stability is more genetic than areal. This means that, if a language has an agreement pattern (except for verbal agreement), its descendants are likely to inherit it and unlikely to lose it in normal circumstances, i.e. except in situations of intensive language contact and widespread bilingualism with languages lacking agreement. Conversely, if a language lacks agreement (again, except for verbal agreement), it is unlikely to develop it spontaneously, i.e. unless it is under strong influence of a language with agreement. Since descendant languages are usually spoken in the same (if somewhat extended) area as the ancestor language, the areal stability of agreement patterns (or lack thereof) may simply be a consequence of their genetic stability. However, as we shall argue in Chapter 10, there are reasons to believe that language contact often plays a role in processes leading to loss of agreement in a language that has it, and even to the development of agreement in a language that had previously lacked it. Hence, areal stability of agreement (or lack of it) may also be a consequence of the following scenarios: If a group of speakers of a language with agreement re-settles in an area where languages without agreement are the norm (for example, if those languages belong to families lacking agreement), intensive language contact will facilitate the loss of agreement in the language of the newcomers. Conversely, if a group of speakers of a language without agreement moves into an area where languages with agreement predominate, their language may acquire agreement through the speech of bilingual speakers imitating the syntactic patterns of those neighboring languages where agreement is a common syntactic rule. Thus, if we assume that each language can be characterized in terms of a (non-verbal) agreement parameter, which can be set to 0 (lack of agreement) or 1 (presence of agreement), then we can state the *Principle of Stability of Agreement*: A language is unlikely to change its value of agreement parameter spontaneously, but it is somewhat likely to change it in situations of intensive language contact with languages having a different value of that parameter. This principle appears to be responsible, then, for the pattern of genetic and areal stability of agreement observable in our data.

9 Typological Correlations in Agreement Systems

In the preceding chapter it was shown that certain agreement patterns are areally biased, in the sense that they are more common in some parts of the world and that pure chance cannot be responsible for the observed areal distribution of these features. However, certain features are very rare in the whole world (e.g. grammatical verbal agreement), while others (e.g. verbal agreement in person) are very common everywhere. Moreover, some combinations of agreement patterns are extremely rare: Languages with adnominal agreement almost always have some verbal agreement as well, while languages with person agreement on verbs do not necessarily have any adnominal agreement. Consequently, very few languages with adnominal agreement and no verbal agreement are found. In this chapter, we will analyze a number of such features and their combinations, and try to determine whether their rarity is statistically unexpected, as well as whether it can be a consequence of different areal biases of features that seldom appear in combination. For example, it may be that languages with adnominal agreement have a different areal bias than languages without verbal agreement. If this were the case, the rarity of languages with adnominal agreement but without verbal agreement would be easily understood. However, it will be shown that areal distributions of features generally cannot explain the incompatibility of a number of agreement patterns.

9.1 Adnominal and Verbal Agreement

Our previous research (Matasović 2014a) has established that languages with adnominal agreement and without verbal agreement were unexpectedly rare among the world's languages.[1] However, the sample analyzed in that research contained only one hundred languages, and it was somewhat biased toward

---

[1] It was Christian Lehmann (1988: 260) who first suggested this as a potential universal ("no language has exclusively internal agreement," where "internal agreement" corresponds to our adnominal agreement). Frans Plank (1994) restated this universal after examining a sample of forty-five languages. Apparently, no counter-examples were considered by either linguist.

the Old World, while languages from the Americas were slightly underrepresented. Therefore, we have repeated the same statistical analysis of the frequency of individual agreement patterns in the sample of 300 languages presented in Chapter 7.

We saw above (see Section 4.5) that the number of languages with adnominal agreement in the sample depends on whether case agreement is considered to be an instance of adnominal agreement or not. Likewise, the number of languages without verbal agreement in the sample depends on whether clitic agreement in person, number and gender is counted as verbal agreement or not (see Section 4.4). Therefore, we have done separate calculations for each of these cases, and we have also checked whether the results are significantly different if languages classified as having marginal agreement are excluded from the calculation. The procedure was then the same in each case: First, we counted the number of languages with adnominal agreement (L_1) and those lacking verb agreement (L_2). Then we calculated the expected number of languages with both of these features (N_E), and this was done by applying the formula $N_E = (L_1/100 \times L_2/100) \times 300$ (and rounding the result to the nearest integer). Basically, this formula says that the expected number of languages with both features is the probability that a language has them (expressed as percentage) multiplied by 300 (the number of languages in the sample). Subsequently a contingency table was constructed with the number of attested and expected languages in the sample having both features (the presence of adnominal agreement and the lack of verbal agreement). Then the chi-square test was applied to the table and the X^2 (chi-square) number was calculated. That number determined the probability that the distribution of attested languages with both features was random. Finally, the probability (p) was calculated. As usual in this type of statistical analysis, it was assumed that probabilities smaller than 0.05 were statistically significant, i.e. that distributions in the sample with a probability lower than 0.05 cannot be due to pure chance.

The analysis of languages in our present 300-language sample fully confirmed the conclusions reached in Matasović (2014a). If case agreement is excluded, in our new sample there are 131 languages (44 percent) with adnominal agreement (henceforth languages of the [+NA] type). Of these, 8 languages have only marginal adnominal agreement (Ineseño Chumash, Hungarian, Kunuz Nubian, Nama, Sinhala, Sirayan, Slave and Wappo). If languages with clitic argument indices are excluded, there are 91 languages (30 percent) without verbal agreement. Those will henceforth be referred as the [−VA] type. In this case, there are 17 languages which have adnominal agreement and lack verbal agreement (the [+NA & −VA] type): Dyirbal, Biri (Pama-Nyungan), Wappo (Yukian), Nama, !Kung (Khoisan), Aghem, Babungo, Bobo, Degema, Grebo, Koromfe, Mbembe, Supyire (Niger-Kordofanian), Hausa (Afro-Asiatic), Yagua (Peba-Yaguan), Bora (Witotoan), and Khasi (Austro-Asiatic). This is highly unexpected, with p < 0.001.[2] If languages with marginal agreement (of either type) are excluded from the calculation, the distribution is even more statistically significant, again with p < 0.001.

Recall that we argued earlier (see Section 4.5) that case agreement is not so different from agreement in Phi-features to justify excluding it from a typological study of agreement phenomena. If languages with case agreement are included in the count of the languages of the [+NA] type, then there are 137 such languages in the database (46 percent, and 4 of these languages have marginal adnominal agreement). In that case, there are three more languages of the [+NA & −VA] type: Cupeño (Uto-Aztecan), Kayardild (Tangkic) and Western Desert (Pama-Nyungan). In these three languages case agreement is the only type of adnominal agreement, and they either lack verbal agreement (Kayardild), or have only clitic verbal agreement (Cupeño and Western Desert have person/number clitics). If we now apply the chi-square test to this new distribution, we again get a statistically significant result, with p < 0.005. If languages with marginal agreement are excluded, the result does not change significantly.

Furthermore, we saw in Section 4.4 that there are few theoretical arguments why languages with clitics (rather than affixes) expressing arguments should not be counted as having verbal person (/number/gender) agreement. Therefore, it appeared reasonable to do a separate statistical analysis of our sample and see if the results change if languages with clitic argument indices are included in the list of languages with verbal agreement. If this is done, then there are 54 languages lacking verbal agreement; again, we first look at what happens if we exclude languages with case agreement from the [+NA] type; in that case, there are 131 languages with adnominal agreement, and 3 languages in the sample belong to the [+NA & −VA type]: Dyirbal, Nama, and Wappo.[3] This distribution is statistically significant, with p < 0.001. And finally, if we include languages with case agreement in the list of languages with adnominal agreement, four languages in the sample can be said to belong to [+NA & −VA] type: Dyirbal, Kayardild, Nama and Wappo. The results of the chi-square tests do not change, and the distribution remains significant, again with p < 0.001. Table 19 summarizes our statistical findings for different methods of counting languages that belong to the [+NA & −VA] type.

Thus we see that languages that can be attributed to the [+NA & −VA] type are unexpectedly rare, whatever method of counting them we apply. It can be

---

[2] As in the 2014 article (Matasović 2014a), all probabilities were calculated by using the chi-square test. The calculation was based on a contingency table with 40 expected languages of the [+NA & −VA] type, with $X^2 = 15.26$.

[3] In Wappo, there is adnominal agreement in number only, and it is marginal.

Table 19 *Rareness of the [+NA & −VA] type*

	Case agreement included	Case agreement excluded
Clitics counted as verbal agreement markers	−VA: 54 lgs. +NA: 137 lgs. [+NA and −VA]: 4 lgs. p < 0.001	−VA: 54 lgs. +NA: 131 lgs. [+NA and −VA]: 3 lgs. p < 0.001
Clitics excluded (only affixes counted as verbal agreement markers)	−VA: 91 lgs. +NA: 137 lgs. [+NA and −VA]: 20 lgs. p < 0.005	−VA: 91 lgs. +NA: 131 lgs. [+NA and −VA]: 17 lgs. p < 0.001

Map 12 Languages with adnominal agreement without verbal agreement in Australia (black)

shown that languages of this unexpected type are found mostly in Central Africa and in Australia (see Maps 12 and 13), so the distribution of such languages is areally very limited.[4] It might be assumed that this is the consequence of different areal distributions of the two features, i.e. that languages with adnominal agreement and those without verbal agreement have different areal distributions. But, on closer inspection, it transpires that this is not the case: Languages without verbal agreement are generally rare, but they are somewhat more common in (Mainland) Southeast Asia, Oceania, in Southern Australia and

---

[4] In Eurasia, a language of this type is Danish, which lost all verbal agreement (except in some archaizing registers), while preserving a two-gender system shown mainly on articles and demonstratives (except in West Jutish dialects, which lost gender altogether). The same applies to Norwegian (Bokmål), which is very close to Danish, especially in the written register (Marm and Sommerfelt 1967). Neither Danish nor Norwegian is in our sample.

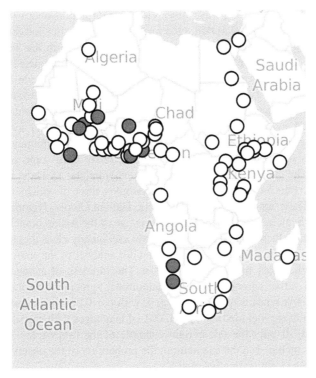

Map 13 Languages with adnominal agreement without verbal agreement in Africa (black)
Only languages with affixal verbal agreement were represented as having verbal agreement on this map.

in parts of Western Africa. Languages with adnominal agreement are significantly more common cross-linguistically, but they are particularly common in western Eurasia, sub-Saharan Africa, many parts of Australia and the Amazon, as well as in northwestern North America. Thus, in at least two large areas (Australia and Western Africa) [+NA] languages and [−VA] languages are reasonably common, and we should expect to find more languages sharing these features than we actually do. The reasons why the [+NA & −VA] type is so rare will be explored in Chapter 10 of this book.

9.2   Grammatical Verbal Agreement and Adnominal Agreement

Our sample shows that grammatical verbal agreement is very rare cross-linguistically, as it is found in under 10 percent of the languages in the sample (29 is the actual number). This percentage should be taken as an approximation, since the sources do not always give reliable information about whether a language has grammatical verbal agreement or not. But after looking at data from 300 languages, we strongly believe that languages with this feature are indeed pretty rare on the global level. More locally, these languages are particularly common in some families and areas, e.g. in parts of Indo-European (Germanic languages, Russian), NE Caucasian (Chechen, Batsbi), as well as in some West African languages mostly from the Niger-Kordofanian family (e.g. Babungo and Koromfe), but grammatical verbal agreement seems to be absent in large parts of the world. Moreover, it appears that grammatical verbal agreement is found only in languages which already have some adnominal agreement. The only certain counter-example is Wandala, a Chadic language, and there are four more possible counter-examples, three of which are contact languages. These are Berbice Dutch Creole, Haitian Creole, Nigerian Pidgin English and Semelai (an Austro-Asiatic language of the Aslian branch, spoken in Malaysia). In these four languages it is not completely clear that they actually have grammatical verbal agreement, but our analysis of the sources shows that this is the most probable hypothesis. The rareness of languages with grammatical verbal agreement without adnominal agreement (henceforth the [+GVA & −NA] type) is quite unexpected, with $p = 0.004$ (if languages with case agreement are included) and $p < 0.001$ (if languages with case agreement are excluded). If only the one certain example of the [+GVA & −NA] type (Wandala) is included in the calculation, the probability of the observed distribution becomes infinitesimally small.

It might be that the rarity of languages of the [+GVA & −NA] type is a consequence of different areal biases in the distribution of the two agreement patterns. Indeed, in at least one area where languages with grammatical verbal agreement are reasonably well attested (Western Europe), languages without adnominal agreement are rare. However, in Western Africa, where we also find a number of languages with grammatical verbal agreement, adnominal agreement is quite common. Therefore, it is doubtful whether the rarity of the [+GVA & −NA] type can be explained purely as the result of different areal biases of grammatical verbal agreement and the lack of adnominal agreement.

9.3   Person Agreement in the NP and in the Verb

It has been claimed that a language cannot have agreement in person in the NP unless it also has person agreement on the verb (Lehmann 1982a: 253, following Keenan 1974: 303). Our data confirm this implicational universal, as there are no languages in our sample with person agreement in possessive NPs and no person agreement on verbs.[5] Although it is dangerous to draw firm and

---

[5] Some languages have person-marking affixes in possessive NPs, while having no verbal agreement (e.g. Eastern Pomo), but unless they also have obligatorily possessed nouns, this

far-reaching conclusions, because data are insufficient for many languages, it appears that person agreement in the NP is reasonably common precisely in those areas (North and South America) where almost all languages have person agreement on the verb. Hence, languages having the former but lacking the latter are bound to be rare, and the fact that we have not found a single language with person agreement in the NP lacking verbal agreement in person might simply be a consequence of the different areal biases in the distribution of the two patterns of agreement. This matter certainly deserves more investigation.

9.4   Agreement and Word Order

As the final possible typological correlation, we have chosen to examine how agreement is related to word order. Since agreement essentially consists in the repetition of grammatical marking of morphosyntactic features, it is necessarily redundant, and its function is not to convey information. Rather, the function of agreement is to be sought in signaling grammatical relations, especially the syntactic structure of the constituents of the clause. In Virgil's phrase *genus unde Latinum, Albanique patres atque altae moenia Romae* "whence [comes] the Latin people, the Alban fathers and the walls of old Rome" (*Aeneid*, I: 6–7) we know that the adjective *altae* 'old' modifies *Romae* because it agrees with that noun (rather than, say, with *patres* 'fathers') in gender, number and case. For the same reason we know that *genus* 'people' is modified by *Latinum* 'Latin' and that *Albani patres* 'Alban fathers' form a single NP. The remarkable freedom of word order in Latin (especially in Roman poetry) is made possible by the extensive use of agreement on both the clause and the NP levels. On the other hand, in Vietnamese (Nguyen 1974), which is a typical isolating language with absolutely no agreement, word order is very rigid. In (118a–c), only one order of elements in the NP is possible (118a):

(118a) *Cái   áo   lụa   đẹp   này*
       PCL   shirt   silk   beautiful that
       'that beautiful silk shirt'

(118b) **Cái đẹp áo   lụa   này*
(118c) **Cái áo   đẹp lụa   này...*

It might be assumed that the presence of agreement would be negatively correlated with the rigidity of word order. If syntactic relations in constituents are indicated by word order, a language is unlikely to develop an agreement system, because such a system would serve no communicative function, i.e.

was not counted as a true agreement pattern (for reasons stated above). Nevertheless, languages such as Eastern Pomo would falsify Lehmann's and Keenan's universal as it was originally formulated.

it would be superfluous. Conversely, if word order is free in a language, and cannot be used to indicate which elements belong to a syntactic constituent, agreement can be used for that purpose, and such a language will probably develop agreement.

Unfortunately for this hypothesis, word order is seldom absolutely free or absolutely rigid. In most languages, some freedom of word order is allowed in at least some syntactic constituents. It is quite doubtful if there are any languages in which word order is absolutely free, i.e., in which there are absolutely no rules determining the order of elements in any constituent. However, some languages appear to be close to that ideal. Vedic Sanskrit had a remarkably free word order, but it is a dead language, with no native speakers who might be interviewed, and most of its texts are in verse, so that certain poetic liberty in word order is expected. On the other hand, a radically free word order has also been reported for Warlpiri, a Pama-Nyungan language of Australia (Bresnan 2001: 6–7), which is alive and very well described in the linguistic literature. In Warlpiri, all the permutations of elements in the clause and in the NP are possible (and, apparently, equally unmarked from the pragmatic point of view):

(119a) *Kurdu-ngku   ka maliki   wita-ngku   wajilipi-nyi*
        child-ERG   PRES dog.ABS   small-ERG   hunt-PRES
        'A small child is hunting a dog'

(119b) *Wajilipi-nyi ka wita-ngku maliki kurdu-ngku*
(119c) *Maliki ka kurdu-ngku wajilipi-nyi wita-ngku...*

(120a) *Maliki-rli Jakamarra-kurlangu*
        dog-ERG   J.-POSS
        'Jakamarra's dog'

(120b) *Jakamarra-kurlangu maliki-rli...*

Warlpiri has a remarkably free word order at both clause and NP levels, and it is also unusual in that it lacks gender/number agreement in the clause, and person/gender/number agreement on verbs. It does, however, have case agreement, which can be used as a cue in determining which elements of the NP belong together. But are there any languages with absolutely no adnominal agreement and free order of elements in the NP? How common is it for a language to have no verbal agreement and also free word order in the clause?

It has long been known that word order patterns are very areally biased. Languages of Eastern Asia are mostly SVO, just like languages of Western Europe and most parts of sub-Saharan Africa, while languages of Northern Eurasia, New Guinea and the Indian Subcontinent tend to have the SOV order.

Verb-initial languages are rather rare everywhere, except in the extreme west of Europe (Insular Celtic), in parts of Africa (Berber languages and some Nilotic languages), as well as in Austronesia, Mesoamerica and western North America (Nichols 1992; Bickel 2007: 241). These three types of languages (SVO, SOV and V-initial) account for more than 95 percent of the world's languages. The order in which the demonstrative precedes the noun in the NP is by far the more common cross-linguistically, but the reverse order is the norm in Africa, SE Asia and parts of Australia and Oceania. The adjective usually precedes the noun in most parts of Eurasia (except in the far west of Europe and in Mainland SE Asia), while the reverse order (N–Adj) is more common in Africa, Australia, Oceania and South America (except in parts of the Andes). All of these areal patterns of word order features are well documented in WALS (Chapters 81–97 by Matthew Dryer and Orin Gensler). It is conceivable that they are somehow connected with the areal patterns evident in the distribution of agreement systems, but this hypothesis has not been tested systematically so far. Could it be the case that languages with adnominal agreement are more common in areas where there are no preferences for the order of adjectives and nouns (or demonstratives and nouns) in the NP? Is it possible that languages with no verbal agreement are common only in areas where one particular order of S, V and O predominates?

A previous study by Anna Siewierska and Dik Bakker (1996) examined 237 languages and tried to determine if there were any correlations between the presence or absence of verbal agreement (for both subject and object) and the type of word order on the sentence level (they examined only the order of S, V and O). The authors found that V2 languages (i.e. the SVO languages, such as English, and the much less frequent OVS type found in Hixkaryana, a Cariban language) were the most likely to lack verbal agreement. In a sense, this is only to be expected, since in such languages the two arguments are clearly distinguished by their pre- and post-verbal positions, and grammatical relations can easily be established by word order only, while verbal agreement markers are redundant.[6] Siewierska and Bakker also discovered that free word order implied the presence of both subject and object agreement on the verb. This correlation was strong in all macro-areas, and, again, this is exactly what we would expect: If word order gives the speakers of a language no cue

---

[6] Of course, dependent-marking patterns for nouns (usually case marking) are also used to establish grammatical relations. Siewierska and Bakker (1996: 136ff.) found that verb-final languages are most likely to have dependent-marking for nouns, while this strategy was much less common for V1 and V2 languages. They explain this by the tendency for languages to establish grammatical relations at the outset, and case marking on S and O facilitate this in SOV (and OSV) languages.

about grammatical relations, agreement has a more important role to play. However, there were only eight languages with free word order (i.e., free order of S, V and O) in their sample.[7] Moreover, the study by Siewierska and Bakker is of limited value to the questions we asked above, since they considered only one agreement type (verbal agreement in person/number) and only one word order parameter (the position of subject, verb and object). Therefore, their study does not tell us anything about the relationship of adnominal agreement and word order.

To see if there is a connection between the freedom of word order and the presence of agreement in languages, we selected 200 languages from our sample for which data about their dominant word order was available.[8] Two word order parameters were selected: the relative orders of nouns and adjectives (N/Adj) in the NP and the relative order of subject, object and verb (S/O/V) in the clause.[9] We then compared the presence/absence of the two main patterns of agreement (i.e. adnominal and verbal agreement) with the variability of the two word order patterns to see whether there are any a priori unexpected correlations. However, the results of this inquiry were mainly negative.

In our 200-language sample, there are 16 languages without a dominant order of nouns and adjectives.[10] The following eight languages have no dominant order of nouns and adjectives and also lack adnominal agreement: Menomini, Totonac, Mam, Trumai, Shipibo-Konibo, Atayal, Tagalog and Lahu. The fact that five of those eight languages are spoken in South and North America might be a consequence of the relative rarity of both features in those areas. However, since exactly half of the languages with free order of adjectives and nouns have adnominal agreement, there is clearly no correlation between these features in the sample: The chi-square test yielded $X^2 = 0.116$ with $p = 0.733$, which is far from statistical significance.

Moreover, 29 languages in the 200-language sample have been classified as having no dominant order of S, O and V. Only three languages have no dominant order of S, O and V and also lack verbal agreement: Fijian, Garrwa and Trumai. This may appear to confirm the statistical correlation between having a free word order on the sentence level and having verbal agreement, but since

---

[7] There were also three languages with "split" word order, in the sense that more than one pattern of order of S, V and O was dominant.

[8] We used the data collected by Matthew S. Dryer for Chapters 81 and 87 of WALS. The selected subset of languages from the sample can be found in our database (they are marked in a separate field).

[9] It appears that there are very, very few languages with free order of demonstratives and nouns in the NP. In Chapter 88 of WALS ("Order of Demonstrative and Noun," by Matthew S. Dryer), which treats this feature, only 67 of 1224 languages in the sample were classified as having a *mixed* order (i.e. not unequivocally any of the orders in which the demonstrative precedes, follows, or both precedes and follows the noun in the NP).

[10] For Tucano (Tucanoan), it is unclear whether it has any adnominal agreement (it may have some marginal number agreement in the NP).

languages without verbal agreement are so rare in the first place, there is in fact no statistically relevant correlation. The value of X^2 is 0.821 with p = 0.365.

Therefore, it is not only the case that languages without agreement and rather free word order are possible, there does not appear to be a statistically significant correlation between the absence of agreement and the presence of dominant word order. However, the data on word order variability we were able to use are not suitable for such a strong conclusion, because they indicate only whether languages have dominant word orders on the clause and NP levels or not. Not having a dominant word order is not the same thing as having a completely free word order. A language in which it is equally grammatical to say *god almighty* and *almighty god* might still disallow discontinuous constituents of the kind that are possible in Latin:

(121) *Omnipoten-s   magn-am   crea-vit   de-us   terr-am*
almighty-NOM.SG great-ACC.SG.F created-PERF.3SG god-NOM.SG earth-ACC.SG.F
'The almighty god created the great earth'

In the preceding example, constituents (*omnipotens deus* 'almighty god' and *magnam terram* 'great earth') can be retrieved only on the basis of agreement, as they are discontinuous and word order cannot be used to establish their boundaries. Our data do not tell us whether languages with "free" word order allow for such discontinuous constituents. Therefore, it still remains to be seen whether there are languages with completely free word order and no agreement, and how common such languages are, if they exist.

Having found no correlation between the presence of free word order (or rather, the absence of a dominant word order) and the presence of agreement on either clause or NP level, we have decided to test the reverse implication: Maybe the absence of agreement in a language implies that the word order is not free, i.e. that the language can be clearly assigned to a type with a dominant word order (SOV, SVO, etc., on the clause level, and AN or NA on the NP level). This would imply that languages with adnominal agreement and a clearly dominant order of adjectives and nouns in the NP (either AN or NA) would be rarer than a priori expected, and the same holds for languages with verbal agreement and a clearly dominant order of S, O and V. It is important to stress that, since languages with a dominant word order pattern are the default in our sample, we do not expect languages with dominant word order and agreement (both verbal and adnominal) to be exceptional. On the contrary, we expect that there will be a lot of such languages, just fewer than there would be if the distribution was random.

Our 200-language sample contains 68 languages with adnominal agreement and a clearly dominant order of adjectives and nouns, and 84 such languages would be expected if the distribution was random. The chi-square test yields weak statistical significance for this distribution, with $X^2 = 5.235$ and p = 0.022.

On the other hand, we have 129 languages with verbal agreement and a clearly identifiable word order of S, V, and O, while 140 such languages are expected a priori. This distribution is not statistically significant, with $X^2 = 2.881$ and $p = 0.09$. Hence, it may be that having a dominant word order in the NP slightly disfavors developing adnominal agreement, but the correlation we found is too weak to assert this with confidence. We must bear in mind that we were able to check only the presence of a dominant order of nouns and adjectives in the NP and that we have no data for the ordering of the other nominal modifiers with respect to the head noun in languages from our sample. At the same time, languages in the sample may have adnominal agreement not just with adjectives, but also with demonstratives, articles, or any other adnominal modifiers. Therefore, the results of this particular statistical analysis may be indicative, but they are not completely reliable.

It remains to be seen if the presence or absence of agreement is correlated with any particular type of word order. It has been suggested (UnivArch no. 1613 after Foster and Hofling 1987: 489) that in VO languages, if the modifier precedes the noun, then there tends to be agreement between the noun and its modifier(s). This pattern can be observed in many Indo-European SVO languages (e.g. Romance, Slavic, Greek, Albanian), in Afro-Asiatic SVO and VSO languages (e.g. Hebrew and Arabic), but also elsewhere, e.g. in Swahili, Yoruba, and Fula (all in different branches of Niger-Kordofanian). There are also many counter-examples: In our sample, it is not only the isolating languages like Cantonese and Mandarin that have VO and Adj-N orders yet lack adnominal agreement. Languages like Gbaya (Ubangi, Niger-Kordofanian), Palauan, Chamorro and Ilocano (Austronesian) and Mapuche (Araucanian) also belong to this type, although they have a considerable amount of morphology. In any case, this statistical universal may be just a consequence of the coincidental correlations of areal distributions of individual features: Languages with adnominal agreement just happen to be found in the same areas as languages with the VO order and prenominal modifiers.

Regarding the areal patterns of particular word order types, one can note that languages without verbal agreement seem to be more common in areas dominated by the SVO and VOS types (sub-Saharan Africa, Mainland SE Asia, parts of Austronesia). However, before rushing to the conclusion that languages with post-verbal objects somehow disfavor verbal agreement, we have to acknowledge that the correlation we observed could be a mere coincidence, and there are many counter-examples: Mongolian, Japanese and Korean[11] all lack verbal agreement and are rigid SOV languages spoken in a contiguous area. In the same manner, we can observe that languages with

---

[11] Note, however, that loss of verbal person agreement in Korean appears to be relatively recent. Middle Korean (until the sixteenth century) still had verbs inflected for person (Sohn 1999: 51f.).

Table 20 *Distribution of languages with adnominal agreement and the order of adjective and noun*

	AN languages (75)	NA languages (109)
Number agreement in NP	44	38
Gender agreement in NP	24	37
Case agreement in NP	15	12

Table 21 *Agreement and word order*

	Adnominal agreement	Verbal agreement
Free word order	no correlation	no correlation
Presence of dominant word order	slightly disfavored (weak correlation)	no correlation

number and case agreement in the NP are slightly more numerous in areas where AN languages predominate, while languages with gender agreement in the NP are more evenly distributed (Table 20). This is probably because the AN order is very common in Northern Eurasia and in Western North America (see Map 87A in WALS: "Order of Adjective and Noun," Dryer 2013), while gender is rather rare in those two areas, as we saw above. The only area where both the AN order and gendered languages are found is the Indian Subcontinent. On the other hand, gender is very common in sub-Saharan Africa, parts of Amazonia and in Northern Australia, the areas where NA languages predominate. The question why case agreement appears to be relatively more common in languages with AN order must remain open. We could speculate that indicating the syntactic function of the NP at its beginning facilitates processing, hence case marking of the adjective preceding the noun in the NP should be a cognitively favored pattern. However, it may be that the distribution we see is just a consequence of two independent areal biases: Case agreement, as we saw above, is virtually limited to a small number of families in Europe and India (Indo-European) and Australia (Pama-Nyungan), and those areas just happen also to contain many languages with AN as the dominant order of adjective and noun in the NP.

Therefore, although some correlation between the absence of agreement and the rigidity of word order might be supposed on theoretical grounds, no such correlation is manifested in our data. Likewise, it does not seem to be the case that having a dominant word order disfavors the development of agreement in languages. If there is a correlation between having a dominant word order in the NP and lacking adnominal agreement, as our analysis suggests, it is certainly not strong. Table 21 summarizes our results in this section.

10 Diachronic Patterns in the Development of Agreement

The prehistory of the large majority of the world's languages is completely unknown. No wonder, then, that we can only speculate how different agreement patterns developed in most languages in our sample, and that any attempt to establish cross-linguistic regularities in the evolution of agreement systems must remain conjectural. However, all synchronic patterns in the distribution of linguistic features must have diachronic explanations, i.e. there must exist diachronic processes that brought them about. These explanations may not be the whole story: Neurolinguistic factors, such as ease of processing, may influence the relative frequency of certain patterns, and there may be other reasons why the distribution of the features is exactly as we see it on a map. But no explanation can be complete unless it includes an account of how that distribution came to be as it is, i.e. unless it offers a plausible history of the developments that led to the current situation. In what follows, we shall attempt to offer a number of historical hypotheses that could serve as an explanation why the geographical distribution of certain agreement patterns appears to be a priori unexpected. Needless to say, it will be very speculative, and it will rely heavily on the reconstructable (pre-)history of the languages and language families of Eurasia, under the assumption that conclusions drawn from them can be applied to the rest of the world, where, historically, we are pretty much in the dark.

In the preceding chapters it was established that the following facts about the areal distribution of agreement patterns need an explanation:

1. A language is likely to have adnominal agreement only if it also has some verbal agreement (Section 9.1).
2. A language is likely to have grammatical verbal agreement only if it also has some adnominal agreement (Section 9.2).
3. Languages with gender agreement are common in SW Eurasia, sub-Saharan Africa, Northern Australia and parts of Amazonia, but rare elsewhere (Chapter 8).
4. Other types of adnominal agreement (case and number agreement) have roughly the same areal distribution as the distribution of languages with

gender agreement, although case agreement and adnominal number agreement[1] are rarer than adnominal gender agreement (Chapter 8).

10.1   Origins of Agreement

Agreement is a diachronically very stable phenomenon (Nichols 1992, 1995; see Section 8.7 above). We seldom find languages that lack agreement but are in the process of acquiring it. Moreover, in the absence of evidence to the contrary, it is a priori probable that different patterns of agreement have different paths of development. In Matasović (2014a), it was suggested that there is a principled difference between the two kinds of agreement, and that this difference is manifested in the way these two patterns develop in languages. Adnominal agreement spontaneously arises only in languages that already have verbal agreement. Verbal agreement, on the other hand, arises by a well-documented process of cliticization of independent pronouns to verbs, and this process is facilitated by pragmatic factors (focalization/topicalization of free pronouns). Essentially, verbal agreement involves syntactic re-analysis, a very common process in historical syntax (Harris and Campbell 1995): Referring expressions that are used in pragmatically marked constructions and are structurally elements of the sentence but not the clause become re-interpreted as elements of the clause while the construction loses its pragmatic markedness. A construction is pragmatically marked if it explicitly expresses the information status of certain constituents, e.g. if they are topical (representing old information, elements of the discourse assumed by the speaker to be identifiable by the listener), or focal (representing new information, new elements of the discourse to which the speaker wishes to draw the listener's attention).

The development of bound agreement markers from free referring expressions in this scenario can be sketched as follows (the examples arc formulated in an imaginary language with words interpreted by English morphemes):

(122)   *[The man, [he sing]$_{CLAUSE}$]$_{SENTENCE}$ →   [[The man he-sing]$_{CLAUSE}$]$_{SENTENCE}$*

After the re-analysis, the word *he-sing* (meaning 'he sings') essentially shows verbal agreement with the subject of the clause (*the man*), and the pragmatically marked construction has become unmarked. It has been argued that this account of the development of verbal agreement, going back to the work of Talmy Givón (1976),[2] cannot explain the cliticization and development into agreement markers of the first and second person pronouns, which are

---

[1] That is, adnominal number agreement that is not included in the gender agreement system.
[2] Cf. also Mithun (1990).

less topical in discourse than third person pronouns. To address this problem, Mira Ariel (2000) offered an accessibility-based account of the development of person agreement, which is thought to be driven by the speaker's desire to use phonologically reduced, bound markers to refer to highly accessible discourse referents. In her view, pronouns may develop directly into verbal person affixes (without first being topicalized), and this applies especially to the highly accessible first and second person pronouns. This is in line with the cross-linguistic tendency that first and second person are more often overtly expressed by agreement markers than third person pronouns. Note that it is irrelevant for our theory which concrete type of grammaticalization process is more common cross-linguistically, and whether Givón's or Ariel's approach is more fruitful in explaining the origin of person agreement markers in individual languages. All that matters is that the development of person agreement is pragmatically motivated in the way that the development of adnominal agreement is not.

In a sense, then, the development of verbal agreement does not really require an explanation: It is ubiquitous, extremely common, and apparently a prerequisite for the development of adnominal agreement in any language. What we need to understand is how and why adnominal agreement develops only under certain conditions and why those conditions seem to be fulfilled only in some areas, and not in others.

We argued above that pragmatic factors which facilitate the development of verbal agreement do not exist with respect to adnominal agreement. Rather, adnominal agreement appears to arise "parasitically" on a pre-existing agreement pattern in a different domain: If a language already has syntactic structures with verbal agreement (as illustrated above: *[[The man he-sings]* $_{CLAUSE}]_{SENTENCE}$), then it can develop the same pattern in the NP, by introducing agreement (say, in number) through re-analysis of pronouns in apposition:

(123)   *those, [(the) men]$_{NP}$* → *[those men]$_{NP}$*

After the re-analysis, the demonstrative is interpreted as being in the same NP as the noun, hence it agrees with it in number. If a language distinguishes different pronouns for different classes of nouns (say, an animate and an inanimate class), then such a re-analysis will bring about agreement not just in number but also in gender:

(124)   *those.animate, [(the) men]$_{NP}$* → *[those.animate men]$_{NP}$*

The crucial point is that there is no motivation for such appositive constructions to be re-analyzed as NPs with agreement. While topicalizing constructions gradually lose their markedness, which leads to re-analysis of free pronouns as agreement markers, appositive demonstratives in language can easily co-exist with NPs in which nouns are modified by uninflected demonstrative pronouns, as in Kabardian:

(125)   *ā-xa-r,   ā pśāśa-xa-r*
        this-PL-ABS   this girl-PL-ABS
        'they, (namely) those girls'

The first occurrence of the pronoun *ā-* in (125) is appositive and inflected for number and case, while the second one is part of the NP (*ā pśāśa-xa-r* 'those girls') and does not agree in number and case with the head noun. We can imagine that a language such as Kabardian could develop a rule of number (and case?) agreement in the NP, but there is no functional motivation for it to do so. However, the rule could develop "parasitically," by copying the pattern that already exists elsewhere in the language, namely, in its rich system of verbal agreement. The construction **ā-xa-r pśāśa-xa-r*, which now has to be marked with an asterisk as ungrammatical, would then become regular.

There are several mechanisms by which agreement can spread from the clausal domain to the NP, besides the re-analysis of demonstratives in apposition. It has been argued that, in some languages, gender agreement arose by re-analysis of classifiers as gender markers (Greenberg 1978), and precisely this process seems to be occurring in some Daly languages of Northern Australia (Corbett 2006: 268). Typically, in this scenario, the number of classifiers is reduced[3] (either by phonological merger of their shape or by semantic changes) and they start to be repeated after different elements in an NP, thus creating agreement. In one language of the Daly group, Ngan'gityemerri (Corbett 2006: 268, after Reid 1997: 177), six noun classes have optional free classifiers modifying the head noun in the NP:

(126)   *(tyin)   gan'gan   (tyin)   kinyi*
        WOOMERA fish.spear WOOMERA this
        'this fish spear-type woomera'

Woomera is a stick for throwing various spears and *tyin* is the classifier for woomeras. When it is first used in (126), it behaves as a classifier, but its second use looks like gender agreement. However, both uses of this morpheme are optional, so Ngan'gityemerri does not have a gender agreement system yet. But if the repeated use of *tyin* (and other 'classifiers') in such constructions becomes obligatory, it will have one.

---

[3] Of course, this is not to deny that there are languages in which the number of genders approaches the typical number of classifiers (Fedden and Corbett 2017). However, such languages are rare cross-linguistically.

We have already mentioned the suggestion that the gender agreement in Dyirbal (Pama-Nyungan) arose in a similar way (see Section 8.5). The same process may be taking place in a number of Amazonian languages, where languages with classifiers and those with gender systems often co-exist, and several languages have both a classifier system *and* a gender system (e.g. Warekena, an Arawakan language, cf. Aikhenvald 1998).[4] In Hup, a Makú language which is under strong Tucanoan influence (Epps 2006: 204), an incipient gender system may be in the process of forming from classifiers, and shape-based classifiers are grammaticalizing from native words for plant parts, e.g. Hup *yŭhum-tat* 'avocado fruit' vs. *yŭhum-teg* 'avocado tree' (where *tat* and *teg* are Hup words for 'fruit' and 'tree', respectively, which have become classifiers).

A special role in the development of gender agreement markers from classifiers is probably played by the so-called "repeater constructions," in which a phrase meaning 'two X' is constructed as 'two X X', where a word can behave as its own classifier. Such a construction is found in Lao, where *taw⁴* 'vase' is its own classifier (Goddard 2005: 98; numerals indicate tones):

(127) *Mii²   taw⁴ dòòk⁵-maj⁴   cak²   taw⁴?*
       there.is vase flower-plant how.many vase
       'How many vases are there?'

In a language with such a construction, a "repeater" classifier with a sufficiently general meaning, e.g. 'woman', could easily be re-analyzed as a gender marker and abstracted from quantified contexts, thus creating a gender agreement system. There are, then, several possibilities for a classifier system to develop into a gender system, but it is difficult to prove that this is the way in which many gender systems actually developed.

Claudi (1985: 58ff.) considers another hypothesis for the development of gender. In East Nilotic, the feminine marker *na-* can be traced back to the noun **nyaa-* 'girl', and, apparently, gender agreement arose through re-interpretation of genitive constructions, i.e. *daughter.of-X* developed into FEM-*X*, where FEM is the feminine marker. Note that **nyaa-* was not a classifier (Nilotic languages do not have classifiers), but just a common noun. The same lexical element also came to be used as a pronoun for referring to females and, when used attributively, it started to agree with the natural gender of the referent. A similar process is assumed for Zande, a language of the Ubangian group of Niger-Kordofanian

---

[4] Blench (2015) speculates that elaborate gender systems of Niger-Congo and some Australian languages developed from earlier classifier systems, which were reduced to affixes. He also thinks that petrified classifiers/noun class affixes may be discerned in some Sino-Tibetan and Austronesian languages. This hypothesis would certainly need further elaboration and supporting evidence.

(Claudi 1985, especially 138ff.), in which new gender markers appear to have developed from nouns referring to general concepts of 'animal', 'woman' and the like. In any case, in order to have agreement, the new gender markers had to be obligatorily repeated before different elements of the NP, and our contention is that this was likely to occur only if the language(s) already had a rule requiring the repetition of grammatical morphemes (i.e. agreement) in the clause.

The development in Zande and similar languages can be summarized as follows:

(128)   *[that girl.of woman]*_{NP} → *[that-girl.of woman]*_{NP} → *[that-FEM.woman]*_{NP}

A similar process may have brought about gender agreement in Sarcee and other Athabaskan languages. In Sarcee, the demonstrative (used to indicate location near the speaker) distinguishes the form *dìní* (human sg.) from *dìyí* (non-human sg./pl.), cf. the opposition between *dìní ts'ìkáʔī* 'this woman' from *dìyí tsí* 'this paint' (Rijkhoff 2002: 79). The human form of the pronoun is very similar to the noun *dìná* 'person, people', which may be its historical origin. If that is correct, an appositive construction meaning 'the person (namely) the woman' developed into an NP in which the former appositive noun was re-interpreted as a demonstrative pronoun agreeing in gender with the head noun.

The development of gender markers from nouns with general reference (as in Zande and, perhaps, in Sarcee) is not so dissimilar to the development of gender markers from classifiers (as in Daly languages). In both cases the starting point is presumably nominal, i.e. a referring expression with general reference that may or may not be part of a system of classifiers.[5] In both cases the nominal element is first reduced to a modifier of the noun or NP, and then to a pure agreement marker. The intermediate stage may be one in which the nominal element has become pronominal and is used attributively to mark definiteness and/or deixis. The development of deictic elements from nouns is well known in the literature on diachronic syntax and grammaticalization. In many languages of the Far East, personal pronouns (especially those of the 1st and 2nd person) were nouns with general reference, e.g. one of the Japanese pronouns meaning 'I', *boku*, was a noun meaning 'servant' (Lehmann 1982b: 41). Similar processes are attested elsewhere, e.g. in Spanish, where the honorific 2nd person sg. pronoun *usted* is reduced from the phrase *vuestra merced*

---

[5] Kiessling (2013: 61) claims that "semantic and morphosyntactic arguments suggest that the Niger-Congo noun class markers and their concords have their ultimate lexical origin in nouns for basic-level concepts such as 'person', 'people', 'animal', 'thing', 'tree', 'fruit' and 'water', in nouns for body parts such as 'eye' and for social functions such as 'child', 'mother', 'father', and 'husband' which were used as head nouns in associative constructions or as class-terms in compounds" – however, he does not reconstruct those lexical items. This should be "the next step." For a reconstruction of Proto-Bantu verbal gender markers, see Nurse (2007).

'your grace', and in Polish, where the second person honorific pronoun *pan* (fem. *pani*, pl. *państwo*) developed from the noun meaning 'sir'. It would not be surprising if such processes, accompanied by cliticization of pronouns to deictic markers on nouns or verbs, could lead to the establishment of gender agreement systems in a variety of languages.

However, these are probably not the only paths by which a system of adnominal agreement can arise. Quite likely, it is also possible for an adnominal gender system to develop "parasitically" on a pre-existing case agreement system. For this to happen, it is enough that animate and inanimate referents have different case marking: say, that a language has differential object marking based on animacy, or that a language has a rule prohibiting inanimate subjects of transitive clauses, as in Hittite (Indo-European) and Diegueño (Yuman branch of Hokan, cf. Langdon 1970). If, in such a language, case marking spreads from nouns to adnominal adjectives, case agreement will at the same time become gender agreement based on animacy, since inanimate nouns and their modifiers will have different marking in the NP when compared with animates. This is, indeed, the most likely scenario for how gender agreement arose in Proto-Indo-European (Matasović 2014b): In Early Proto-Indo-European, inanimates did not distinguish the nominative and the accusative (both being unmarked), while animates had a special case ending *-s* in the nominative.[6] Adjectives were originally not distinguishable from nouns (they shared the same morphology), and demonstratives were uninflected: There are still traces of uninflected demonstrative particles in early Indo-European languages, such as *-c* < *-k'e* in Latin *hi-c, hae-c, ho-c* 'this' (in Lithuanian, on the other hand, this particle yielded a fully inflected pronoun *šìs* m. 'this', *šì* f. 'this'). However, at a certain point, inflected demonstrative pronouns were created, and they started agreeing with the head noun in case/number/gender in the NP. At that time the proto-language distinguished only common and neuter genders, and the semantic feature distinguishing the two genders was animacy. At a later stage, the opposition of feminine and masculine genders was created within the animate class, but this development did not affect the Anatolian languages (such as Hittite), which was the first to branch off (for details cf. Matasović 2004 and 2014b). It is impossible to say how common this type of development is cross-linguistically, but it can only happen in languages in which adnominal modifiers are the chief locus of gender agreement. In the majority of languages with gender, where verbs are marked for gender as well, this scenario will work only if gender agreement further spreads to verbs via infinite forms, such as participles. This is what happened in Russian during the historical period, when the past tense forms were created from earlier participles, which were

---

[6] This case ending may have expressed the ergative case in (very) Early Proto-Indo-European, but this is not the point in the present discussion.

inflected for gender (but not person), cf. Russian *(On) byl* '(He) was' vs. *(Ona) byla* '(She) was' and *(Ja) byl* 'I was (male speaker)', *(Ja) byla* 'I was (female speaker)'. The development of adnominal agreement in Proto-Indo-European and in similar languages can be summarized as follows:

(129a)   *[that woman-ACC]$_{NP}$ → [that-ACC woman-ACC]$_{NP}$*

    vs.

(129b)   *[that stone-0]$_{NP}$ → [that-0 stone-0]$_{NP}$*

In this scenario, the development of case agreement immediately triggers gender agreement based on animacy, since animates (*woman*) and inanimates (*stone*) have different case marking to begin with. We can imagine how certain genderless languages, such as Basque, could eventually develop gender in this way. In Basque, local cases of animate and inanimate nouns have different suffixes (Zubiri 2000: 107–9), e.g. the inessive case of *mutil* 'boy' is *mutil-en-gan*, while the same case forms of *Bilbo* 'Bilbao' and *etxe* 'house' are *Bilbo-n* and *etxe-tan* respectively (proper names and common nouns also have different case endings). If Basque developed case agreement (say, by marking case on adnominal adjectives and pronouns), it would automatically develop a rudimentary gender agreement system as well.

"Covert animacy systems" (Nichols 1989a) that sometimes trigger the development of gender agreement can be based not only on different case marking of animate and inanimate nouns but also on different number marking. In many languages only nouns denoting animates (or only humans) can have plural marking, e.g. in Dani (Trans-New Guinea, cf. Barclay 2008) and in Panare (Cariban, cf. Payne and Payne 2013). If, in such a language, number morphemes start to be used after different elements of the NP (e.g. adjectives and demonstratives), the resulting pattern will be gender/number agreement based on the opposition of the features human/non-human (or animate/inanimate). It has been argued that this kind of process is going on in Kiowa (Kiowa-Tanoan, cf. Watkins and McKenzie 1984: 78ff.). It can be summarized as follows:

(130a)   *[that man-PL]$_{NP}$ → [that-PL man- PL]$_{NP}$* 'these men'
(130b)   *[that stone-0]$_{NP}$ → [that stone]$_{NP}$* 'that stone/these stones'

We cannot be sure how common different diachronic paths of creation of adnominal agreement systems are. It may be that, in areas where morphological case is common (especially in Eurasia) the default development is the one sketched above for Proto-Indo-European. Language families with small inventories of genders, especially those in which animacy plays a role in gender assignment, would be good candidates for this scenario, e.g. Dravidian and Munda languages (Andronov 1970; Bhattacharya 1976; Krishnamurti 2003;

Anderson 2008). Since classifier systems usually have dozens of classifiers, language families with elaborate gender systems (with four or more genders), where shape and consistency of referents play a role in gender assignment, could easily have developed gender agreement from earlier classifier systems. This holds, for example, for NE Caucasian (where we find up to nine genders in some languages) and Niger-Kordofanian, where languages of the Atlantic branch have almost thirty genders. The same development is the likely source of gender systems in some Austronesian languages of Papua New Guinea and Indonesia (e.g. Kilivila, spoken on the Trobriand Islands, see Fedden and Corbett 2017: 21–2), where the incipient gender system still has numerous features of classifier systems. However, one also has to take into account that in some languages their small number of genders might be a remnant of an earlier more elaborate system; in fact, it can be shown that the number of genders was greatly reduced in some NE Caucasian languages, e.g. in Archi, which has four genders, or in certain dialects of Tabasaran, which have only two genders. The two-gender system of Afro-Asiatic is also often considered to be a reduction of an earlier more Bantu-like system of several noun classes (Lipinski 1987: 234; Diakonov1988: 58), and the three-gender system of Abkhaz and Abaza (NW Caucasian) has been interpreted as a remnant of a more complex gender system akin to the one found in NE Caucasian (Abdokov 1981; Matasović 2017). Hence, the scenario in which a gender system develops from a classifier system through a gradual reduction of the number of noun classes based on shape/consistency (besides animacy and sex) is always possible.

It is also possible that the areal distribution of languages with adnominal agreement corresponds to certain broad patterns in the ethnography of speaking and the pragmatics of discourse structure. It was noted that discourse in Australian languages typically begins with a generic noun, and then its meaning is narrowed down by the use of a specific noun which may be in apposition:

Australian languages are notable for their freedom of word order. The words in a noun phrase may be separated into two (or, sometimes, more) parts, occurring at different places in the clause. One strategy is to place part of the NP before the verb and the remainder after the verb; the part preceding the verb is typically a generic noun or a deictic, with specific noun or adjective coming after the verb. (Dixon 2002: 59)

Of course, if it is natural to construct the utterance so that it is common to say things like "the animal went downstream (namely) the kangaroo," and nouns are morphologically marked for case, adnominal agreement is very likely to develop. Case agreement will help establish co-reference between different elements of a split NP, and if generic nouns are reduced to the status of classifiers, and then to definite articles, adnominal gender agreement will develop. Indeed, the development of gender in Dyirbal probably followed that historical path, as we suggested above.

On the other hand, if the discourse is typically structured so that the referent is mentioned by a referring NP only once, at the beginning, and then repeatedly omitted because it is retrievable from the context, or if it is cross-referenced by verbal argument indices in a topic chain, it will be very difficult for adnominal agreement to develop in such a language. Iroquoian languages spoken in the eastern parts of North America would seem to be of this type, as well as the NW Caucasian languages such as Kabardian and Abkhaz. If gender/number agreement develops in such languages, it will be marked on verbs rather than adjectives and adnominal demonstratives, and this is indeed what we find in Tuscarora (Iroquoian, Mithun 1974) and Abkhaz (Hewitt 1979). It is not that agreement in such languages could not spread from the clause to the NP: Rather, this is unlikely to happen, since full NPs are uncommon in the discourse, especially when compared with languages of the Indo-European type.

"Exotic" patterns of discourse structuring may even lead to aberrant types of agreement. We have seen above that the person/number/gender agreement in the NP that is found in Nama and some other Khoisan languages is typologically exceptional. The immediate precursor of a language in which the noun obligatorily carries person marking was presumably a language in which it was more common to say "we, the people," "you, the king," or "they, the foreigners" rather than just "we," "you," "they" or "the people," "the king," "the foreigners."

Thus, if there are culturally determined patterns of discourse structuring, it is likely that these patterns will have similar areal distributions as other social norms and cultural traits do. This will then at least partially determine the way different agreement systems develop in languages.

It may well be that spreading the pattern of agreement from the clausal domain to the NP is the most common way a language can develop adnominal agreement. But it is certainly not the only way. Adnominal agreement can also arise in situations of intensive language contact: If L1 has adnominal agreement, while L2 does not, bilingual speakers can "transfer" the adnominal agreement rule from L1 to L2. Such a development occurred in the history of Baltic Finnic languages, which did not have case agreement (just like the other Uralic languages), but acquired it through contacts with their Indo-European neighbors (chiefly Germanic, Baltic and Slavic languages, which inherited adnominal agreement from Proto-Indo-European). Thus in Estonian we have plural agreement in (131b) and case and number agreement in (131c) (Moseley 1994: 45):

(131a)   *minu esimene mulje*
          my   first   impression
          'my first impression'

(131b)   *minu esimese muljed*
         my   first.PL   impression.PL
         'my first impressions'

(131c)   *minu esimeste   muljete*
         my   first.GEN.PL impression.GEN.PL
         'of my first impressions'

A similar process took place in Karaim, a highly endangered Turkic language spoken in Lithuania, which developed number agreement in the NP, probably under influence of Polish and Lithuanian, cf. Karaim *suklančï-lar baxur-lar* (young.man-PL wonderful-PL) 'wonderful young men' (Berta 1998: 315).[7]

In principle, this borrowing of adnominal agreement can happen even if the L2 does not have any verbal agreement, which may be one of the reasons why languages of the type [+NA & −VA] exist, although they are demonstrably rare, as we saw in Chapter 9. In such languages, we would argue, adnominal agreement arose as a result of intensive language contact, or because verbal agreement was lost, while adnominal agreement was not. A typical case would appear to be Bobo, a Mande language spoken in Burkina Faso. Bobo has number agreement in the NP and a very marginal verbal agreement system, consisting only of auxiliaries inflected for tense.[8] The difference between the two tenses is expressed by tone (Le Bris and Prost 1981: 60):

(132a)   *yē   nìmī*
         they.PRES dance
         'They dance'

(132b)   *yè   nìmī*
         they.PST dance
         'They danced'

Bobo is likely to have lost person markers on verbs under the influence of Gur languages, which surround it in Burkina Faso and the neighboring areas of Mali. It has also been suggested that it developed number agreement under the influence of Gur languages (Prost 1983), in which it is common. Thus, in situations of intensive language contact, an adnominal agreement pattern can be borrowed even if verbal agreement is marginal or, possibly, non-existent.

---

[7] This pattern of adnominal agreement seems to be optional at present, as one can find several examples of NPs without number agreement in Kocaoğlu (2006). Note that Turkish, Karaim's close relative, does not have any adnominal agreement (see Chapter 2).

[8] They are called "pronouns," but this would imply that the language has different pronouns in different tenses, so we believe it is preferable to analyse them as auxiliaries.

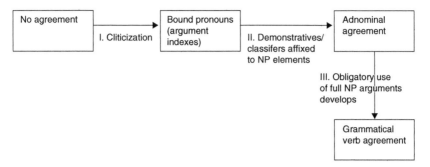

Figure 3 The development of agreement systems

We have already mentioned in Chapter 6 how Tagalog acquired marginal gender agreement in loanwords from Spanish – adjectives of Spanish origin agree in gender with the head noun in the NP, while inherited adjectives do not – and the same restriction of adnominal gender agreement applies in a number of other languages, including Munda languages Santali (Ghosh 2008: 12) and Kharia (Peterson 2011: 139), where only loanwords from Indo-Aryan languages show agreement in the NP. Hayek (2006: 171) reports that in the Austronesian language Tetun Dili, spoken on East Timor, a small group of nouns and adjectives borrowed from Portuguese obligatorily shows gender, e.g. *tiu* 'uncle', *tia* 'aunt', *mestre* 'male teacher', *mestra* 'female teacher', *bonitu* 'handsome m.', *bonita* 'pretty f.'. Such examples could probably be multiplied, but systematic research of these phenomena is lacking. It is conceivable that in some languages this kind of agreement rule spread from the borrowed to the inherited lexicon, but at present, this development cannot be demonstrated in any language.

Finally, if our data are to be trusted, it seems that grammatical verbal agreement can develop only in languages that already have adnominal agreement. This appears to be a kind of "transfer" of a syntactic pattern from one domain, where it is functionally motivated, to another, where functional motivation is weaker or non-existent. If the structure of the NP requires that grammatical information is redundantly repeated, the same principle can be applied to the structure of the clause. The development of the agreement systems is summarized in Figure 3.

Note that the development of agreement systems sketched on Figure 3 can be broken off at any point, i.e. it is not necessary that all languages eventually develop grammatical verb agreement. Moreover, all agreement patterns can be lost at any time, due to phonological attrition of markers or to syntactic changes. This means that a language having bound pronouns/argument indices can lose them irrespective of whether it has adnominal agreement, grammatical verbal agreement, or neither of these two agreement patterns.

If these claims about the origin of different agreement patterns are true, then they suffice to explain the statistical typological correlations we observed in our sample, namely, why languages with adnominal agreement almost always also have verbal agreement, and why grammatical verbal agreement is so rare. Moreover, since case agreement, where it develops at all, tends to be parasitic on gender/number agreement, it is clear why its areal distribution corresponds closely to the distribution of languages with gender(/number) adnominal agreement. The only exceptions are Africa, where languages with the morphological category of case are rare, and (parts of) Southern Australia, where case agreement is found without gender agreement. The reason for this has to do with the ways agreement patterns can be lost, to which we shall now turn.

10.2   Loss of Agreement

All agreement patterns can be lost, and there are generally two mechanisms by which this can happen: Firstly, phonological changes can lead to erosion of morphemes expressing agreement, and, secondly, syntactic changes can bring about the generalization of one form showing agreement, which replaces all others. This second type of loss would seem to be particularly common in situations of language contact. If L1 has agreement and L2 lacks it, speakers of an L2 may tend to generalize the use of only one form of agreeing words while learning an L1 as a second language. However, in most situations that can reasonably be reconstructed, agreement is not lost without a trace; rather, it is reduced to a marginal pattern, as in most of the following examples.

Gender was lost in Cappadocian Greek probably under the influence of the Turkish adstratum and superstratum, as this dialect has been surrounded by speakers of Turkish, which does not have gender; thus, rather than having the three gendered forms of adjectives and articles of Classical and Modern Greek, Cappadocian Greek has only one form in the singular:[9] *do kalon do andra* 'the good man' vs. *do kalon do neka* 'the good woman' and *do kalon do pei* 'the good child'; however, number agreement was preserved, so the plurals of the preceding NPs are *da kalan da andres, da kalan da nekes* and *da kalan da peija*, respectively (Karatsareas 2009).

In Armenian, the gender system inherited from Proto-Indo-European was lost before its first historical attestation in the fifth century AD. It is probable that the loss of gender in Armenian should also be attributed to some substratum influence. One possible candidate is Urartean, a language spoken in Armenia in the early first millennium BC, whose only known relative is Hurrian, also an extinct language of ancient Anatolia. Both Urartean and Hurrian were

---

[9] The gendered forms of Modern Greek are *o* (m.), *i* (f.) and *to* (n.) for the article and *kalos* (m.), *kali* (f.) and *kalo* (n.) for the adjective.

genderless languages, and we know that Armenian has borrowed many words from Urartean. In Classical Armenian (fifth century AD), final syllables were generally lost by apocope, but different nominal, adjectival and pronominal stems can still be distinguished by their inflection, e.g. *azg* 'people' has the genitive sg. *azg-i* and corresponds to the Proto-Indo-European feminine ā-stems (the type of Latin *terra*, Gen. *terrae* 'land'), while *get* 'river' has the genitive *get-oy* and corresponds to the Proto-Indo-European masculine/neuter o-stems (the type of Latin *lupus*, Gen. sg. *lupī* 'wolf'). However, there is no rule of agreement of o-stem adjectives with o-stem nouns, or ā-stem adjectives and ā-stem nouns, i.e. all traces of gender agreement were lost (Meillet 1936). As in Cappadocian Greek, not all adnominal agreement was lost: Adjectives still agree with the head noun in case and number if they are postposed, but not if they are preposed (Schmitt 1981: 159):

(133)   *bazowm*   *gorc-s*   *bari-s*
         many   deed-ACC.PL   good-ACC.PL
         'many good deeds'

In (133), the preposed adjective *bazowm* does not show case/number agreement, but the postposed adjective *bari-s* does.[10]

In NE Caucasian, languages that lost gender (Udi, Lezgian, Agul and some dialects of Tabasaran) are spoken on the southern fringes of the NE Caucasian speaking area and are in long-standing contact with the speakers of the Turkic language Azeri (which does not have gender) and Iranian languages that had lost gender very early. In Lezgian (Alekseev 2003), the inherited system of prefixes showing gender was lost, but there is no evidence for the general loss of initial syllables. Rather, words inflected for one particular gender were generalized, and earlier gender markers still exist as petrified forms. The development in Agul was very similar (Magometov 1970). Thus, the development leading to gender loss in those NE Caucasian languages almost certainly involved syntactic changes rather than phonological attrition of gender markers alone.

Outside Eurasia, contact-induced loss of gender, as a typical agreement pattern, is reported for many languages. Aikhenvald (2006: 18) mentions Tangale, a Chadic language, that lost gender distinctions as a result of contact with Adamawa languages, and generalized the inherited Afro-Asiatic feminine form of adjectives and demonstratives. The loss of gender in some Kru languages may have been due to contact with South Mande languages, which are genderless and belong to a very distant branch of Niger-Kordofanian (see above). Similarly, the loss of gender in Arawak languages Mawayana, Amuesha and

---

[10] Compare the similar agreement pattern in Georgian, discussed in Chapter 6.

perhaps Chamicuro, is probably due to the influence of surrounding languages that have no gender, and the absence of gender in Jivaroan may be due to the influence of the neighboring Quechuan and Aymaran languages (Aikhenvald 2012: 280).

Just as gender agreement in the NP can be lost in contact situations, so a language can lose verbal agreement in person/number/gender due to areal pressure. This can probably explain why we find a number of languages very close to the [+NA & −VA] type in West Africa. Typically, these languages have some gender/number agreement in the NP, but their verbs are not inflected for gender/number/person. Usually, they have person marking clitics or words with a very fixed position in the clause that fall under our definition of "argument indices," but under a strictly morphological interpretation of verbal agreement, they would have to be analyzed as having adnominal agreement and lacking verbal agreement (see Section 4.4). A typical case is Supyire, a Gur language spoken in Mali and Ivory Coast. It has gender/number agreement in the NP and generally uninflected verbs, but it also has two sets of pronouns: "declarative" and "non-declarative" (Carlson 1994: 151–4). The latter have a very fixed position in the clause and are used in commands, prohibitives, exclamations, etc., and can be viewed as inflected auxiliaries showing person agreement (although this is not the only possible analysis). However this may be, it is fair to say that verbal agreement is rather marginal in Supyire, while adnominal agreement is well developed for number and gender (Carlson 1994: 192):

(134)   *u*   *pyà-ngi*
        this.CL.1.SG   child-DEF.CL.1
        'this/that child'

(135)   *pi*   *cyèe-bíí*
        these.CL.1PL   women-DEF.CL.1
        'these women'

(136)   *li*   *kû-ni*
        this.CL.3   road-DEF.CL.3
        'this road'

The interesting thing about Supyire is that this language has been under strong areal influence of Mande languages, which typically do not have any verbal agreement, or have only inflected auxiliaries (Garber 1987). Supyire is separated from the other Senufo (Gur) languages by a strip of area where Mande languages are spoken (Carlson 1994: 3). Even though it is not a perfect example of a [+NA & −VA] language type, we see how such a language could have arisen under areal pressure of languages without agreement: Verbal agreement can be lost even as adnominal agreement stays intact.

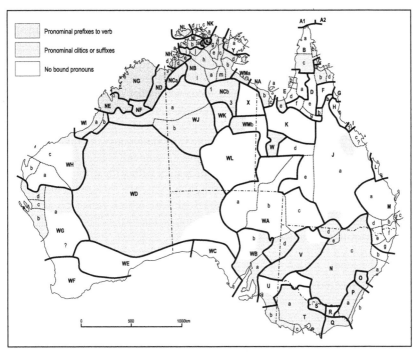

Map 14 Languages with bound pronouns in Australia
(Adopted from Dixon 2002: 340 and reproduced with permission.)

We can speculate even further, and assume that Pama-Nyungan languages
(in Australia) with adnominal agreement (usually in case) and without verbal
agreement originally had bound argument indices, but lost it, while preserving adnominal agreement systems in which noun and its modifiers are case
marked. There is no way to prove this hypothesis, because the comparative
and historical grammar of Pama-Nyungan is still not developed enough, and
it is at present unknown whether Proto-Pama-Nyungan had verbal agreement
or not.[11] However, if we look at Dixon's map of Australian languages with
bound pronouns (Dixon 2002: 340, adopted here as Map 14), we can see that
languages that lack them (and thus, by definition, also lack verbal agreement)
are found in a rather compact area in the center of the continent, while those
that have them are located chiefly in the periphery, both in the west (e.g.
Nhanta, Marrngu), in the southeast (e.g. Muruwari, Dharuk, Dharrawal) and

---

[11] Alpher (1990) reconstructs Proto-Pama-Nyungan verbal paradigms without bound pronouns
(argument indices) and Dixon (2002), who does not believe in Pama-Nyungan as a genetic
unit, thinks that verbs in Proto-Australian were uninflected.

in the north (e.g. Warlpiri). The large area in western Australia near the center of the continent, where bound pronouns are found, is populated by the speakers of a single language (actually a dialect continuum). This is Western Desert Language (WD), which happens to have bound pronouns and which probably spread quite recently over a vast and hitherto sparsely inhabited area, where earlier languages were submerged by the newcomers (Veth 2000). Now, it is a standard principle of dialect geography that languages spoken on the periphery tend to be archaic, while those in the center of an area are more likely to be innovative; the application of this principle to Pama-Nyungan would imply that Proto-Pama-Nyungan had bound pronouns (argument indices), which were subsequently lost in a part of those languages, including those that now belong to the [+NA & –VA] type. Although strictly unprovable, this speculation is the best we can offer to explain why case agreement without verbal agreement is common in Australia (chiefly in Pama-Nyungan, but also in Tangkic languages (e.g. Kayardild), which may be distantly related to Pama-Nyungan).

To conclude this chapter, we can say that the key to our understanding of how the current distribution of different agreement patterns arose lies in the different diachronic paths by which different types of agreement tend to be acquired or lost. What we have suggested here should serve only as a guide for further study. In any case, the typologist's job is to discover which language types exist (with respect to certain features) and how they are distributed across the globe. The questions why precisely these types exist and why they are so distributed should be left to historical and theoretical linguists.

11   Conclusions

The largest part of this book had a purely descriptive task: It attempted to draw a map of how one interesting linguistic phenomenon is distributed among the world's languages. If the book has any merit, it is if it has achieved this task and provided the linguistic community with a reliable map of the cross-linguistic distribution of different systems of agreement. However, in drawing that map we had to make sure we were comparing the same phenomenon across different languages, and this proved to be a theoretically difficult endeavor. Although we have adopted Corbett's (2006) approach to agreement, the door was left open to different frameworks, including the one that regards case agreement as parallel to agreement in gender, number and person. Moreover, by looking at data from individual languages in some detail, we believe that we have been able to contribute to the general typology of agreement systems, as well as providing reliable information on which patterns of agreement tend to be widespread and common in languages and which patterns are rather marginal and limited in their distribution.

Our investigation revealed a number of empirical generalizations in need of historical and/or theoretical explanation: Firstly, we have discovered that adnominal agreement is considerably more limited in its incidence and distribution than verbal agreement, and that languages almost universally have adnominal agreement only if they also have verbal agreement (but not vice versa). Secondly, case agreement was found to be areally limited and, just like gender agreement, associated with certain language families. Both gender and case agreement are genetically and areally very stable patterns, but our analysis showed that their genetic stability is more prominent. Thirdly, grammatical verbal agreement has proved to be the rarest pattern of all, occurring almost universally in languages that already have extensive agreement in the NP.

Explanations of these findings could only be sketched in the last chapter of this book, and they are admittedly speculative. Nevertheless, we believe that the key to our understanding of the actual distribution of agreement patterns in languages of the world lies in the different historical processes that led to this distribution. Since the history of the large majority of the world's languages is unknown, in most cases we can only guess at how agreement patterns in individual languages developed. However, we have argued that, cross-linguistically, the developments of adnominal and verbal agreement tend to follow different historical pathways, and we have provided several examples to support this claim. Basically, the development of verbal agreement is a pragmatically well-motivated and common phenomenon, while the development of adnominal agreement occurs only if certain pre-conditions are met. It involves the copying and spread of a pre-existent syntactic process from one domain (the clause) to another (the NP), and it may be triggered both by internal processes in a language and by syntactic borrowing; the latter scenario is probably responsible for the areally limited distribution of languages with adnominal agreement among the languages of the world.

Over the last couple of decades, the number of good descriptive grammars of languages spoken by small communities in faraway places has increased dramatically. Thanks to the efforts of many field linguists, we now know more about linguistic diversity in general, and also about how languages can differ in terms of a single feature, or a set of related features, such as the presence and functioning of an agreement system. However, researchers tend to focus on individual languages and on how such languages contribute to linguistic typology. Therefore, larger patterns and empirical generalizations are in danger of being left unnoticed. After all, the task of science is not just the observation and recording of facts but the discovery of patterns and rules connecting those facts and explaining why those patterns and rules exist in the first place. There is still a lot of work that needs to be done before we can fully appreciate all of the general patterns in the distribution of linguistic features, let alone understand why those patterns exist and how they came into being. But this book is, hopefully, a modest effort in that direction.

Appendix: Languages in the Database

For the sake of space, only some fields from the database were included in the following table; the full database, with comments on how individual languages were described and coded, is available at www.ffzg.hr/~rmatasov/Matasovic-Agreement.pdf. In the table, "AA" = adnominal agreement, "VA" = verbal agreement, and "G, N, C, P" indicate "gender, number, case and person," respectively. "YES-M" indicates that the language has been classified as having a feature, but marginally, and "YES-C" in the columns with data on verbal agreement indicates that a language has clitic agreement in the respective category. References are missing for languages in which the author of the present book judges himself to be competent enough.

LANGUAGE	CODE	FAMILY	AREA	AA-G	AA-N	AA-C	VA-P	VA-N	VA-G	REFERENCES
Abkhaz	abk	NW Caucasian	Eurasia	NO	NO	NO	YES	YES	YES	Hewitt 1979
Acehnese	ace	Austronesian	Australia and Oceania	NO	NO	NO	YES-C	YES-C	NO	Durie 1985
Afrikaans	afr	Indo-European	Africa and Middle East	NO	YES	NO	YES	YES	NO	Donaldson 1993
Aghem	agh	Niger-Kordofanian	Africa and Middle East	YES	YES	NO	NO	YES-C	YES-C	Hyman 1979
Ainu	ain	Isolate	Eurasia	NO	NO	NO	YES	YES	NO	Shibatani 1990, Tamura 2000
Akan	akn	Niger-Kordofanian	Africa and Middle East	NO	NO	NO	YES	YES	NO	Marfo 2005, Redden et al. 1963.
Alaaba	alw	Afro-Asiatic	Africa and Middle East	YES	YES	YES	YES	YES	YES	Schneider-Blum 2007
Alamblak	ala	Sepik Hill	Australia and Oceania	YES	YES	NO	YES	YES	YES	Bruce 1984, Edmiston 1997
Albanian	aln	Indo-European	Eurasia	YES	YES	YES	YES	YES	NO	Zymberi 1993
Ambulas	abt	Sepik	Australia and Oceania	YES	YES	NO	YES	YES	YES	Wilson 1980
Amele	ame	Trans-New Guinea	Australia and Oceania	NO	NO	NO	YES	YES	NO	Roberts 1987
Apache	apc	Athabaskan	North America	NO	NO	NO	YES	YES	NO	Hojier 1946
Arabic (Egyptian variety)	arz	Afro-Asiatic	Africa and Middle East	YES	YES	NO	YES	YES	YES	Menu 2002
Arapaho	aph	Algic	North America	NO	NO	NO	YES	YES	YES	Cowell & Moss 2008
Arapesh	arp	Torricelli	Australia and Oceania	YES	YES	NO	YES	YES	YES	Fortune 1940
Arawak	arw	Arawakan	South America	NO	NO	NO	YES	YES	YES	Pet 2011, De Goeje 2009
Armenian (Eastern variety)	hye	Indo-European	Eurasia	NO	NO	NO	YES	YES	NO	Dum-Tragut 2009

Language	code	Family	Area								Reference
Atayal	ata	Austronesian	Eurasia	NO	NO	NO	NO	YES-C	YES-C	NO	Rau 1992
A'tong	aot	Sino-Tibetan	Eurasia	NO	NO	NO	NO	NO	NO	NO	Van Breugel 2014
Aymara	ayc	Aymaran	South America	NO	NO	NO	YES	YES	YES	NO	Adelaar 2004
Babungo	bab	Niger-Kordofanian	Africa and Middle East	YES	YES	NO	YES-C	YES-C	YES-C	YES-C	Schaub 1985
Bambara	bam	Niger-Kordofanian	Africa and Middle East	NO	NO	NO	NO	NO	NO	NO	Dumestre 2003
Basque	eus	Isolate	Eurasia	NO	NO	NO	YES	YES	YES	NO	Zubiri 2000, de Rijk 2008
Batsbi (Tsova-Tush)	tso	NE Caucasian	Eurasia	YES	YES	YES	YES	YES	YES	YES	Dešeriev 1953
Baure	baq	Arawakan	South America	YES	NO	NO	YES	YES	YES	NO	Danielsen 2007
Beja	bej	Afro-Asiatic	Africa and Middle East	YES	YES	YES	YES	YES	YES	YES	Wedekind et al. 2007, 2008
Belhare	byw	Sino-Tibetan	Eurasia	NO	NO	NO	YES	YES	YES	NO	Bickel 1996, 2003
Bella Coola	bco	Salishan	North America	YES	YES	YES	YES	YES	YES	NO	Davis & Saunders 1997
Bengali	ben	Indo-European	Eurasia	NO	NO	NO	NO	YES	YES	NO	Hudson 1965, Bykova 1981
Berbice Dutch Creole	bdc	Indo-European	South America	NO	NO	NO	YES-C	YES-C	YES-C	NO	Kouwenberg 1994
Bilinarra	bnr	Pama-Nyungan	Australia and Oceania	NO	YES	NO	YES	YES	YES	YES	Meakins & Nordlinger 2014
Biloxi	bll	Siouan	North America	NO	NO	NO	YES	YES	YES	NO	Einaudi 1974
Biri	bii	Pama-Nyungan	Australia and Oceania	NO	YES	YES	YES-C	YES-C	YES-C	NO	Terrill 1998
Blackfoot	bla	Algic	North America	NO	NO	NO	YES	YES	YES	YES	Frantz 1991
Bobo	bbo	Niger-Kordofanian	Africa and Middle East	YES	YES	NO	YES-C	YES-C	YES-C	NO	Dienst 2004, Le Bris & Prost 1981, Morse 1976
Bora	bor	Witotoan	South America	YES	YES	YES-C	YES-C	YES-C	YES	NO	Thiesen & Weber 2012
Brahui	brh	Dravidian	Eurasia	YES	YES	YES-M	YES	YES	YES	NO	Andronov 1980
Burmese	mya	Sino-Tibetan	Eurasia	NO	NO	NO	NO	NO	NO	NO	N'un 1963, Omel'janovič 1971
Burushaski	bsk	Isolate	Eurasia	YES	YES	YES	YES	YES	YES	YES	Klimov & Edel'man 1970, Munshi 2006
Cantonese	cnt	Sino-Tibetan	Eurasia	NO	NO	NO	NO	NO	NO	NO	Matthews & Yip 1994

(continued)

157

LANGUAGE	CODE	FAMILY	AREA	AA-G	AA-N	AA-C	VA-P	VA-N	VA-G	REFERENCES
Carib	car	Cariban	South America	NO	NO	NO	YES	YES	NO	Derbyshire 1999, Courtz 2007
Cavineña	cav	Tacanan	South America	NO	NO	NO	YES	YES	NO	Guillaume 2008
Cham	chw	Austronesian	Eurasia	NO	NO	NO	NO	NO	NO	Thurgood 2014
Chamorro	cha	Austronesian	Australia and Oceania	NO	NO	NO	YES	YES	NO	Topping 1973
Chechen	che	NE Caucasian	Eurasia	YES	YES	YES	NO	YES	YES	Molochieva 2010, Vinogradov 1967, Nichols 2007, Matsiev 1995: 34.
Chemehuevi	ute	Uto-Aztecan	North America	NO	YES	YES-M	YES	YES	NO	Press 1979
Chichewa	cic	Niger-Kordofanian	Africa and Middle East	YES	YES	NO	YES	YES	YES	Mchombo 2006
Chinook	cku	Chinookan	North America	YES	YES	NO	YES	YES	YES	Hymes 1955, Mithun 1999: 96–8
Chipewyan	chp	Athabaskan	North America	NO	NO	NO	YES	YES	NO	Richardson 1968
Choctaw	cho	Muskogean	North America	NO	NO	NO	YES	YES	NO	Davies 1981, Broadwell 2006
Chrau	chr	Austro-Asiatic	Eurasia	NO	NO	NO	NO	NO	NO	Thomas 1971
Chukchi	ckt	Chukchi-Kamchatkan	Eurasia	NO	YES	YES-M	YES	YES	NO	Skorik 1961, Dunn 1999
Creole Réunionnais	rcf	Indo-European	Africa and Middle East	NO	NO	NO	YES-C	YES-C	NO	Staudacher-Valliamée 2004
Croatian	hrv	Indo-European	Eurasia	YES	YES	YES	YES	YES	NO	
Cubeo	cub	Tucanoan	South America	YES	YES	NO	YES	YES	YES	Morse & Maxwell 1999
Cupeño	cup	Uto-Aztecan	North America	NO	NO	YES	YES-C	YES-C	NO	Hill 2005
Dagaare	dga	Niger-Kordofanian	Africa and Middle East	NO	NO	NO	NO	NO	NO	Bodomo 1997
Dani (Western variety)	dni	Trans-New Guinea	Australia and Oceania	NO	NO	NO	YES	YES	NO	Barclay 2008
Degema	deg	Niger-Kordofanian	Africa and Middle East	YES	YES	NO	YES-C	YES-C	NO	Kari 2004

Language	Code	Family	Region							Reference
Desano	des	Tucanoan	South America	YES	NO	NO	YES	YES	YES	Miller 1999
Dhimal	dhi	Sino-Tibetan	Eurasia	NO	NO	NO	YES	YES	NO	King 2009
Diegueño	dih	Hokan	North America	YES	NO	NO	YES	YES	NO	Langdon 1970
Dime	dim	Afro-Asiatic	Africa and Middle East	YES	YES	NO	YES	NO	NO	Seyoum 2008
Dogon (Jamsay variety)	dgm	Niger-Kordofanian	Africa and Middle East	YES	YES	NO	YES	YES	NO	Heath 2008
Duungidjawu	duu	Pama-Nyungan	Australia and Oceania	NO	NO	NO	NO	NO	NO	Kite & Wurm 2004
Dyirbal	dbl	Pama-Nyungan	Australia and Oceania	YES	NO	YES	NO	NO	NO	Dixon 1972
Eastern Pomo	peb	Pomoan	North America	NO	NO	NO	NO	NO	NO	McLendon 1975
Enets	ene	Altaic	Eurasia	NO	NO	NO	YES	YES	NO	Tereščenko 1966, Künnap 1999
English	eng	Indo-European	Eurasia	NO	NO	NO	YES	YES	YES	
Ewe	ewe	Niger-Kordofanian	Africa and Middle East	NO	YES	NO	YES-C	YES-C	NO	Fiaga 1997, Ameka 1991
Fijian (Boumaa variety)	fij	Austronesian	Australia and Oceania	NO	NO	NO	NO	NO	NO	Dixon 1988
Finnish	fin	Uralic	Eurasia	NO	YES	YES	YES	YES	NO	Englund & Wolf 1960
Fon (Fongbe)	fon	Niger-Kordofanian	Africa and Middle East	NO	NO	NO	NO	NO	NO	Fadairo 2001, Lefevre & Brousseau 2001
French	fra	Indo-European	Eurasia	YES	YES	NO	YES	YES	NO	
Fula	fub	Niger-Kordofanian	Africa and Middle East	YES	YES	NO	YES	YES	NO	Koval' & Zubko 1986,
Gaagudju	gaa	Gaagudju	Australia and Oceania	YES	NO	NO	YES	YES	YES	Harvey 2002
Gaahmg	tbi	Nilo-Saharan	Africa and Middle East	NO	YES	YES	YES	YES	NO	Stirtz 2011
Garrwa (Western variety)	grr	Garrwan	Australia and Oceania	NO	NO	NO	NO	NO	NO	Mushin 2012

(continued)

LANGUAGE	CODE	FAMILY	AREA	AA-G	AA-N	AA-C	VA-P	VA-N	VA-G	REFERENCES
Gbaya	gbk	Niger-Kordofanian	Africa and Middle East	NO	NO	NO	YES-C	YES-C	NO	Roulon-Doko 1997
Ge'ez	gez	Afro-Asiatic	Africa and Middle East	YES	YES	YES?	YES	YES	YES	Starinin 1967
Georgian	kat	Kartvelian	Eurasia	NO	YES	YES	YES	YES	NO	Hewitt 1996
German	ger	Indo-European	Eurasia	YES	YES	YES	YES	YES	NO	
Goemai	goe	Afro-Asiatic	Africa and Middle East	NO	NO	NO	NO	NO	NO	Hellwig 2011
Gooniyandi	goo	Bunuban	Australia and Oceania	NO	NO	NO	YES	YES	NO	McGregor 1990
Grebo	grb	Niger-Kordofanian	Africa and Middle East	NO	YES	NO	YES-C	YES-C	NO	Innes 1966
Greek	ell	Indo-European	Eurasia	YES	YES	YES	YES	YES	NO	
Guarani	gua	Tupian	South America	NO	NO	NO	YES	YES	NO	Gregores & Suáres 1967
Haitian Creole	hcr	Indo-European	North America	NO	NO	NO	YES-C	YES-C	NO	Sylvain 1979
Hakka	hak	Sino-Tibetan	Eurasia	NO	NO	NO	NO	NO	NO	Hashimoto 2010
Halkomelem (Upriver variety)	hur	Salishan	North America	YES	NO	NO	YES	YES	NO	Galloway 1993
Hausa	hau	Afro-Asiatic	Africa and Middle East	YES	YES	NO	YES-C	YES-C	YES-C	Smirnova 1982, Jaggar 2001
Hawaiian	haw	Austronesian	Australia and Oceania	NO	NO	NO	NO	NO	NO	Ebert & Pukui 1979
Hdi	hdi	Afro-Asiatic	Africa and Middle East	NO	NO	NO	YES-C	YES-C	NO	Frajzyngier 2002
Hebrew	heb	Afro-Asiatic	Africa and Middle East	YES	YES	NO	YES	YES	YES	Meyer 1966
Hindi	hin	Indo-European	Eurasia	YES	YES	YES	YES	YES	YES	McGregor 1986
Hixkaryana	hix	Cariban	South America	NO	NO	NO	YES	YES	NO	Derbyshire 1979

Language	Code	Family	Region							Reference
Hualapai	hlp	Hokan	North America	NO	NO	NO	YES	YES	NO	Watahomigie et al. 2001
Hungarian	hun	Uralic	Eurasia	NO	YES-M	YES-M	YES	YES	NO	Rounds 2001
Hup	hpd	Makú	South America	NO	NO	NO	YES	YES	NO	Epps 2008
Icelandic	ice	Indo-European	Eurasia	YES	YES	YES	YES	YES	NO	Welmers 1973, Heine & Nurse 2000
Igbo	ibo	Niger-Kordofanian	Africa and Middle East	NO	NO	NO	YES-C	YES-C	NO	
Ilocano	ilo	Austronesian	Australia and Oceania	NO	NO	YES	YES	YES	NO	Rubino 2000
Indonesian	ind	Austronesian	Australia and Oceania	NO	NO	NO	NO	NO	NO	Kwee 1965, Sneddon 1996
Ineseño Chumash	cin	Isolate	North America	YES-M	NO	NO	YES	YES	NO	Applegate 1972
Ingush	ing	NE Caucasian	Eurasia	YES	YES	YES	NO	YES	YES	Nichols 2011
Iraqw	irq	Afro-Asiatic	Africa and Middle East	NO	YES	NO	YES	NO	YES	Mous 1993
Irish	gle	Indo-European	Eurasia	YES	YES	YES	YES	YES	NO	Ó Siadhail 1989
Italian	ita	Indo-European	Eurasia	YES	YES	YES	YES	YES	NO	
Japanese	jap	Altaic	Eurasia	NO	NO	NO	NO	NO	NO	Kuno 1973
Jaqaru	jaq	Aymaran	South America	NO	NO	YES	NO	YES	NO	Hardman 2000
Jarawara	jwr	Arauan	South America	YES	NO	YES	YES	YES	YES	Dixon 2004
Jingpho	jng	Sino-Tibetan	Eurasia	NO	NO	NO	NO	NO	NO	Qiangxia & Diehl 2003
Jingulu (Djingili)	jig	Mirndi	Australia and Oceania	YES	NO	YES	YES	YES	NO	Pensalfini 1997, 2003
Jiwarli (Mangala)	mem	Pama-Nyungan	Australia and Oceania	NO	YES	YES	YES	YES	NO	Austin 2001
Kabardian	kbd	NW Caucasian	Eurasia	NO	NO	NO	YES	YES	NO	Matasović 2010
Kana	kan	Niger-Kordofanian	Africa and Middle East	NO	NO	NO	YES	YES	NO	Ikoro 1996
Karen (Sgaw variety)	ksg	Sino-Tibetan	Eurasia	NO	NO	NO	NO	NO	NO	Gilmore 1898
Kayardild	gyd	Tangkic	Australia and Oceania	NO	NO	YES	NO	NO	NO	Evans 1995
Kazakh	kaz	Altaic	Eurasia	NO	NO	NO	YES	YES	NO	Kajdarov 1997

(continued)

LANGUAGE	CODE	FAMILY	AREA	AA-G	AA-N	AA-C	VA-P	VA-N	VA-G	REFERENCES
Ket	ket	Yeniseian	Eurasia	YES	YES	NO	YES	YES	YES	Vajda 2004
Khalkha	khk	Altaic	Eurasia	NO	NO	NO	NO	NO	NO	Vietze 1974
Kharia	khr	Austro-Asiatic	Eurasia	NO	NO	NO	YES-C	YES-C	NO	Peterson 2011
Khasi	kha	Austro-Asiatic	Eurasia	YES	NO	NO	YES-C	YES-C	NO	Nagaraja 1985
Khmer	khm	Austro-Asiatic	Eurasia	NO	NO	NO	NO	NO	NO	Huffman 1970, Smyth 1995
Khwarshi	khv	NE Caucasian	Eurasia	YES	YES	YES	NO	YES	YES	Khalilova 2009
Kinyarwanda	kin	Niger-Kordofanian	Africa and Middle East	YES	YES	NO	YES	YES	YES	Kimenyi 1980
Kiowa	kio	Kiowa-Tanoan	North America	NO	NO	NO	YES	YES	NO	Watkins & McKenzie 1984
Kisi	kis	Niger-Kordofanian	Africa and Middle East	YES	YES	NO	YES	YES	NO	Tucker Childs 1988, 1995
Kiwai	kiw	Kiwaian	Australia and Oceania	NO	NO	NO	YES	YES	NO	Ray 1931
Kongo	kon	Niger-Kordofanian	Africa and Middle East	YES	YES	NO	YES	YES	YES	De Clercq 1960
Korean	kor	Altaic	Eurasia	NO	NO	NO	NO	NO	NO	Sohn 1999
Koromfe	krf	Niger-Kordofanian	Africa and Middle East	YES	YES	NO	YES-C	YES-C	YES-C	Rennison 1997
Kotiria	gvc	Tucanoan	South America	YES	YES	NO	YES	YES	YES	Stenzel 2013
Koyra Chiini	kch	Nilo-Saharan	Africa and Middle East	NO	NO	NO	NO	NO	NO	Heath 1999
Kryz	kry	NE Caucasian	Eurasia	YES	YES	NO	NO	YES	YES	Authier 2009
Kulina	xpk	Arauan	South America	YES	YES	NO	YES	YES	YES	Dienst 2014
Kulung	klg	Sino-Tibetan	Eurasia	NO	NO	NO	YES	YES	NO	Tolsma 2006
Kung (!Kung, Kung-Ekoka, !Xu)	knw	Khoesan	Africa and Middle East	YES	YES	NO	YES-C	YES-C	NO	Snyman 1970, König 2009
Kutenai	kut	Isolate	North America	NO	NO	NO	NO	NO	NO	Morgan 1992
Kuuk Thaayorre	thd	Pama-Nyungan	Australia and Oceania	NO	NO	NO	NO	NO	NO	Gaby 2006

Kwakw'ala	kwk	Wakashan	North America	NO	NO	NO	YES	YES	NO	Boas 1947
Kwanyama (Ndonga variety)	ndo	Niger-Kordofanian	Africa and Middle East	YES	YES	NO	YES	YES	YES	Halme 2004
Kwaza	kwz	Isolate	South America	YES	NO	NO	YES	YES	YES	Van der Voort 2004
Lahu	lah	Sino-Tibetan	Eurasia	NO	NO	NO	NO	NO	NO	Matisoff 1973
Lakhota (Lakota)	lkt	Siouan	North America	NO	NO	NO	YES	NO	NO	Rood & Taylor 1996
Lao	lao	Tai-Kadai	Eurasia	NO	NO	NO	NO	NO	NO	Enfield 2008
Lavukaleve	lav	Solomons East Papuan	Australia and Oceania	YES	YES	NO	YES	YES	YES	Terrill 1999
Lepcha	lep	Sino-Tibetar	Eurasia	NO	NO	NO	NO	NO	NO	Plaisier 2007
Lezgian	lez	NE Caucasian	Eurasia	NO	NO	NO	YES	YES	NO	Haspelmath 1993
Lisu	lis	Sino-Tibetan	Eurasia	NO	NO	NO	NO	NO	NO	Bradley 2003
Lithuanian	lit	Indo-European	Eurasia	YES	YES	YES	YES	YES	NO	
Logbo (Logba)	lgq	Niger-Kordofanian	Africa and Middle East	YES	YES	NO	YES	YES	YES	Dorvlo 2008: 7–8.
Luiseño	lui	Uto-Aztecan	North America	NO	YES	YES	YES	YES	NO	Steele 1990
Luwo (Luo)	luo	Nilo-Saharan	Africa and Middle East	YES	YES	NO?	YES	YES	NO	Storch 2014, Odhiambo & Malherbe 2008
Maasai	maa	Nilo-Saharan	Africa and Middle East	YES	YES	YES	YES	YES	NO	Payne 1998
Ma'di	mad	Nilo-Saharan	Africa and Middle East	NO	NO	NO	YES-C	NO	NO	Blackings & Fabb 2003
Maidu	mne	Maiduan	North America	NO	NO	NO	YES	YES	NO	Shipley 1964
Makalero	mjb	Trans-New Guinea	Australia and Oceania	NO	NO	NO	NO	YES	NO	Huber 2011
Malagasy	plt	Austronesian	Africa and Middle East	NO	NO	NO	NO	NO	NO	Parker 1883
Mali	mli	Baining	Australia and Oceania	YES	YES	YES	YES	YES	YES	Stebbins 2011
Mam	mam	Mayan	North America	NO	NO	NO	YES	YES	NO	England 1983

(continued)

LANGUAGE	CODE	FAMILY	AREA	AA-G	AA-N	AA-C	VA-P	VA-N	VA-G	REFERENCES
Mambay	mcs	Niger-Kordofanian	Africa and Middle East	NO	NO	NO	YES-C	YES-C	NO	Anonby 2011
Manambu	mle	Ndu	Australia and Oceania	YES	YES	NO	YES	YES	YES	Aikhenvald 2008
Manchu	mnc	Altaic	Eurasia	NO	NO	NO	NO	NO	NO	Gorelova 2002
Mandarin	cmn	Sino-Tibetan	Eurasia	NO	NO	NO	NO	NO	NO	Norman 1988
Mangarai (Mangarayi)	myi	Mangarayi	Australia and Oceania	YES	YES	YES	YES	YES	NO	Merlan 1982
Mani (Bullom So)	buy	Niger-Kordofanian	Africa and Middle East	YES	YES	NO	YES	YES	YES	Tucker Childs 2011: 135ff.
Maori	mri	Austronesian	Australia and Oceania	NO	NO	NO	NO	NO	NO	Biggs 1973
Mapuche (Mapudungun)	arn	Araucanian	South America	NO	NO	NO	YES	YES	NO	Smeets 2008
Marathi	mhi	Indo-European	Eurasia	YES	YES	YES	YES	YES	YES	Vaman Dhongde & Wali 2009, Pandharipande 1997
Maricopa	mar	Hokan	North America	NO	NO	NO	YES	YES	NO	Gordon 1986
Maybrat	may	West Papuan	Australia and Oceania	YES	YES	NO	YES	YES	YES	Dol 2007
Mbembe	mfn	Niger-Kordofanian	Africa and Middle East	NO	YES	NO	YES-C	YES-C	NO	Kemmermann 2015
Menomini	men	Algic	North America	NO	NO	NO	YES	YES	YES	Bloomfield 1962
Mian	mpt	Trans-New Guinea	Australia and Oceania	YES	YES	NO	YES	YES	YES	Fedden 2011
Miao (Blue variety)	hmo	Miao-Yao	Eurasia	NO	NO	NO	NO	NO	NO	Harriehausen 1990
Miao (White variety)	mww	Miao-Yao	Eurasia	NO	NO	NO	NO	NO	NO	Mottin 1978, Harriehausen 1990
Mixtec (Chalcatongo variety)	mig	Oto-Manguean	North America	NO	NO	NO	YES	YES	YES	Macaulay 1996
Mochica	mcc	Isolate	South America	NO	NO	NO	YES	YES	NO	Hovdhaugen 2004

(continued)

Language	Code	Family	Area						Reference
Mocovi	mcv	Guaicuruan	South America	YES	NO	YES	YES	NO	Grondona 1998.
Mohawk	moh	Iroquoian	North America	NO	NO	YES	YES	YES	Bonvillain 1973
Mokilese	mok	Austronesian	Australia and Oceania	NO	NO	NO	NO	NO	Harrison 1976
Mordvin (Erzya variety)	moe	Uralic	Eurasia	NO	NO	YES	YES	NO	Zaicz 1997, Djordjević & Léonard 2006.
Moseten	mos	Mosetenan	South America	YES	YES	YES	YES	YES	Sakel 2002
Motuna	mot	East Bougainville	Australia and Oceania	YES	YES	YES	YES	YES	Onishi 2012
Movima	mzp	Movima	South America	YES	NO	YES	YES	YES	Haude 2006
Nahuatl (Classical variety)	nhn	Uto-Aztecan	North America	NO	NO	YES	YES	NO	Sullivan 1983, Andrews 2003
Nama (Khoekhoe)	naq	Khoesan	Africa and Middle East	YES-M	YES-M	NO	NO	NO	Olpp 1977, Hagman 1977
Navajo	nav	Athabaskan	North America	NO	NO	YES	YES	NO	Goossen 2000, Young & Morgan 1972
Nenets	yrk	Uralic	Eurasia	NO	NO	YES	YES	NO	Almazova 1961
Nepali	nep	Indo-European	Eurasia	YES	NO	YES	YES	YES	Acharya 1991
Newari	new	Sino-Tibetan	Eurasia	NO	NO	YES	YES	NO	Korolev 1989, Genetti 2007
Nganasan	nga	Uralic	Eurasia	NO	NO	YES	YES	NO	Helimski 1998
Ngarla	nlr	Pama-Nyungan	Australia and Oceania	NO	NO	YES	YES	NO	Westerlund 2007
Ngiti	nti	Nilo-Saharan	Africa and Middle East	NO	NO	YES-C	YES-C	NO	Kutsch Lojenga 1993
Nigerian Pidgin	npi	(Pidgin)	Africa and Middle East	NO	NO	YES-C	YES-C	NO	Faraclas 1996
Nootka (Nitinaht)	noo	Wakashan	North America	NO	NO	YES	YES	NO	Davidson 2002
Nubian (Kumuz variety)	kzh	Nilo-Saharan	Africa and Middle East	NO	YES-M	YES	YES	NO	Abdel-Hafiz 1988
Nung	nun	Tai-Kadai	Eurasia	NO	NO	NO	NO	NO	Saul & Wilson 1980
Ojibwa	oji	Algic	North America	YES	NO	YES	YES	YES	Valentine 2001

LANGUAGE	CODE	FAMILY	AREA	AA-G	AA-N	AA-C	VA-P	VA-N	VA-G	REFERENCES
Oneida	one	Iroquoian	North America	NO	NO	NO	YES	YES	YES	Abbott 2000, 2006
Oriya	oya	Indo-European	Eurasia	YES	YES	YES	YES	YES	NO	Ray 2003
Otomi	ots	Oto-Manguean	North America	NO	NO	NO	YES	YES	NO	Voigtlander & Echegoyen 1985
Palauan	pau	Austronesian	Australia and Oceania	NO	NO	NO	YES	YES	NO	Josephs 1975
Panare	pnr	Cariban	South America	YES	NO	NO	YES	NO	NO	Payne & Payne 2013
Pashto	psh	Indo-European	Eurasia	YES	YES	YES	YES	YES	YES	Grjunberg & Èdel'man 1987
Pipil	pip	Uto-Aztecan	North America	NO	NO	NO	YES	YES	NO	Campbell 1985
Pirahã	pir	Mura-Pirahã	South America	NO	NO	NO	NO	NO	NO	Everett 1986
Polish	pol	Indo-European	Eurasia	YES	YES	YES	YES	YES	YES	
Portuguese (Brasilian variety)	por	Indo-European	South America	YES	YES	NO	YES	YES	NO	
Quechua (Huallaga variety)	qvh	Quechuan	South America	NO	NO	NO	YES	YES	NO	Weber 1989
Quechua (Cuzco-Collao variety)	qcu	Quechuan	South America	NO	NO	NO	YES	YES	NO	Cusihuamán 1976
Quileute	qui	Chemaquan	North America	YES	YES	NO	YES	YES	YES	Andrade 1933, Mithun 1999: 96
Rama	ram	Chibchan	North America	NO	NO	NO	NO	NO	NO	Grinevald 1990
Rundi (Kirundi)	rnd	Niger-Kordofanian	Africa and Middle East	YES	YES	NO	YES	YES	YES	Meeussen 1959
Russian	rus	Indo-European	Eurasia	YES	YES	YES	YES	YES	YES	
Sabanes (Sabané, Nambikuára)	nab	Nambiquaran	South America	NO	NO	NO	YES	YES	NO	De Araujo 2004
Samoan	smo	Austronesian	Australia and Oceania	NO	NO	NO	YES-C	YES-C	NO	Marsack 1962
Sandawe	sad	Khoesan	Africa and Middle East	YES	YES	NO	YES	YES	YES	Eaton 2010
Sango	san	Niger-Kordofanian	Africa and Middle East	NO	NO	NO	NO	NO	NO	Samarin 1967, Thornell 1997

(continued)

Language	Code	Family	Region								Reference
Savosavo	svs	Solomons East Papuan	Australia and Oceania	YES	YES	NO	YES	YES	YES	YES	Wegener 2012
Semelai	sml	Austro-Asiatic	Eurasia	NO	NO	NO	NO	YES-C	YES-C	NO	Kruspe 2004
Shipibo-Konibo	shk	Panoan	South America	NO	NO	NO	NO	NO	NO	NO	Valenzuela 1997
Shona	shn	Niger-Kordofanian	Africa and Middle East	YES	YES	NO	YES	YES	YES	YES	Brauner 1995
Shoshone	sho	Uto-Aztecan	North America	NO	NO	NO	NO	YES	YES	NO	Miller 1996
Sidamo	sid	Afro-Asiatic	Africa and Middle East	YES	YES	YES	YES	YES	YES	YES	Kawachi 2007
Sikuani	skn	Guahiban	South America	NO	NO	NO	NO	YES	YES	YES	Queixalós 2000
Sinhala	snh	Indo-European	Eurasia	YES-M	NO	NO	NO	NO	NO	YES-M	Gair & Paolillo 1997, Matzel 1966, Chandralal 2010
Sirayan (Siraya)	sry	Austronesian	Eurasia	YES-M	NO	NO	NO	YES-C	YES-C	NO	Adelaar 2011
Slave	sla	Athabaskan	North America	NO	NO	NO	NO	YES	YES	YES	Rice 1989
So	so	Kuliak	Africa and Middle East	NO	NO	NO	NO	YES	YES	NO	Carlin 1993
Somali	som	Afro-Asiatic	Africa and Middle East	YES	YES	NO	YES	YES	YES	YES	Saeed 1999, Berchem 1991
Spanish	spa	Indo-European	Eurasia	YES	YES	NO	YES	YES	YES	NO	
Supyire	sup	Niger-Kordofanian	Africa and Middle East	YES	YES	NO	YES	YES-C	YES-C	NO	Carlson 1994
Swazi (Swati)	swt	Niger-Kordofanian	Africa and Middle East	YES	YES	NO	YES	YES	YES	YES	Ziervogel 1952
Tagalog	tgl	Austronesian	Australia and Oceania	NO	NO	NO	NO	NO	NO	NO	Schachter & Otanes 1972, Castle & McGonnell 2003
Tahitian	tah	Austronesian	Australia and Oceania	NO	NO	NO	NO	NO	NO	NO	Tryon 1970
Tajik	taj	Indo-European	Eurasia	NO	NO	NO	NO	YES	YES	NO	Oranskij 1963
Tamashek	tsk	Afro-Asiatic	Africa and Middle East	YES	YES	NO	YES	YES	YES	YES	Heath 2005
Tamazight	ber	Afro-Asiatic	Africa and Middle East	YES	YES	NO	YES	YES	YES	YES	Abdel-Massih 1971, Sadiqi 1997

LANGUAGE	CODE	FAMILY	AREA	AA-G	AA-N	AA-C	VA-P	VA-N	VA-G	REFERENCES
Tamil	tam	Dravidian	Eurasia	NO	NO	NO	YES	YES	YES	Schiffman 1999, Andronov 1987
Tarascan (Purépecha)	pur	Isolate	North America	NO	NO	YES	YES	YES	NO	LeCron Foster 1969
Tariana	tae	Arawakan	South America	YES	YES	NO	YES	YES	NO	Dixon & Aikhenvald 1999
Teiwa (Tewa)	twe	Teiwa	Australia and Oceania	NO	NO	NO	YES	YES	NO	Klamer 2010
Telugu	te	Dravidian	Eurasia	NO	NO	NO	YES	YES	YES	Krishnamurti 1998, Krishnamurti & Gwynn 1985
Tepehua (Huehuetla)	tee	Totonacan	North America	NO	NO	NO	YES	YES	NO	Kung 2007
Thai	tha	Tai-Kadai	Eurasia	NO	NO	NO	NO	NO	NO	Smyth 2002
Tibetan (Standard Spoken variety)	tmo	Sino-Tibetan	Eurasia	NO	NO	NO	NO	NO	NO	Denwood 1999
Timucua	tmc	Isolate	North America	NO	NO	NO	YES	YES	NO	Granberry 1993
Tinrin	tin	Austronesian	Australia and Oceania	NO	NO	NO	YES-C	YES-C	NO	Osumi 1995
Tiriyo (Trio)	tri	Cariban	South America	NO	NO	NO	YES	YES	NO	Carlin 2004, Meira 1999
Tiwi	tiw	Tiwian	Australia and Oceania	YES	YES	NO	YES	YES	YES	Osborne 1974
Toba	tob	Guaicuruan	South America	NO	NO	NO	YES	YES	NO	Manelis Klein 1973
Tongan	tng	Austronesian	Australia and Oceania	NO	NO	NO	YES-C	YES-C	NO	Devane 2008, Fell 1918
Totonac (Misantla variety)	tot	Totonacan	North America	NO	NO	NO	YES	YES	NO	Mackay 1991
Trumai	tru	Isolate	South America	NO	NO	NO	NO	NO	NO	Guirardello 1999
Ts'amakko	tsb	Afro-Asiatic	Africa and Middle East	YES	YES	NO	YES	YES	YES	Sava 2005
Tsimshian (Coast variety)	tsi	Tsimshianic	North America	NO	YES	NO	YES	YES	NO	Dunn 1979
Tsou	tso	Austronesian	Eurasia	NO	NO	NO	NO	NO	NO	Zeitoun 2005

Name	Code	Family	Region							Reference
Tucano	tuo	Tucanoan	South America	NO	NO?	NO	YES	YES	YES	Dixon & Aikhenvald 1999: 400
Tunica	tun	Isolate	North America	YES	YES	YES	YES	YES	YES	Haas 1941, Mithun 1999
Tupi	tup	Tupian	South America	NO	NO	NO	YES	YES	NO	Anchieta 1933
Turkish	tur	Altaic	Eurasia	NO	NO	NO	YES	YES	NO	Čaušević 1996
Tuscarora	tus	Iroquoian	North America	NO	NO?	NO	YES	YES	YES	Mithun 1974
Tuvaluan	tvl	Austronesian	Australia and Oceania	NO	NO	NO	YES	YES	NO	Besnier 2000
Tzeltal (Oxchuc variety)	tzb	Mayan	North America	NO	NO	NO	YES	YES	NO	Polian 2006
Urarina	urm	Isolate	South America	NO	NO	NO	YES	YES	NO	Olawsky 2006
Uru	uru	Uru-Chipayan	South America	NO	NO	NO	YES	YES	NO	Hannss 2008
Uyghur	uig	Altaic	Eurasia	NO	NO	NO	YES	YES	NO	Abdurehim 2014
Vai	vai	Niger-Kordofanian	Africa and Middle East	NO	NO	NO	NO	NO	NO	Welmers 1976
Vietnamese	vie	Austro-Asiatic	Eurasia	NO	NO	NO	NO	NO	NO	Nguyen 1974
Wambaya	wam	Mirndi	Australia and Oceania	YES	YES	YES	YES	YES	YES	Nordlinger 1998
Wandala	mfi	Afro-Asiatic	Africa and Middle East	NO	NO	YES	YES	YES	NO	Frajzyngier 2012
Wappo	wao	Wappo-Yukian	North America	NO	YES-M	NO	NO	NO	NO	Radin 1929, Thompson et al. 2006
Warao	wra	Isolate	South America	NO	YES	NO	YES	YES	NO	Romero-Figueroa 1997
Warekena	wrk	Arawakan	South America	YES	NO	YES	YES	YES	YES	Aikhenvald 1998
Wari' (Chapacuva)	pav	Chapacura-Wanham	South America	YES	YES	YES	YES	YES	YES	Everett & Kern 1997
Warlpiri	wbp	Pama-Nyungan	Australia and Oceania	NO	NO	YES	YES	YES	NO	Reece 1970
Warrongo (Warrungu)	wgu	Pama-Nyungan	Australia and Oceania	NO	NO	YES	YES	YES	YES	Tsunoda 2011
Waunana	wau	Choco	South America	NO	NO	YES	YES	YES	YES	Loewen 1954
Welsh	wel	Indo-European	Eurasia	YES	YES	YES	YES	YES	NO	Fortescue 1984
West Greenlandic	kal	Eskimo-Aleut	North America	NO	YES	YES-C	YES	YES	YES	
Western Desert (Pitjantjatjara variety)	wdo	Pama-Nyungan	Australia and Oceania	NO	NO	YES-C	YES-C	YES-C	NO	Douglas 1964, Jones 2011

(continued)

LANGUAGE	CODE	FAMILY	AREA	AA-G	AA-N	AA-C	VA-P	VA-N	VA-G	REFERENCES
Wichita	wic	Caddoan	North America	NO	NO	NO	YES	YES	YES-M	Rood 1976
Wintu	wit	Wintuan	North America	NO	NO	NO	YES	YES	NO	Pitkin 1984
Wolof	wol	Niger-Kordofanian	Africa and Middle East	YES	YES	NO	YES	YES	YES	Diagné 1971, Ngom 2003
Worora	wro	Wororan	Australia and Oceania	YES	NO	YES?	YES	YES	YES	Love 2000
Xhosa	xho	Niger-Kordofanian	Africa and Middle East	YES	YES	NO	YES	YES	YES	Kirsch et al. 2004
Yagua	yag	Peba-Yaguan	South America	YES	YES	NO	YES-C	YES-C	NO	Payne & Payne 1990
Yakut	ykt	Altaic	Eurasia	NO	NO	NO	YES	YES	NO	Ubrjatova 1966
Yanomami	ynm	Yanomaman	South America	NO	NO	NO	YES	YES	NO	Dixon & Aikhenvald 1999: 341–51
Yate (Fulniô)	fun	Macro-Jê	South America	YES	YES	NO	YES	YES	NO	Meland & Meland 2009, Dixon & Aikhenvald 1999
Yeyi	yey	Niger-Kordofanian	Africa and Middle East	YES	YES	NO	YES	YES	YES	Seidel 2008
Yimas	yee	Lower Sepik	Australia and Oceania	YES	YES	NO	YES	YES	YES	Foley 1991
Yintyingka	yin1	Pama-Nyungan	Australia and Oceania	NO	NO	NO	YES-C	YES-C	NO	Verstraete & Rigsby 2015
Yoruba	yor	Niger-Kordofanian	Africa and Middle East	NO	NO	NO	NO	NO	NO	Jakovleva 1963, Bamgbose 1966
Zapotec (Coatlan-Loxicha variety)	zap	Oto-Manguean	North America	NO	NO	NO	YES-C	YES-C	NO	Beam de Azcona 2004
Zaza	diq	Indo-European	Eurasia	YES	YES	YES	YES	YES	NO	Todd 1985
Zulu	zul	Niger-Kordofanian	Africa and Middle East	YES	YES	NO	YES	YES	YES	Oxotina 1961
Zuni	zun	Zuni	North America	NO	NO	NO	YES	YES	NO	Newman 1965

References

Abaev, V. I. (ed.) 1981. *Osnovy iranskogo jazykoznania*, Moscow: Nauka.

Abbott, Clifford 2000. *Oneida*, Munich: Lincom.

　2006. *Oneida Teaching Grammar*, Green Bay, WI: University of Wisconsin.

Abbi, Anvita 2013. *A Grammar of the Great Andamanese Language. An Ethnolinguistic Study*, Leiden: Brill.

Abbott, Miriam 1991. "Macushi," in Derbyshire and Pullum (eds), 23–160.

Abdel-Hafiz, Ahmed Sokarno 1988. *A Reference Grammar of Kunuz Nubian*, PhD dissertation, SUNY, Buffalo.

Abdel-Massih, Ernest T. 1971. *A Reference Grammar of Tamazight*, Ann Arbor, MI: The University of Michigan Press.

Abdokov, A. I. 1981. *Vvedenie v sravnitel'no-istoričeskuju morfologiju abxazsko-adygskix i naxsko-dagestanskix jazykov*, Nal'čik: Kabardino-balkarskij Gosudarst-vennyj Universitet.

Abdurehim, Esmael 2014. *The Lopnor Dialect of Uyghur*, Helsinki: Unigrafia.

Aboh, Enoch 2010. "The Morphosyntax of the Noun Phrase," in Enoch Aboh and James Essegbey (eds), *Topics in Kwa Syntax*, Berlin: Springer, 11–38.

Abondolo, Daniel (ed.) 1997. *The Uralic Languages*, London: Routledge.

Acharya, Jayaraj. 1991. *A Descriptive Grammar of Nepali and an Analysed Corpus*, Washington, DC: Georgetown University Press.

Adelaar, Alexander 2011. *Siraya: Retrieving the Phonology, Grammar and Lexicon of a Dormant Formosan Language*, Berlin: Mouton De Gruyter.

Adelaar, Willem 2004. *The Languages of the Andes*, Cambridge: Cambridge University Press.

Aikhenvald, Alexandra 1998. "Warekena," in Derbyshire and Pullum (eds), 225–440.

　2000. *Classifiers. A Typology of Noun-classification Devices*, Oxford: Oxford University Press.

　2006. "Grammars in Contact. A Cross-Linguistic Perspective," in Aikhenvald and Dixon (eds), 1–66.

　2008. *The Manambu Language of East Sepik, Papua New Guinea*, Oxford: Oxford University Press.

　2012. *The Languages of the Amazon*, Oxford: Oxford University Press.

Aikhenvald, Alexandra and Dixon, Robert M. W. (eds) 2006. *Grammars in Contact. A Cross-Linguistic Typology*, Oxford: Oxford University Press.

Alekseev, Mixail 2003. *Sravnitel'no istoričeskaja morfologija naxsko-dagestanskix jazykov*, Moscow: Academia.

Allen, Keith 1977. "Classifiers," *Language* 53: 284–310.

Almazova, A. V. 1961. *Samoučitel' neneckogo jazyka*, Leningrad: Učpedgiz.

Alpher, Barry 1990. "Some Proto-Pama-Nyungan Paradigms: A Verb in the Hand Is Worth Two in the Phylum," in G. N. O'Grady and D. T. Tryon (eds), *Studies in Comparative Pama-Nyungan*, Dept. of Linguistics, Canberra: The Australian National University, 155–71.

Ameka, Felix Kofi 1991. *Ewe: Its Grammatical Constructions and Illocutionary Devices*, PhD thesis, Canberra: Australian National University.

Anchieta, José de 1933. *Arte da gramática da língua mais usada na costa do Brasil*. Rio de Janeiro: Imprensa Nacional.

Anderson, Gregory D. S. (ed.) 2008. *The Munda Languages*, London: Routledge.

Andrade, Manuel J. 1933. "Quileute," in Franz Boas (ed.), *Handbook of American Indian Languages 3*, New York: Columbia University Press, 151–292.

Andrews, J. Richard 2003. *An Introduction to Classical Nahuatl*, Norman, OK: University of Oklahoma Press.

Andronov, M. S. 1970. *Dravidian Languages*, Moscow: Nauka.

1980. *The Brahui Language*, Moscow: Nauka.

1987. *Grammatika tamil'skogo jazyka*, Moscow: Nauka.

Anonby, Erik J. 2011. *A Grammar of Mambay: An Adamawa Language of Chad and Cameroon*, Cologne: Rüdiger Köppe Verlag.

Applegate, Richard Brian 1972. *Ineseño Chumash Grammar*, PhD dissertation, University of California, Berkeley.

Ariel, Mira 2000. "The Development of Person Agreement Markers: From Pronoun to Higher Accessibility Markers," in Suzanne Kemmer and Michael Barlow (eds), *Usage-based Models of Language*, Stanford, CA: CSLI, 197–261.

Aristava, Š. K. 1968. *Grammatika abxazskogo jazyka*, Suhumi: Alašara.

Austin, Peter 2001. "Word Order in a Free Word Order Language: The Case of Jiwarli," in Jane Simpson, David Nash, Mary Laughren, Peter Austin and Barry Alpher (eds), *Forty Years on: Ken Hale and Australian Languages*, Canberra: Pacific Linguistics, 205–323.

Austin, Peter and Bresnan, Joan 1996. "Non-Configurationality in Australian Aboriginal Languages," *Natural Language and Linguistic Theory* 14: 215–68.

Authier, Gilles 2009. *Grammaire kryz, langue d'Azerbaidjan*, Louvain: Peeters.

Baerman, Matthew and Brown, Dunstan 2013. "Syncretism in Verbal Person/Number Marking," in WALS (Chapter 29).

Baerman, Matthew and Corbett, Greville 2013. "Person by Other Means," in Dik Bakker and Martin Haspelmath (eds), *Languages Across Boundaries. Studies in Memory of Anna Siewierska*, Berlin: De Gruyter, 1–15.

Baker, Brett J. 2002. "How Referential Is Agreement? The Interpretation of Polysynthetic Dis-Agreement Morphology in Ngalakgan," in Nicholas Evans and Hans-Jürgen Sasse (eds), *Problems of Polysynthesis* (Studia Typologica 4), Berlin: Akademie Verlag, 51–85.

Baker, Mark 1996. *Of Parameters and Polysynthesis: The Polysynthesis Parameter*, Oxford: Oxford University Press.

Bakker, Dik 2011. "Language Sampling," in Jae-Jung Song (ed.), *Handbook of Linguistic Typology*, Oxford: Oxford University Press, 101–27.

Bakker, Peter 1997. *A Language of Our Own: The Genesis of Michif, a Mixed Cree-French Language of the Canadian Métis*, Oxford: Oxford University Press.

Bamgbose, Ayo 1966. *A Grammar of Yoruba*, Cambridge: Cambridge University Press.

Barclay, Peter 2008. *A Grammar of Western Dani*, Munich: Lincom.

Barker, Muhammad A. R. 1964. *Klamath Grammar*, Berkeley,CA: The University of California Press.

Barlow, Michael 1992. *A Situated Theory of Agreement*, London: Routledge.

Beam de Azcona, Rosemary Grace 2004. *A Coatlán-Loxicha Zapotec Grammar*, PhD dissertation, University of California, Berkeley.

Berchem, Jörg 1991. *Referenzgrammatik des Somali*. Cologne: Omimee.

Berta, Árpád 1998. "West Kipchak Languages," in Johanson and Csató (eds), 301–17.

Bertinetto, Pier Marco 2009. "Ayoreo (Zamuco): A Grammatical Sketch," *Quaderni del laboratorio di linguistica 8* (http://linguistica.sns.it/QLL/QLL/QLL09.htm, accessed June 15, 2017).

Besnier, Niko 2000. *A Grammar of Tuvaluan*, London: Routledge.

Bhattacharya, Sudhibhushan 1976. "Gender in the Munda Languages," *Oceanic Linguistics Special Publications*, No. 13, Austroasiatic Studies Part 1: 189–211.

Bickel, Balthasar 1996. *Aspect, Mood and Time in Belhare*, Zurich: University of Zurich.

  2003. "Belhare," in Thurgood and LaPolla (eds), 546–70.

  2007. "Typology in the 21st century: Major current developments," *Linguistic Typology* 11: 239–51.

Bickel, Balthasar and Nichols, Johanna 2009. "The geography of case," in Andrej Malchukov and Andrew Spencer (eds), *The Oxford Handbook of Case*, Oxford: Oxford University Press, 478–93.

  2013. "Obligatory Possessive Inflection," in WALS (Chapter 58).

Biggs, Bruce 1973. *Let's Learn Maori*, Auckland, NZ: Auckland University Press.

Blackings, Mairi and Fabb, Nigel 2003. *A Grammar of Ma'di*, Berlin: Mouton De Gruyter.

Blake, Barry 1994. *Case*, Cambridge: Cambridge University Press.

Blench, Roger 2015. "The Origins of Nominal Classification Markers in MSEA Languages: Convergence, Contact and Some African Parallels," in N. J. Enfield, Bernard Comrie (eds), *The Languages of Mainland Southeast Asia. The State of the Art*, Berlin: Mouton De Gruyter, 558–85.

Bloomfield, Leonard 1962. *The Menominee Language*, New Haven, CT: Yale University Press.

Boas, Franz 1947. *Kwakiutl Grammar*, Chicago, IL: Edwards Brothers.

Bodomo, Adams 1997. *The Structure of Dagaare*, Stanford: CSLI Publications.

Bond, Oliver, Corbett, Greville G. Chumakina, Marina and Brown, Dunstan (eds) 2016. *Archi: Complexities of Agreement in Cross-Theoretical Perspective*, Oxford: Oxford University Press.

Bonvillain, Nancy 1973. *A Grammar of Akwesasne Mohawk*, Ethnology Division Paper, 8. 8. Ottawa: National Museum of Man.

Bowern, Claire 2012. *A Grammar of Bardi*, Berlin: De Gruyter.

Boyeldieu, Pascal 1982. *Deux études laal (Moyen-Chari, Tchad)*, Berlin: Reimer.

Bradley, David 2003. "Lisu," in Thurgood and LaPolla (eds), 222–35.

Brauner, Sigmund 1995. *A Grammatical Sketch of Shona Including Historical Notes*, Cologne: Rüdiger Koppe.

Bresnan, Joan 2001. *Lexical-Functional Syntax*, Oxford: Blackwell.

Bresnan, Joan and Mchombo, Sam 1987. "Topic, Pronoun, and Agreement in Chichewa," *Language* 63: 741–82.

Broadwell, George A. 2006. *A Choctaw Reference Grammar*, Lincoln: The University of Nebraska Press.

Brown, Dunstan P. and Chumakina, Marina 2013. "What There Might Be and What There Is: An Introduction to Canonical Typology," in Dunstan P. Brown, Marina Chumakina and Greville G. Corbett (eds), *Canonical Morphology and Syntax*; Oxford: Oxford University Press, 1–19.

Bruce, Les 1984. *The Alamblak Language of Papua New Guinea (East Sepik)*, Canberra: The Dept. of Linguistics, Australian National University.

Bykova, E. M. 1981. *The Bengali Language*, Moscow: Nauka.

Camacho, José A. 2013. *Null Subjects*, Cambridge: Cambridge University Press.

Campbell, Lyle 1985. *The Pipil Language of El Salvador*, Berlin: De Gruyter.

Campbell, Lyle and Grondona, Verónica 2012. *The Indigenous Languages of South America. A Comprehensive Guide*, Berlin: De Gruyter.

Campbell, Lyle, Kaufman, Terrence and Smith-Stark, Thomas 1986. "Meso-America as a Linguistic Area," *Language* 62: 530–70.

Carlin, Eithne B. 1993. *The So Language*, Cologne: Institut für Afrikanistik.

  2004. *A Grammar of Trio, a Cariban Language of Suriname*, Frankfurt: Peter Lang.

Carlson, Robert 1994. *A Grammar of Supyire*, Berlin: Mouton De Gruyter.

Castle, Corazon Salvacion and McGonnell, Laurence 2003. *Tagalog*, London: Hodder & Stoughton.

Chandralal, Dileep 2010. *Sinhala*, Amsterdam: Benjamins.

Chomsky, Noam 2000. "Minimalist Inquiries: The Framework," in Martin Roger et al. (eds), *Step by Step: Essays on Minimalist Syntax in Honor of Howard Lasnik*, Cambridge, MA: MIT Press, 89–156.

Chung, Sandra 1994. "Wh-Agreement and 'Referentiality' in Chamorro," *Linguistic Inquiry* 25(1): 1–44.

Claudi, Ulrike 1985. *Zur Entstehung von Genussystemen. Überlegungen zu einigen theoretischen Aspekten, verbunden mit einer Fallstudie des Zande*, Hamburg: Buske.

Collins, Chris and Gruber, Jeffrey S. 2014. *A Grammar of ≠Hõã*, Cologne: Rüdiger Köppe.

Comrie, Bernard 1981. *The Languages of the Soviet Union*, Cambridge: Cambridge University Press.

Corbett, Greville 1991. *Gender*, Cambridge: Cambridge University Press.

  1997. "Constraints on agreement," in *Proceedings of the 16th International Congress of Linguists*, Oxford: Pergamon, paper no. 0518 (retrieved from www.surrey.ac.uk/LIS/SMG/GREVS%20PUBLICATIONS/Constraints%20On%20Agreement.pdf, accessed June 15, 2017).

  2000. *Number*, Cambridge: Cambridge University Press.

  2006. *Agreement*, Cambridge: Cambridge University Press.

  2007. "Gender and Noun Classes," in Timothy Shopen (ed.), *Language Typology and Syntactic Description. Vol. III, Grammatical Categories and the Lexicon*, Cambridge: Cambridge University Press, 241–79.

  2012. *Features*, Cambridge: Cambridge University Press.

  2013a. "Number of genders," in WALS (Chapter 30).

  2013b. "Sex-based and non-sex-based gender systems," in WALS (Chapter 31).

  2013c. "Systems of gender assignment," in WALS (Chapter 32).

Courtz, Hendrik 2007. *A Carib Grammar and Dictionary*, Toronto: Magoria Books.

Cowell, Andrew and Moss Sr., Alonzo 2008. *The Arapaho Language*, Boulder, CO: University Press of Colorado.

Creissels, Denis 2000. "Typology," in Heine and Nurse (eds), 231–58.

2006. "A Typology of Subject and Object Markers in African Languages," in F. K. Erhard Veltz (ed.), *Studies in African Linguistic Typology*, Amsterdam: Benjamins, 43–70.

Crowley, Terry 1983. "Uradhi," in Robert M. W. Dixon and Barry J. Blake (eds), *Handbook of Australian Languages, Vol. 3*, Amsterdam: Benjamins, 306–54.

1998. *Pacific Languages. An Introduction*, Honolulu: University of Hawaii Press.

Cusihuamán Antonio G. 1976. *Gramatica Quechua Cuzco-Collao*, Lima: Instituto de estudios Peruanos.

Čaušević, Ekrem 1996. *Gramatika turskoga jezika*, Zagreb: Hrvatska Sveučilišna Naklada.

Dahl, Östen 2009. "An Exercise in a Posteriori Language Sampling," *STUF – Language Typology and Universals* 61(3): 208–20.

Dahlstrom, Amy 1991. *Plains Cree Morphosyntax*, outstanding dissertations in linguistics, New York: Garland.

Danielsen, Swintha 2007. *Baure: An Arawak Language of Bolivia*, Leiden: Research School CNWS.

Davidson, M. 2002. *Studies in Southern Wakashan (Nootkan) Grammar*, PhD dissertation, SUNY Buffalo.

Davies, Wiliam Daniel 1981. *Choctaw Clause Structure*, PhD dissertation, University of California San Diego.

Davis, Philip W. and Saunders, Ross 1997. *A Grammar of Bella Coola*, Missoula, MT: The University of Montana Press.

De Araujo, Gabriel Antunes 2004. *A Grammar of Sabané, a Nambikwaran Language*, Utrecht: LOT.

De Clercq, Louis 1960. *Grammaire du kiyombe*, Brussels: Goemaere.

De Goeje, Claudius Henricus 2009. *The Arawak Language of Guiana*, Cambridge: Cambridge University Press.

Demuth, Katherine, Faraclas, Nicholas and Marchese, Lynell 1986. "Niger-Congo Noun Class and Agreement Systems in Language Acquisition and Historical Change," in Colette Craig (ed.), *Noun Classes and Categorization*, Amsterdam: Benjamins, 453–71.

Denwood, Philip 1999. *Tibetan*. Amsterdam: John Benjamins.

Derbyshire, Desmond 1979. *Hixkaryana*, Amsterdam: North Holland.

1999. "Carib," in Dixon and Aikhenwald (eds), 23–64.

de Rijk, Rudolf P. G. 2008. *Standard Basque*, Cambridge, MA: The MIT Press.

Dešeriev, Junus Dešerievič 1953. *Batsbijskij jazyk: fonetika, morfologija, sintaksis, leksika*. Moscow: Izdatel'stvo Akademii nauk SSSR.

Devane, Melissa 2008. *The Syntax and Semantics of the Tongan Noun Phrase*, MA thesis, William and Mary College, Williamsburg.

Diagné, Pathé 1971. *Grammaire de wolof moderne*, Paris: Présence Africaine.

Diakonov, I. M. 1988. *Afrasian Languages*, Moscow: Nauka.

Dienst, Stephan 2004. *Nominalmorphologie und Numerus im Bobo (Mande)*, Working Papers 34, Mainz: Johannes Gutenberg-Universität.

2014. *A Grammar of Kulina*, Berlin: Mouton De Gruyter.

Dixon, Robert M. W. 1972. *The Dyirbal Language of North Queensland*, Cambridge: Cambridge University Press.

1988. *A Grammar of Boumaa Fijian*, Chicago, IL: The University of Chicago Press.

2002. *Australian Languages*, Cambridge: Cambridge University Press.

2004. *The Jarawara Language of Southern Amazonia*, Oxford: Oxford University Press.

Dixon, Robert M. W. and Aikhenvald, Alexandra (eds) 1999. *The Amazonian Languages*, Cambridge: Cambridge University Press.

Djordjević, Ksenija and Léonard, Jean-Léo 2006. *Parlons mordve*, Paris: L'Harmattan.

Dol, Philomena 2007. *A Grammar of Maybrat: A Language of the Bird's Head Peninsula, Papua Province, Indonesia*, Canberra: The Australian National University.

Donaldson, Bruce C. 1993. *A Grammar of Afrikaans*, Berlin: De Gruyter.

Dorvlo, Kofi 2008. *A Grammar of Logba (Ikpana)*, Utrecht: LOT.

Douglas, Wilfrid H. 1964. *An Introduction to the Western Desert Language*. (Oceania Linguistics Monographs, 4.) Sydney: The University of Sydney, Australia.

Dryer, Matthew S. 1989. "Large Linguistic Areas and Language Sampling," *Studies in Language* 13: 257–92.

1992. "The Greenbergian Word Order Correlations," *Language* 68: 81–138.

2013. "Coding of Nominal Plurality," in WALS (Chapter 33).

Dumestre, Gérard 2003. *Grammaire fondamentale du bambara*, Paris: Karthala.

Dum-Tragut, Jasmine 2009. *Armenian*, Amsterdam: Benjamins.

Dunn, John Asher 1979. *A Reference Grammar for the Coast Tsimshian Language*, Ottawa: National Museums of Canada.

Dunn, Michael J. 1999. *A Grammar of Chukchi*, PhD dissertation, Australian National University, Canberra.

Durie, Mark 1985. *A Grammar of Acehnese on the Basis of the Dialect of North Aceh*, Dordrecht: Foris.

Eaton, Helen 2010. *A Sandawe Grammar*, Dallas, TX: SIL International.

Édel'man, D. I. 1990. *Sravnitel'naja grammatika vostočnoiranskix jazykov. Morfologija. Èlementy sintaksisa*, Moscow: Nauka.

Édel'man, D. I. (ed.) 1999. *Dardskie i nuristanskie jazyki*, Moscow: Indrik.

Edmiston, Patrick 1997. *Alamblak Discourse Features*, Ukarumpa: Summer Institute of Linguistics.

Efimov, V. A. 1975. "Obščie čerty èvoljucii kategorii roda v iranskix jazykax," in *Iranskoe jazykoznanie*, Moscow: Nauka, 23–34.

Einaudi, Paula Ferris 1974. *A Grammar of Biloxi*, PhD dissertation, University of Colorado.

Elbert, Samuel H. and Pukui, Mary Kawena 1979. *Hawaiian Grammar*, Honolulu: University of Hawaii Press.

Emenau, Murray 1956. "India as a linguistic area," *Language* 32: 3–16.

Enfield, Nick J. 2008. *A Grammar of Lao*, Berlin: Mouton De Gruyter.

England, Nora C. 1983. *A Grammar of Mam, a Mayan Language*, Austin, TX: University of Texas Press.

Englund, Robert and Wolf, Werner 1960. *Finnische Sprachlehre*, Heidelberg: Groos.

Epps, Patience 2006. "The Vaupés Melting Pot: Tucanoan Influence on Hup," in Aikhenvald and Dixon (eds), 267–89.

2008. *A Grammar of Hup*, Berlin: De Gruyter.

Evans, Nicholas 1995. *A Grammar of Kayardild*, Berlin: Mouton De Gruyter.

1999. "Why Argument Affixes in Polysynthetic Languages Are Not Pronouns: Evidence from Bininj Gun-wok," *Sprachtypologie und Universalienforschung* 52: 225–81.

2003a. "Introduction," in Nicholas Evans (ed.), *The Non-Pama-Nyungan Languages of Northern Australia*, Canberra: Australian National University, 1–25.

2003b. "Typologies of Agreement: Some Problems from Kayardild," *Transactions of the Philological Society* 101(2): 203–34.

2005. "Australian Languages Reconsidered: A Review of Dixon (2002)," *Oceanic Linguistics* 41(1): 216–60.

Everett, Daniel L. 1986. "Pirahã," in Derbyshire and Pullum (eds), 200–325.

Everett, Daniel and Kern, Barbara 1997. *Wari': The Pacaas Novos Language of Western Brazil*, London: Routledge.

Fadairo, Dominique 2001. *Parlons fon*, Paris: L'Harmattan.

Faraclas, Nicholas G. 1996. *Nigerian Pidgin*, London: Routledge.

Fedden, Sebastian 2011. *A Grammar of Mian*, Berlin: Mouton De Gruyter.

Fedden, Sebastian and Corbett, Greville 2017. "Gender and Classifiers in Concurrent Systems: Refining the Typology of Nominal Classification," *Glossa* 2(1): 1–47.

Feldman, Harry 1986. *A Grammar of Awtuw*, Canberra: The Australian National University.

Fell, J. R. 1918. *A Tonga Grammar*, London: Society for Promoting Christian Knowledge.

Fiaga, Kwasi 1997. *Grammaire eve*, Paris and Lomé: Haho.

Foley, William A. 1986. *The Papuan Languages of New Guinea*, Cambridge: Cambridge University Press.

1991. *The Yimas Language of New Guinea*, Stanford, CA: Stanford University Press.

Fortescue, Michael 1984. *West Greenlandic*, London: Croom Helm.

Fortune, R. F. 1940. *Arapesh*, New York: J. J. Augustin.

Foster, Joseph F. and Hofling, Charles A. 1987. "Word Order, Case, and Agreement," *Linguistics* 25: 475–99.

Frajzyngier, Zygmunt (with Erin Shay) 2002. *A Grammar of Hdi*, Berlin: Mouton De Gruyter.

2012. *A Grammar of Wandala*, Berlin: Mouton De Gruyter.

Frank, W. J. 1999. *Nuer Noun Morphology*, MA thesis submitted to SUNY Buffalo, Buffalo, CO.

Frantz, Donald B. 1991. *Blackfoot Grammar*, Toronto: University of Toronto Press.

Gaby, A. R. 2006. *A Grammar of Kuuk Thaayorre*, PhD dissertation, University of Melbourne.

Gair, James W. and Paolillo, John C. 1997. *Sinhala*, Munich: Lincom.

Galloway, Brent D. 1993. *A Grammar of Upriver Halkomelem*, Berkeley, CA: The University of California Press.

Garber, Anne Elisabeth 1987. *Tonal Analysis of Senufo: Sucite dialect*, Urbana-Champaign, IN: University of Indiana Press.

Genetti, Carol 2007. *A Grammar of Dolakha Newar*, Berlin: Mouton De Gruyter.

Ghosh, Arun 2008. "Santali," in Anderson (ed.), 10–24.

Gil, David 2013. "Adjectives without Nouns," in WALS (Chapter 61).

Gildersleeve, B. L. and Lodge, Gonzalez 1895. *Latin Grammar*, London: Macmillan.

Gilmore, David 1898. *A Grammar of the Sgaw Karen Language*, Rangoon.

Givón, Talmy 1976. "Topic, Pronoun, and Grammatical Agreement," in Charles N. Li (ed.), *Subject and Topic*, New York: Academic Press, 149–88.

Goddard, Cliff 1982. "Case Systems and Case Marking in Australian Languages: A New Interpretation," *Australian Journal of Linguistics* 2: 167–96.

2005. *The Languages of East and Southeast Asia*, Oxford: Oxford University Press.

Gordon, Lynn 1986. *Maricopa Morphology and Syntax*, Berkeley, CA: University of California Press.

Gorelova, Liliya M. 2002. *Manchu Grammar*, Leiden: Brill.

Goossen, Irvy 2000. *Diné Bizaad: Speak, Read, Write Navajo*, Flagstaff, AZ: Salina Bookshelf.

Granberry, Julian 1993. *A Grammar and Dictionary of the Timucua Language*, Tuscaloosa, AL: The University of Alabama Press.

Greenberg, Joseph H. 1963. "Some Universals of Grammar with Particular Reference to the Order of Meaningful Elements," in Joseph H. Greenberg (ed.), *Universals of Language*, Cambridge, MA: MIT Press, 73–113.

1978. "How Does a Language Acquire Gender Markers," in J. Greenberg et al. (eds), *Universals of Human Language, Vol. III*, Stanford, CA: Stanford University Press, 43–82.

Gregersen, Edgar A. 1977. *Language in Africa. An Introductory Survey*, New York: Gordon & Breach.

Gregores, Eva and Suáres, Jorge 1967. *A Description of Colloquial Guarani*, The Hague: Mouton.

Grinevald, Colette G. 1990. *A Grammar of Rama*. Report to National Science Foundation.

Grjunberg, Aleksandr L. and Èdel'man, D. I. 1987. *Afganskij jazyk. Osnovy iranskogo jazykoznanija, novoiranskije jazyki*. Moscow: Nauka.

Grondona, Verónica María 1998. *A Grammar of Mocovi*, PhD dissertation, University of Pittsburgh.

Guillaume, Antoine 2008. *A Grammar of Cavineña*, Berlin: Mouton De Gruyter.

Guirardello, Raquel 1999. *A Reference Grammar of Trumai*, PhD dissertation, University of Texas, Houston.

Haas, Mary R. 1941. *A Grammar of the Tunica Language*, New York: Augustin.

Hagège, Claude 2000. *Halte à la mort des langues*, Paris: Éditions Odile Jacob.

Hagman, Roy S. 1977. *Nama Hottentot Grammar*. Bloomington, IN: Indiana University Press.

Halme, Riikka 2004. *A Tonal Grammar of Kwanyama*, Cologne: Köppe.

Hammarström, Harald and Donohue, Mark 2014. "Some Principles on the Use of Macro-Areas in Typological Comparison," *Language Dynamics and Change* 4(1): 167–87.

Hannss, Katja 2008. *Uchumataqu: The Lost Language of the Urus of Bolivia. a Grammatical Description of the Language as Documented between 1894 and 1952*, Leiden: CNWS.

Hantgan, Abbie 2013. *Aspects of Bangime Phonology, Morphology and Morphosyntax*, PhD dissertation, Department of Linguistics, Indiana University.

Hardman, Martha J. 2000. *Jaqaru*, Munich: Lincom.

Harriehausen, Bettina 1990. *Hmong Njua. Syntaktische Analyse einer gesprochener Sprache mithilfe datenverarbeitungstechnischer Mittel und sprachvergleichende Beschreibung des südostasiatischen Sprachraumes*, Tübingen: Niemeyer.

Harris, Alice C. and Campbell, Lyle 1995. *Historical Syntax in Cross-Linguistic Perspective*, Cambridge: Cambridge University Press.

Harrison, Sheldon P. 1976. *Mokilese Reference Grammar*. With the assistance of Salich Y. Albert, Honolulu: University of Hawaii.

Harvey, Mark 2002. *A Grammar of Gaagudju*, Berlin: Mouton De Gruyter.

Harvey, Mark and Reid, Nicholas (eds) 1997. *Nominal Classification in Aboriginal Australia*, Amsterdam: John Benjamins.

Hashimoto, Mantaro 2010. *The Hakka Dialect: A Linguistic Study of Its Phonology, Syntax and Lexicon*, Cambridge: Cambridge University Press.

Haspelmath, Martin 1993. *A Grammar of Lezgian*, Berlin: De Gruyter.

    1999. "Long-Distance Agreement in Godoberi (Daghestanian) Complement Clauses," in Greville G. Corbett (ed.), *Agreement* (Special issue of *Folia Linguistica* 33/2), 131–51.

    2013a. "Argument Indexing: A Conceptual Framework for the Syntactic Status of Bound Person Forms," in D. Bakker and M. Haspelmath (eds), *Languages Across Boundaries. Studies in Memory of Anna Siewierska*, Berlin: De Gruyter, 197–226.

    2013b. "Occurrence of Nominal Plurality," in WALS (Chapter 33).

Haude, Katharina 2006. *A Grammar of Movima*, Nijmegen: Nijmegen University.

Hayek, John 2006. "Language Contact and Convergence in East Timor. The Case of Tetun Dili," in Aikhenvald and Dixon (eds), 162–78.

Heath, Jeffrey 1978. *Linguistic Diffusion in Arnhem Land*, Canberra: Australian Institute of Aboriginal Studies.

    1999. *A Grammar of Koyra Chiini. Songhay of Timbuktu*, Berlin: Mouton De Gruyter.

    2005. *A Grammar of Tamashek (Tuareg of Mali)*, Berlin: Mouton De Gruyter.

    2008. *A Grammar of Jamsay*, Berlin: Mouton De Gruyter.

Heine, Bernd and Nurse, David (eds) 2000. *African Languages. An Introduction*, Cambridge: Cambridge University Press.

Helimski, Eugene 1998. "Nganasan," in Abondolo (ed.), 480–515.

Hellwig, Birgit 2011. *A Grammar of Goemai*, Berlin: De Gruyter.

Hewitt, George 1979. *Abkhaz*, London: Routledge.

    1996. *Georgian: A Learning Grammar*, London: Routledge.

    2004. *Introduction to the Study of the Languages of the Caucasus*, Munich: Lincom.

Hill, Jane 2005. *A Grammar of Cupeño*, Berkeley, CA: University of California Press.

Hoijer, Harry 1946. "Chiricahua Apache," in Cornelius Osgood (ed.), *Linguistic Structures of Native America*, New York: Viking Fund Inc. (Johnson Reprint Corp. New York), 55–84.

Holzknecht, Susanne 1989. *The Markham Languages of Papua New Guinea*, Canberra: Pacific Linguistics.

Hovdhaugen, Even 2004. *Mochica*, Munich: Lincom.

Huang, C.-T. James 1984. "On the Distribution and Reference of Empty Pronouns," *Linguistic Inquiry* 15: 531–74.

Huber, Juliette 2011. *A Grammar of Makalero*, Utrecht: LOT.

Hudson, D. F. 1965. *Bengali*, London: The English Universities Press.

Huffman, Frank E. 1970. *Modern Spoken Cambodian*, Ithaca, NY: Cornell University.

Hurskainen, Arvi 2000. "Noun classification in African languages," in Unterbeck and Rissanen (eds), 665–87.

Hyman, Larry (ed.) 1979. *Aghem Grammatical Structure. With special reference to noun classes, tense-aspect and focus marking*, Southern California Occasional Papers in Linguistics No. 7, June 1979, Los Angeles: University of Southern California.

Hymes, Dell Hathaway 1955. *The Language of the Kathlamet Chinook*, PhD dissertation, Indiana University.

Ibragimov, G. X. 1990. *Caxurskij jazyk*, Moscow: Nauka.

Idiatov, Dmitry 2010. "Person-Number Agreement on Clause Linking Markers in Mande," *Studies in Language* 34(4): 832–68.

Iggesen, Oliver 2013. "Number of cases," in WALS (Chapter 49).

Ikoro, Suanu M. 1996. *A Grammar of Kana*, Leiden: Research School CNWS.

Innes, G. 1966. *An Introduction to Grebo*, London: School of Oriental and African Studies.

Irwin, Barry 1974. *Salt-Yui Grammar*, Canberra: Pacific Linguistics.

Jaggar, Philip J. 2001. *Hausa*, Amsterdam: Benjamins.

Jakobi, Angelika 1989. *A Fur Grammar*, Hamburg: Buske.

Jakovleva, V. K. 1963. *Jazyk joruba*, Moscow: Nauka.

Janhunen Juha 2000. "Grammatical Gender from East to West," in Unterbeck and Rissanen (eds), 689–708.

Johanson, Lars and Csató, Eva Á. (eds) 1998. *The Turkic Languages*, Routledge: London.

Jones, Barbara 2011. *A Grammar of Wangkajunga, a Language of the Great Sandy Desert of North Western Australia*, Canberra: Pacific Linguistics. Australian National University.

Josephs, Lewis S. 1975. *Palauan Reference Grammar*, Honolulu: University of Hawaii Press.

Kajdarov, A. T. 1997. "Kazakskij jazyk," in E. R. Tenišev (ed.), *Jazyki mira: Tjurkskie jazyki*, Moscow: Indrik, 242–54.

Karatsareas, Petros 2009. "The Loss of Grammatical Gender in Cappadocian Greek," *Transactions of the Philological Society* 107: 196–230.

Kari, Ethelbert Emmanuel 2004. *A Reference Grammar of Degema*, Cologne: Rüdiger Köppe.

Kawachi, Kazuhiro 2007. *A Grammar of Sidaama (Sidamo), a Cushitic Language of Ethiopia*, PhD dissertation, SUNY Buffalo, NY.

Keenan, Edward 1974. "The Functional Principle: Generalizing the Notion of 'Subject-of'," *Chicago Linguistic Society* 10: 298–310.

Kemmermann, Doris Richter (Genannt) 2015. *A Grammar of Mbembe*, Leiden: Brill.

Khalilova, Zaira 2009. *A Grammar of Khwarshi*, Leiden: LOT.

Kiessling, Ronald. 2013. "On the Origin of Niger-Congo Nominal Classification," in Ritsuko Kikusawa and Lawrence A. Reid, *Historical Linguistics 2011*, Amsterdam: Benjamins, 43–65.

Kilarski, Marcin 2013. *Nominal Classification: A History of Its Study from the Classical Period to the Present*, Amsterdam: Benjamins.

Kimenyi, Alexandre 1980. *A Relational Grammar of Kinyarwanda*, Berkeley, CA: University of California Press.

King, John T. 2009. *A Grammar of Dhimal*, Leiden: Brill.

Kirsch, Beverley et al. 2004. *Teach Yourself Xhosa*, London: Hodder Arnold.

Kite, Suzanne and Wurm, Stephen 2004. *The Duungidjawu Language of Southeast Queensland: Grammar, Texts and Vocabulary*, Canberra: Australian National University.

Klamer, Marian 2010. *A Grammar of Teiwa*, Berlin: Mouton De Gruyter.

(ed.) 2014. *The Alor-Pantar Languages. History and Typology*, Berlin: Language Sciences Press.

Klimov, G. A. 1986. *Vvedenie v kavkazskoe jazykoznanie*, Moscow: Nauka.

Klimov, G. A. and Edel'man, D. I. 1970. *Jazyk burušaski*, Moscow: Nauka.

Kocaoğlu, Timur 2006. *Karay. The Trakai Dialect*, Munich: Lincom.

König, Christa 2009. "!Xun," in Gerrit J. Dimmendaal (ed.), *Coding Participant Marking: Construction Types in Twelve African Languages*, Amsterdam: Benjamins, 23–54.

Korolev, N. I. 1989. *Nevarskij jazyk*, Moscow: Nauka.

Kouwenberg, Silvia 1994. *A Grammar of Berbice Dutch Creole*, Berlin: Mouton De Gruyter.

Koval', A. I. and Zubko, G. B. 1986. *Jazyk fula*, Moscow: Nauka.

Krejnovič, E. A. 1961. "Immenye klassy i grammatičeskie sredstva ix vyraženij v ketskom jazyke," *Voprosy jazykoznanija* 2(1961): 106–16.

Krishnamurti, Bhadriraju 1998. "Telugu," in Sanford Steever (ed.), *The Dravidian Languages*, London: Routledge, 202–40.

2003. *The Dravidian Languages*, Cambridge: Cambridge University Press.

Krishnamurti, Bhadriraju and Gwynn, John P. L. 1985. *A Grammar of Modern Telugu*. Oxford: Oxford University Press.

Kruspe, Nicole 2004. *A Grammar of Semelai*, Cambridge: Cambridge University Press.

Kung, Susan S. 2007. *A Descriptive Grammar of Huehuetla Tepehua*, PhD dissertation, University of Texas at Austin.

Künnap, Ago 1999. *Enets*, Munich: Lincom.

Kuno, Susumu 1973. *The Structure of the Japanese Language*, Cambridge, MA: The MIT Press.

Kutsch Lojenga, Constance 1993. *Ngiti. A Central-Sudanic Language of Zaire*, Cologne: Rüdiger Köppe Verlag.

Kwee, John B. 1965. *Indonesian*, London: Hodder & Stoughton.

Langdon, Margaret 1970. *A Grammar of Diegueño*, Berkeley, CA: The University of California Press.

Lapointe, Steven G. 1988. "Toward a Unified Theory of Agreement," in Michael Barlow and Charles A. Ferguson (eds), *Agreement in Natural Language: Approaches, Theories, Descriptions*. Stanford, CA: CSLI Publications, 67–88.

Le Bris, Pierre and Prost, André 1981. *Dictionnaire bobo-francais*, Paris: SELAF.

LeCron Foster, Mary 1969. *The Tarascan Language*, Berkeley, CA: University of California Press.

Lefebvre, Claire and Brousseau, Anne-Marie 2001. *A Grammar of Fongbe*, Berlin: Mouton De Gruyter.

Legate, Julie A. 2014. "Split Ergativity Based on Nominal Type," *Lingua* 148: 183–212.

Lehmann, Christian 1982a. "Universal and Typological Aspects of Agreement," in Hansjakob Seiler and Franz J. Stachowiak (eds), *Apprehension: Das sprachliche Erfassen von Gegenständen*. Tübingen: Narr, II, 201–67.

1982b. "Thoughts on Grammaticalization. A Programmatic Sketch," *Arbeiten des Kölner Universalienprojekts* 48, University of Cologne.

1988. "On the Function of Agreement," in Michael Barlow and Charles A. Ferguson (eds), *Agreement in Natural Language: Approaches, Theories, Descriptions*. Stanford, CA: CSLI Publications, 55–65.

Lehmann, Christian and Moravcsik, Edith 2000. "Noun," in Geert Booij, Christian Lehmann and Joachim Mugdan (eds), *Morphology: A Handbook on Inflection and Word Formation*, Berlin: Mouton De Gruyter, 732–57.

Lipinski, Edward 1987. *Semitic Languages: An Outline of a Comparative Grammar*, Louvain: Peeters.

Loewen, Jacob Abram 1954. *Waunana Grammar: A Descriptive Analysis*, PhD dissertation, University of Washington.

Loos, Eugene B. 1999. "Pano," in Dixon and Aikhenvald (eds), 226–60.

Love, J. R. B. 2000. *The Grammatical Structure of the Worora Language of North-Western Australia*. Munich: Lincom Europa.

Lowe, Ivan 1999. "Nambiquara," in Dixon and Aikhenvald (eds), 269–91.

Lüdtke, Helmut 1974. "Die Mundart von Ripatransone – ein sprachtypologisches Kuriosum," *Acta Universitatis Carolinae, Philologica* 5/1974: 173–7.

Macaulay, Monica 1996. *A Grammar of Chalcatongo Mixtec*, Berkeley, CA: University of California Press.

Mackay, Carolyn Joyce 1991. *A Grammar of Misantla Totonac*, PhD dissertation, University of Texas, Austin.

Magometov, A. A. 1970. *Agul'skij jazyk*, Tbilissi: Mecniereba.

Manelis Klein, Harriet E. 1973. *A Grammar of Argentine Toba: Verbal and Nominal Morphology*, PhD dissertation, Columbia University, New York.

Marfo, Charles 2005. *Aspects of Akan Grammar and the Phonology–Syntax Interface*, PhD dissertation, Hong Kong University.

Marm, Ingvald and Sommerfelt, Alf 1967. *Norwegian*, London: Hodder & Stoughton.

Marsack, C. C. 1962. *Samoan*, London: Teach Yourself Books.

Masica, Colin P. 1976. *Defining a Linguistic Area: South Asia*, Chicago, IL: University of Chicago Press.

Maslova, Elena 2003. *Tundra Yukaghir*, Munich: Lincom.

Mason, J. Alden 1918. *The Language of the Salinan Indians*, Berkeley, CA: University of California Press.

Matasović, Ranko 2004. *Gender in Indo-European*, Heidelberg: Winter.

  2010. *A Grammar of East Circassian (Kabardian)*, http://deenes.ffzg.hr/~rmatasov.

  2014a. "Adnominal and verbal agreement: Areal distribution and typological correlations," *Linguistic Typology* 18(2): 171–214.

  2014b. "Nominal Agreement in Proto-Indo-European from the Areal and Typological Point of View," in Sergio Neri and Roland Schuhmann (eds), *Studies on the Collective and Feminine in Indo-European from a Diachronic and Typological Perspective*, Leiden: Brill, 133–55.

  2017. "The Origin of Gender in Northwest Caucasian," paper presented at the conference "Historical Linguistics of the Caucasus," École Pratique des Hautes Études, Paris, April 2017; to appear in *Filologija*. Pre-print is available at www.academia.edu.

Matisoff, James 1973. *A Grammar of Lahu*, Berkeley, CA: University of California Press.

Matsiev, A. G. 1995. *A Short Grammatical Outine of the Chechen Language*, Kensington, MA: Dunwoody Press.

Matthews, Stephen and Yip, Virginia 1994. *Cantonese: A Comprehensive Grammar*. New York: Routledge.

Matzel, Klaus 1966. *Einführung in die singhalesische Sprache*, Wiesbaden: Harrassowitz.

McElhanon, Kenneth A. 1973. *Towards a Typology of the Finisterre-Huon Languages, New Guinea*, Canberra: Pacific Linguistics.

McGregor, Robert S. 1986. *Outline of Hindi Grammar*, Oxford: Oxford University Press.

McGregor, William B. 1990. *A Functional Grammar of Gooniyandi*, Amsterdam: Benjamins.

Mchombo, Sam 2006. *Syntax of Chichewa*, Cambridge: Cambridge University Press.

McLean, Greg L. 2014. *A Sketch of the Central Mfumte Grammar*, Yaoundé: SIL.

McLendon, Sally 1975. *A Grammar of Eastern Pomo*, Berkeley, CA: University of California Press.

Meakins, Felicity and Nordlinger, Rachel 2014. *A Grammar of Bilinarra: An Australian Aboriginal Language of the Northern Territory*, Berlin: De Gruyter.

Meeussen, A. E. 1959. *Essai de grammaire rundi*, Tervuren: Musée Royal du Congo Belge.

Meillet, Antoine 1936. *Esquisse d'une grammaire de l'arménien classique*, Vienna: Mekhitaristes.

Meira, Sergio 1999. *A Grammar of Tiriyó*, PhD dissertation, University of Texas, Houston.

Meland, Douglas and Meland, Doris 2009. *Fulniô (Yahthe) Syntax Structure: Preliminary Version*, Anápolis: Associação Internacional de Linguística – SIL Brasil.

Menu, Bernadette 2002. *Petite grammaire de l'égyptien hiérogyphique*, Paris: Geuthner.

Merlan, Francesca 1982. *Mangarayi*, London: Croom Helm.

1983. *Ngalakan Grammar, Texts and Vocabulary*, Canberra: Pacific Linguistics.

Meyer, Rudolf 1966. *Hebräische Grammatik I–IV*, Berlin: De Gruyter.

Miller, Marion 1999. *Desano Grammar*, Dallas, TX: Summer Institute of Linguistics.

Miller, Wick R. 1996. "Sketch of Shoshone, a Uto-Aztecan Language," in Ives Goddard (ed.), *Handbook of American Indians. Volume 17: Languages*, Washington, DC: Smithsonian Institute, 693–720.

Mithun, Marianne 1974. *A Grammar of Tuscarora*, PhD dissertation, Yale University.

1986. "The Convergence of Noun Classification Systems," in Colette Craig (ed.), *Noun Classes and Categorization*, Amsterdam: Benjamins, 379–97.

1990. "The Development of Bound Pronominal Paradigms," in W. P. Lehmann and Helen-Jo Jakusz Hewitt (eds), *Language Typology 1988. Typological Models in Reconstruction*, Amsterdam: Benjamins, 85–104.

1999. *The Languages of Native North America*, Cambridge: Cambridge University Press.

2003. "Pronouns and Agreement: The Information Status of Pronominal Affixes," *Transactions of the Philological Society* 101(2): 235–78.

Molochieva, Zarina 2010. *Tense, Aspect, and Mood in Chechen*, PhD dissertation, Leipzig University.

Moravcsik, Edith A. 1978. "Agreement," in Joseph H Greenberg (ed.), *Universals of Human Language: IV: Syntax*, Stanford, CA: Stanford University Press, 331–74.

1988. "Agreement and Markedness," in Michael Barlow and Charles A. Ferguson (eds), *Agreement in Natural Language: Approaches, Theories, Descriptions*. Stanford, CA: CSLI Publications, 89–106.

Morgan, Lawrence R. 1992. *A Description of the Kutenai Language*, MS, version 1.2.2, University of California, Berkeley.

Morse, Mary Lynn 1976. *A Sketch of the Phonology and Morphology of Bobo*, PhD dissertation, Columbia University, New York.

Morse, Nancy L. and Maxwell, Michael B. 1999. *Cubeo Grammar*, Arlington, TX: Summer Institute of Linguistics.

Moseley, Christopher 1994. *Colloquial Estonian*, London: Routledge.

Mottin, Jean 1978. *Eléments de grammaire Hmong Blanc*, Munich: Don Bosco Press.

Mous, Marten 1993. *A Grammar of Iraqw*, Hamburg: Helmut Buske Verlag.

Munshi, Sadaf 2006. *Jammu and Kashmir Burushaski: Language, Language Contact, and Change*, PhD dissertation, University of Texas.

Mushin, Ilana 2012. *A Grammar of (Western) Garrwa*, Berlin: Mouton De Gruyter.

Muysken, Peter 2003. "The Grammatical Elements in Negerhollands: Loss, Retention, Reconstitution," in J. Koster and H. van Riemsdijk (eds), *Germania et alia : A Linguistic Webschrift for Hans den Besten*, Groningen: University of Groningen.

Nagaraja, Kumar S. 1985. *Khasi: A Descriptive Analysis*, Poona: Deccan College.

Newman, Stanley 1965. *Zuni Grammar*, Albuquerque, NM: The University of New Mexico Press.

Ngom, Fallou 2003. *Wolof*, Munich: Lincom.

Nguyen, Dinh Hoa 1974. *Colloquial Vietnamese*, London: Routledge.

Nichols, Johanna 1989a. "The Origin of Nominal Classification," *Proceedings of the Fifteenth Annual Meeting of the Berkeley Linguistics Society (1989)*: 409–20.

1989b. "The Nakh Evidence for the History of Gender in Nakh-Daghestanian," in H. I. Aronson (ed.), *The Non-Slavic Languages of the USSR: Linguistic Studies*, Chicagom IL: Chicago Linguistic Society, 158–73.

1992. *Linguistic Diversity in Space and Time*, Chicago, IL: The University of Chicago Press.

1995. "Diachronically Stable Structural Features," in H. Andersen (ed.), *Historical Linguistics 1993*, Amsterdam: Benjamins, 337–55.

2003. "Diversity and Stability in Language," in Brian D. Joseph and Richard D. Janda (eds), *The Handbook of Historical Linguistics*, Oxford: Blackwell, 283–310.

2007. "Chechen Morphology (with Notes on Ingush)," in Alan S. Kaye (ed.), *Morphologies of Asia and Africa (including the Caucasus)*, Winona Lake, IN: Eisenbrauns, 1173–92.

2011. *Ingush Grammar*, Berkeley, CA: University of California Press (available online at http://escholarship.org/uc/item/3nn7z6w5).

Nordlinger, Rachel 1998. *A Grammar of Wambaya, Northern Territory (Australia)*. (Pacific Linguistics, Series C, 140.) Canberra: Australian National University.

Norman, Jerry 1988. *Chinese*, Cambridge: Cambridge University Press.

N'un, Maun Maun 1963. *Birmanskij jazyk*, Moscow: Izdatel'stvo vostočnoj literatury.

Nurse, Derek 2007. "Did the Proto-Bantu Verb Have a Synthetic or an Analytic Structure?" *SOAS Working Papers in Linguistics* 15: 239–56.

Oates, Lynette F. 1988. *The Muruwari Language*, Canberra: Pacific Linguistics.

Odhiambo, Neddy and Malherbe, Michel 2008. *Parlons luo*, Paris: L'Harmattan.

Olawsky, Knut J. 2006. *A Grammar of Urarina*, Berlin: Mouton De Gruyter.

Olpp, Johannes 1977. *Nama Grammatika*, Windhoek.

Omel'janovič, N. V. 1971. *Samoučitel' birmanskogo jazyka*, Moscow: Izdatel'stvo "Meždunarodnye otnošenija".

Onishi, Masayuki 2012. *A Grammar of Motuna*. Munich: Lincom Europa.

Oranskij, I. M. 1963. *Iranskie jazyki*, Moscow: Nauka.

Osborne, Charles R. 1974. *The Tiwi Language*, Canberra: Australian Institute of Aboriginal Studies.

Ó Siadhail, Micheál 1989. *Modern Irish*, Cambridge: Cambridge University Press.

Osumi, Midori 1995. *Tinrin Grammar*, Honolulu: The University of Hawaii Press.

Oxotina, N. V. 1961. *Jazyk zulu*, Moscow: Nauka.

Pandharipande, Rajeshwari V. 1997. *Marathi*. (Descriptive Grammar Series.) London: Routledge.

Parker, George W. 1883. *A Concise Grammar of the Malagasy Language*, London: Trübner & Co.

Payne, Doris 1998. "Maasai Gender in Typological Perspective," *Studies in African Linguistics* 27: 15–175.

Payne, Thomas E. and Payne, Doris L. 1990. "Yagua," in Derbyshire and Pullum (eds), 249–474.

   2013. *A Typological Grammar of Panare: A Cariban Language of Venezuela*, Leiden: Brill.

Pensalfini, Robert J. 1997. *Jingulu Grammar, Dictionary, and Texts*, PhD dissertation, MIT, Cambridge, MA.

   2003. *A Grammar of Jingulu. An Aboriginal Language of the Northern Territory*, Canberra: The Australian National University.

Pet, Willem A. 2011. *A Grammar Sketch and Lexicon of Arawak (Lokono Dian)*, SIL: www-01.sil.org/silepubs/Pubs/928474543236/e-Books_30_Pet_Arawak_Suriname.pdf (accessed June 15, 2017).

Peterson, John 2011. *A Grammar of Kharia*, Leiden: Brill.

Pitkin, Harvey 1984. *Wintu Grammar*, Berkeley, CA: University of California Press.

Plaisier, Heleen 2007. *A Grammar of Lepcha*, Leiden: Brill.

Plank, Frans 1991. Review of Michael Barlow and Charles A. Ferguson (eds), *Agreement in Natural Language. Approaches, Theories, Descriptions, Stanford*: Center for the Study of Languages and Information (1988), *Journal of Linguistics* 27: 532–42.

   1994. "What Agrees with What, in What, Generally Speaking," *EUROTYP Working Papers* 7(23): 39–58.

Plaster, Keith and Polinsky, Maria 2007. "Women Are Not Dangerous Things: Gender and Categorization," *Harvard Working Papers in Linguistics* 12: 1–44.

Polian, Gilles 2006. *Éléments de grammaire du tseltal*, Paris: L'Harmattan.

Polinsky, Maria 2003. "Non-Canonical Agreement Is Canonical," *Transactions of the Philological Society* 101(2): 279–312.

Polinsky, Maria and Potsdam, Eric 2001. "Long-Distance Agreement and Topic in Tsez," *Natural Language and Linguistic Theory* 19: 583–646.

Press, Margaret L. 1979. *Chemehuevi: A Grammar and Lexicon*, Los Angeles, CA: University of California Press.

Prost, André, 1983. "Essai de description grammaticale du dialecte Bobo de Tansila, Haute-Volta", *Mandenkan* 5: 1–99.

Qingxia, Dai and Diehl, Lon 2003. "Jingpho," in Graham Thurgood and Randy LaPolla J. (eds), *The Sino-Tibetan Languages*, London: Curzon Press, 401–8.

Queixalós, Francisco 2000. *Syntaxe sikuani (Colombie)*, Louvain: Peeters.

Radin, Paul 1929. *A Grammar of the Wappo Language*, Berkeley, CA: University of California Press.

Rau, Der-Hwa Victoria 1992. *A Grammar of Atayal*, PhD dissertation, Ithaca, NY: Cornell University.

Ray, Sidney K. 1931. *A Grammar of the Kiwai Language, Fly Delta, Papua*, Sidney: Baker.

186   References

Ray, Tapas S. 2003. "Oriya," in George Cardona and Dhanesh Jain (eds), *The Indo-Aryan Languages*, London: Routledge, 444–76.

Redden, James E. et al. 1963. *Twi Basic Course*, Washington DC: Foreign Service Institute.

Reece, Laurie 1970. *Grammar of the Walibri Language of Central Australia*. (Oceania Linguistic Monographs, 13.) Sydney: s.n.

Reid, Nicholas 1997. "Class and Classifier in Ngan'gityemmeri," in Mark Harvey and Nicholas Reid (eds), *Nominal Classification in Aboriginal Australia* (Studies in Language Companion Series 37), Amsterdam: John Benjamins, 165–228.

Renault, Robert 1987. "Genre grammatical et typologie linguistique," *Bulletin de la Société de linguistique* 82: 339–63.

Rennison, John R. 1997. *Koromfe*, London: Routledge.

Rice, Keren 1989. *A Grammar of Slave*, Berlin: Mouton De Gruyter.

Richardson, Murray 1968. *Chipewyan Grammar*. Cold Lake, Alberta: Northern Canada Evangelical Mission.

Rießler, Michael 2011. *Typology and Evolution of Adjective Attribution Marking in the Languages of Northern Eurasia*. PhD Dissertation, Leipzig University.

Rießler, Michael 2016. *Adjective Attribution*, Berlin: Language Science Press.

Rijkhoff, Jan 2002. *The Noun Phrase*, Oxford: Oxford University Press.

Roberts, John R. 1987. *Amele*, London: Croom Helm.

Rodrigues, Aryon D. 1999. "Macro-Jê," in Dixon and Aikhenvald (eds), 165–206.

Romero-Figeroa, Andrés 1997. *A Reference Grammar of Warao*, Munich: Lincom Europa.

Rood, David S. 1976. *Wichita Grammar*, New York: Garland.

Rood, David S. and Taylor, Allan R. 1996. *Sketch of Lakhota, a Siouan Language*, in *Handbook of North American Indians*, Vol. 17, Washington DC: The Smithsonian Institution, 440–82.

Roulon-Doko, Paulette 1997. *Parlons gbaya*, Paris: L'Harmattan.

Rounds, Carol 2001. *Hungarian: An Essential Grammar*, London: Routledge.

Royen, Gerlach 1929. *Die nominalen Klassifikationssysteme in der Sprachen der Erde*, Vienna: Holzer und Söhne.

Rubino, Carl 2000. *Ilocano Dictionary and Grammar: Ilocano–English, English–Ilocano*, Honolulu: University of Hawaii Press.

Ruhlen, Merritt 1991. *A Guide to the World's Languages. Volume 1: Classification*, Stanford, CA: Stanford University Press.

Ryding, Karin C. 2014. *Arabic: A Linguistic Introduction*, Cambridge: Cambridge University Press.

Sadiqi, Fatima 1997. *Grammaire du berbère*, Paris: L'Harmattan.

Saeed, John 1999. *Somali*, Amsterdam: Benjamins.

Sakel, Jeanette 2002. *A Grammar of Mosetén*, Berlin: Mouton de Gruyter.

Salminen, Tapani 2012. *Tundra Nenets*, www.helsinki.fi/~tasalmin/sketch.html (accessed June 15, 2017).

Samarin, William J. 1967. *A Grammar of Sango*, The Hague: Mouton.

Sanžeev, G. D. 1956. "Sledy grammatičeskogo roda v mongol'skix jazykax," *Voprosy Jazykoznanija* 5: 73–4.

Saul, Janice E. and Wilson, Nancy Freiberger 1980. *Nung Grammar*. (SIL Publications in Linguistics, 62.) Dallas, TX: Summer Institute of Linguistics and University of Texas at Arlington.

Savà, Graziano 2005. *A Grammar of Ts'amakko*, Cologne: Rüdiger Köppe.

Schachter, Paul and Otanes, Fe T. 1972. *Tagalog Reference Grammar*, Berkeley, CA: University of California Press.

Schapper, Antoinette 2010. "Neuter Gender in Eastern Indonesia," *Oceanic Linguistics* 49: 407–35.

Schaub, William 1985. *Babungo*, London: Croom Helm.

Schiffman, Harold F. 1999. *A Reference Grammar of Spoken Tamil*, Cambridge: Cambridge University Press.

Schlachter, Wolfgang 1958. "Die Kongruenz des attributiven Adjektivs im Finnischen," *Münchener Studien zur Sprachwissenschaft* 12: 19–38.

Schmitt, Rüdiger 1981. *Grammatik des Klassisch-armenischen*, Innsbruck: Innsbrucker Beiträge zur Sprachwissenschaft.

Schneider-Blum, Gertrud 2007. *A Grammar of Alaaba*, Cologne: Rüdiger Köppe Verlag.

Seidel, Frank 2008. *A Grammar of Yeyi: A Bantu Language of Southern Africa*, Cologne: Rüdiger Köppe.

Seki, Lucy 1999. "The Upper Xingu as an Incipient Linguistic Area," in Dixon and Aikhenvald (eds), 417–30.

Senft, Gunter 1986. *Kilivila: The Language of the Trobriand Islanders* (Mouton Grammar Library 3), Berlin: Mouton De Gruyter.

Seyoum, Mulugeta 2008. *A Grammar of Dime*, Utrecht: LOT.

Sherzer, Joel 1973. "Areal Linguistics in North America," in T. Sebeok (ed.), *Current Trends in Linguistics, Vol. 10*, The Hague: Mouton, 749–95.

Shibatani, Masayoshi 1990. *The Languages of Japan,* Cambridge: Cambridge University Press.

Shipley, William B. 1964. *A Grammar of Maidu*, Berkeley, CA: University of California Press.

Siewierska, Anna 1999. "From Anaphoric Pronoun to Grammatical Agreement Marker: Why Objects Don't Make It," *Folia Linguistica* 33 (1–2): 225–51.

2004. *Person*, Cambridge: Cambridge University Press.

Siewierska, Anna and Bakker, Dik 1996. "The Distribution of Subject and Object Agreement and Word Order Type," *Studies in Language* 20(1): 115–61.

Skorik, P. Ja. 1961. *Grammatika čukotskogo jazyka*, I, Moscow: AN SSSR.

1968. "*Čukotskij jazyk*," in V. V. Vinogradov (ed.), *Jazyki narodov SSSR, T. 5, Mongol'skie, tunguso-man'čurskie i paleoaziatskie jazyki*, Moscow: Nauka, 248–70.

Smeets, Ineke 2008. *A Grammar of Mapuche*, Berlin: Mouton De Gruyter.

Smirnova, M. A. 1982. *The Hausa Language*, London: Routledge.

Smyth, David 1995. *Colloquial Cambodian*, London: Routledge.

2002. *Thai: An Essential Grammar*, London: Routledge.

Sneddon, James N. 1996. *Indonesian: A Comprehensive Grammar*, London: Routledge.

Snyman, Jannie W. 1970. *The !Xũ (!Kung) Language*, Cape Town: A. A. Balkema.

Sohn, Ho-Min, 1999. *The Korean Language*, Cambridge: Cambridge University Press.

Soukka, Maria 2000. *A Descriptive Grammar of Noon: A Cangin Language of Senegal*, Munich: Lincom.

Starinin, V. P. 1967. *Èfiopskij jazyk*, Moscow: Nauka.

Staudacher-Valliamée, Gillette 2004. *Grammaire du créole réunionnais*, La Réunion: Université de La Réunion.

Stebbins, Tonya N. 2011. *Mali (Baining) Grammar. A Language of the East New Britain Province, Papua New Guinea*, Canberra: The Australian National University.

Steele, Susan 1990. *Agreement and Anti-Agreement: A Syntax of Luiseño*, Dordrecht: Kluwer.

Steever, Sanford B. (ed.) 1988. *The Dravidian Languages*, London: Routledge.

Stenzel, Kristine 2013. *A Reference Grammar of Kotiria (Wanano)*, Lincoln, NE: The University of Nebraska Press.

Stirtz, Timothy 2011. *A Grammar of Gaahmg, a Nilo-Saharan Language of Sudan*, Utrecht: LOT.

Stolper, Matthew W. 2008. "Elamite," in Roger D. Woodard (ed.), *The Ancient Languages of Mesopotamia, Egypt, and Aksum*, Cambridge: Cambridge University Press, 60–95.

Storch, Anne 2014. *A Grammar of Luwo: An Anthropological Approach*, Amsterdam: Benjamins.

Suárez, Jorge A. 1983. *The Mesoamerican Indian Languages*, Cambridge: Cambridge University Press.

Sullivan, Thelma D. 1983. *Compendio de la gramática náhuatl*, Mexico City: UNAM.

Sylvain, Suzanne 1979. *Le créole haïtien*. Geneva: Slatkine.

Tamura, Suzuko 2000. *The Ainu Language*, Tokyo: Sanseido.

Tauberschmidt, Gerhard 1999. *A Grammar of Sinaugoro: An Austronesian language of the Central province of Papua New Guinea*, Canberra: Pacific Linguistics.

Tereščenko, N. M. 1966. "Èneckij jazyk," in V. I. Lytkin and E. K. Majtinskaja (eds), *Jazyki narodov SSSR. Volume 3: Finno-Ugorskie jazyki i samodijskie jazyki*, Moscow: Nauka, 438–57.

Terrill, Angela 1998. *Biri*, Munich: Lincom Europa.

1999. *A Grammar of Lavukaleve*, Berlin: Mouton De Gruyter.

Testelec, Yakov G. 1998. "Word Order in Kartvelian Languages," in Anna Siewierska (ed.), *Constituent Order in the Languages of Europe*, Berlin: Mouton De Gruyter, 649–79.

Thackston, W. M. 2006. *Kurmanji Kurdish: A Reference Grammar with Selected Readings*, New York: Renas Media.

Thiesen, Wesley and Weber, David 2012. *A Grammar of Bora with Special Attention to Tone*, Dallas, TX: SIL International.

Thomas, David D. 1971. *Chrau Grammar*, Honolulu: University of Hawaii Press.

Thomason, Sarah G. and Kaufman, Terrence 1988. *Language Contact, Creolization, and Genetic Linguistics*, Berkeley, CA: University of California Press.

Thompson, Sandra A. et al. 2006. *A Reference Grammar of Wappo*, Berkeley, CA: University of California Press.

Thornell, Christina 1997. *The Sango Language and Its Lexicon*, Lund: Lund University Press.

Thurgood, Graham 2014. *A Grammatical Sketch of Hainan Cham*, Berlin: Mouton De Gruyter.

Thurgood, Graham and LaPolla, Randy (eds) 2003. *The Sino-Tibetan Languages*, London: Routledge.

Todd, Terry Lynn 1985. *A Grammar of Dimili, also known as Zaza*, Ann Arbor, MI: The University of Michigan Press.

Tolsma, Gerard J. 2006. *A Grammar of Kulung*, Leiden: Brill.

Topping, Donald M. 1973. *Chamorro Reference Grammar*, Honolulu: University of Hawaii Press.

Topuria, G. V. 1994. "Zur Geschichte der grammatischen Klassen in den ostkaukasischen Sprachen," in Ronald Bielmeier (ed.), *Studia Indogermanica et Caucasica. Festschrift für K. H. Schmidt zum 65. Geburtstag*, Berlin: De Gruyter: 524–34.

Troike, Rudolph 1981. "Subject-Object Concord in Coahuilteco," *Language* 57: 658–73.

1996. "Coahuilteco (Pajalate)," in I. Goddard (ed.), *Languages. Handbook of North American Indians*, Washington DC: The Smithsonian Institution, 644–65.

Tryon, Darrell T. 1970. *Conversational Tahitian*. Berkeley, CA: University of California Press.

Tsunoda, Tasaku 2011. *A Grammar of Warrongo*, Berlin: Mouton De Gruyter.

Tucker, Archibald N. and Bryan, Margaret A. 1966. *Linguistic Analyses: The Non-Bantu Languages of North-Eastern Africa*, Oxford: Oxford University Press.

Tucker Childs, Gordon 1988. *The Phonology and Morphology of Kisi*, PhD dissertation, University of California, Berkeley.

1995. *A Grammar of Kisi*, Berlin: De Gruyter.

2011. *A Grammar of Mani*, Berlin: Mouton De Gruyter.

Tuite, Kevin 1997. *Svan*, Munich: Lincom Europa.

Ubrjatova, E. I. 1966. "Jakutskij jazyk," in V. V. Vinogradov (ed.), *Jazyki narodov SSSR. Volume 2: tjurkskie jazyki*, Moscow/Leningrad: Nauka, 403–27.

UnivArch = *The Universals Archive* (Konstanz University), http://typo.uni-konstanz. de/archive/intro/index.php (accessed June 15, 2017).

Unterbeck, Barbara and Rissanen, Matti (eds) 2000. *Gender in Grammar and Cognition*, Berlin and New York: Mouton de Gruyter.

Upadhyay, Shiv R. 2009. "The Sociolinguistic Variation of Grammatical Gender Agreement in Nepali," *Journal of Pragmatics* 41: 564–85.

Vajda, Edward J. 2004. *Ket*, Munich: Lincom.

Valentine, J. Randolph 2001. *Nishnaabemwin Reference Grammar*. Toronto: University of Toronto Press.

Valenzuela, Pilar M. 1997. *Basic Verb Types and Argument Structures in Shipibo-Conibo*, MA thesis, University of Oregon.

Vaman Dhongde, Ramesh and Wali, Kashi 2009. *Marathi*, Amsterdam: Benjamins.

Van Breugel, Seino 2014. *A Grammar of Atong*, Leiden: Brill.

Van der Voort, Hein 2004. *A Grammar of Kwaza*, Berlin: Mouton De Gruyter.

Van Driem, George 1987. *A Grammar of Limbu*, Berlin: De Gruyter.

2001. *Languages of the Himalayas*, Leiden: Brill.

Van Valin, Robert D., Jr. 2005. *Exploring the Syntax–Semantics Interface*, Cambridge: Cambridge University Press.

2008. "RPs and the Nature of Lexical and Syntactic Categories in Role and Reference Grammar," in Robert D. Van Valin, Jr. (ed.), *Investigations of the Syntax–Semantics–Pragmatics Interface*, Amsterdam: John Benjamins, 161–78.

Van Valin, Robert D., Jr. and LaPolla, Randy 1997. *Syntax. Structure, Meaning and Function*, Cambridge: Cambridge University Press.

Verstraete, Jean-Cristophe and Rigsby, Bruce 2015. *A Grammar and Lexicon of Yintyingka*, Berlin: Mouton De Gruyter.

Veth, Peter 2000. "Origins of the Western Desert Language: Convergences in Linguistic and Archaeological Space and Time Models," *Archaeology in Oceania* 35(1): 11–19.

Vietze, Hans-Peter 1974. *Lehrbuch der mongolischen Sprache*, Leipzig: VEB.

Vinogradov, V. V. (ed.) 1967. *Jazyki narodov SSSR, IV: Iberijsko-kavkazskie jazyki*, Moscow: AN SSSR.

Voigtlander, Katherine and Echegoyen, Artemisa 1985. *Luces contemporaneas del otomi. Gramática del otomí de la sierra*, México, DF: Instituto Lingüístico de Verano.

Von Humboldt, Wilhelm 1963. *Schriften zur Sprachphilosophie*, Darmstadt: Wissenschaftliche Buchgesellschaft.

Vossen, Rainer (ed.) 2012. *The Khoesan languages*, London: Routledge.

Vydrine, Valentin 2009. "Areal Features in South Mande and Kru Languages," in Georg Ziegelmeyer and Norbert Cyffer (eds), *When Languages Meet: Language Contact and Change in West Africa*, Cologne: Rüdiger Köppe, 91–116.

WALS = Dryer, Matthew S. and Haspelmath, Martin (eds) 2013. *The World Atlas of Language Structures*, Oxford: Oxford University Press, also available online at http: wals.info (accessed June 15, 2017).

Watahomigie, Lucille J., Bender, Jorigine, et al. 2001. *Hualapai Reference Grammar. Revised and Expanded Edition*, Kyoto: Endangered Languages of the Pacific.

Watkins, Laurel J. and McKenzie, Parker 1984. *A Grammar of Kiowa*. Studies in the anthropology of North American Indians. Lincoln, NE: University of Nebraska Press.

Weber, David J. 1989. *A Grammar of Huallaga (Huánaco) Quechua*, Los Angeles, CA: University of California Publications in Linguistics.

Wechsler, Stephen 2015. "The Syntactic Role of Agreement," in Tibor Kiss and Artemis Alexiadou (eds), *Syntax: Theory and Analysis*, Berlin: De Gruyter, 309–42.

Wedekind, Klaus, Wedekind, Charlotte and Abuzeinab, Musa 2007. *A Learner's Grammar of Beja (East Sudan)*, Cologne: Rüdiger Köppe.

2008. *Beja Pedagogical Grammar*, www.afrikanistik-aegyptologie-online.de/archiv/2008/1283/.

Wegener, Claudia 2012. *A Grammar of Savosavo*, Berlin: Mouton De Gruyter.

Welmers, William 1973. *African Language Structures*, Berkeley, CA: University of California Press.

1976. *A Grammar of Vai*, Los Angeles, CA: UCLA Press.

Westerlund, Torbjörn 2007. *A Grammatical Sketch of Ngarla: A Language of Western Australia*, MA thesis, Uppsala University.

Wichmann, Søren 2013. "A Classification of Papuan Languages," *Language and Linguistics in Melanesia*, Special Issue 2012, Harald Hammarström and Wilco van den Heuvel (eds), *History Contact and Classification of Papuan Languages*, Part Two, 313–86.

Wilson, Patricia R. 1980. *Ambulas Grammar* (Workpapers in Papua New Guinea Languages 26), Ukarumpa: Summer Institute of Linguistics.

Wintner, Shuly 2000. "Definiteness in the Hebrew Noun Phrase," *Journal of Linguistics* 36: 319–63.

Young, Robert and Morgan, William 1972. *The Navaho Language*, Salt Lake City, UT: United States Indian Service.

Zaicz, Gábor 1997. "Mordva," in Abondolo (ed.), 184–218.

Zeitoun, Elisabeth 2005. "Tsou," in Alexander Adelaar and Nikolaus P. Himmelmann (eds), *The Austronesian Languages of Asia and Madagascar*, London: Routledge, 259–90.

Ziervogel, Dirk 1952. *A Grammar of Swazi*, Johannesburg: Witwatersrand Press.

Zubiri, Ilari 2000. *Gramática didáctica del euskera*, Bilbo: Didaktiker, S.A.

Zwicky, Arnold 1985. "Heads," *Journal of Linguistics* 21: 1–29.

Zymberi, Isa 1993. *Colloquial Albanian*, London: Routledge.

Language Index

Names of language families and other genetic groupings are italicized.

Subject Index